Rational Emotive Behaviour Therapy

Theoretical Developments

Edited by Windy Dryden

Brunner-Routledge
Taylor & Francis Group

HOVE AND NEW YORK

First published 2003 by Brunner-Routledge
27 Church Road, Hove, East Sussex BN3 2FA

Simultaneously published in the USA and Canada
by Brunner-Routledge
29 West 35th Street, New York, NY 10001

Brunner-Routledge is an imprint of the Taylor & Francis Group

Typeset in Times by Mayhew Typesetting, Rhayader, Powys
Printed and bound in Great Britain by TJ International Ltd, Padstow, Cornwall
Paperback cover design by Sandra Heath

British Library Cataloguing in Publication Data
A catalogue record for this book is available from the British Library

Library of Congress Cataloging-in-Publication Data
Rational emotive behaviour therapy : theoretical developments /
edited by Windy Dryden
          p. cm. – (Advancing theory in therapy)
Includes bibliographical references and index.
    ISBN 1-58391-272-X
    1. Rational-emotive psychotherapy. I. Dryden, Windy. II. Series.

RC489.R3 R383 2003
616.89'142–dc21

                                                             2002010743

ISBN 1-58391-272-X (hbk)
ISBN 1-58391-273-8 (pbk)

Contents

Series preface

This series focuses on advanced and advancing theory in psychotherapy. Its aims are: to present theory and practice within a specific theoretical orientation or approach at an advanced, postgraduate level; to advance theory by presenting and evaluating new ideas and their relation to the approach; to locate the orientation and its applications within cultural contexts both historically in terms of the origins of the approach, and contemporarily in terms of current debates about philosophy, theory, society and therapy; and, finally, to present and develop a critical view of theory and practice, especially in the context of debates about power, organization and the increasing professionalization of therapy.

It is 50 years since Albert Ellis, the founding father of Rational Emotive Behaviour Therapy (REBT), dissatisfied with psychoanalysis, began research on new techniques in psychotherapy. Originally called 'rational psychotherapy' and later 'rational-emotive therapy' the term REBT reflects the development of this approach which stresses the importance of the interaction of cognitive, emotive and behavioural factors in human lives. Generally viewed as representing 'second-force' (behavioural) psychology, REBT has traditionally inhabited the intellectual and clinical territory between psychoanalysis and humanistic psychology; however, in more recent times, it has clearly influenced and been influenced by other traditions – dialogues which are reflected in this present volume. Indeed, a feature of this present contribution is the consideration of developments both from within REBT as well as from outside the theory, the effect of which is a comprehensive and critical exploration of the therapy. Some readers may well find the text unfamiliar both in content and in layout; however, a close reading will be rewarded by an appreciation – first-time or renewed – of the sophistication of REBT and the commitment of the contributors to developing and advancing its theory and application.

List of contributors

Wouter Backx studied clinical and theoretical psychology and has specialized in Rational Emotive Behaviour Therapy at the Albert Ellis Institute. He is a Fellow of the Albert Ellis Institute and Director of the Dutch REBT affiliate training centre in the city of Haarlem. He is author of several articles and co-author of books on REBT.

Daniel David, PhD, is an Assistant Professor in the Department of Psychology at Babes-Bolyai University in Cluj-Napoca, Romania. He earned his PhD in cognitive psychology (Babes-Bolyai University, Romania), and received postdoctoral training in clinical psychology (Mount Sinai School of Medicine, USA) and in cognitive-behavioral therapy (Albert Ellis Institute of REBT). Dr David is the Director of the Center for Cognitive and Rational-Emotive Behavior Therapy, Cluj-Napoca, Romania, and is the President of the Romanian Association of Hypnosis and Cognitive Behavioral Psychotherapy. He is the Editor of the *Romanian Journal of Cognitive and Behavioral Psychotherapies* and he has published three books and more than 25 articles about cognitive psychology and cognitive-behavioral therapy, in both national and international journals.

Kristene A. Doyle, PhD, is a licensed psychologist, the Training and Development Coordinator and the Coordinator of the Child and Family Services Clinic at the Albert Ellis Institute in New York City. She is an Associate Adjunct Professor at St John's University.

Windy Dryden is Professor of Psychotherapeutic Studies at Goldsmiths College, University of London, and is an international authority on Rational Emotive Behaviour Therapy. He is the author of *Reason to Change: A Rational Emotive Behaviour Therapy (REBT) Workbook*, co-editor (with Laurence Spurling) of *On Becoming a Psychotherapist* and co-author (with Jill Mytton) of *Four Approaches to Counselling and Psychotherapy*, and (with Michael Neenan) of *Life Coaching: A Cognitive-Behavioural Approach*.

Albert Ellis is President of the Albert Ellis Institute in New York, where he still conducts many individual and group psychotherapy sessions, supervises a number of therapists, and gives many public and professional talks and workshops in Rational Emotive Behaviour Therapy. He also presents many workshops and talks nationally and internationally and is consulting editor of a dozen psychological journals. He has published over 700 articles and 68 books on psychotherapy, relationships therapy and sex therapy.

Susan Presby Kodish, PhD, a psychologist and Albert Ellis Institute supervisor, and Bruce I. Kodish, PhD, a physical therapist, both have practices in Pasadena, CA. They are on the teaching, speaking and editorial staffs of the Institute of General Semantics. Together they wrote *Drive Yourself Sane: Using the Uncommon Sense of General Semantics*. Bruce wrote *Back Pain Solutions: How to Help Yourself With Posture-Movement Therapy and Education*.

James McMahon, PsyD, PhD, is President of MATES Foundation, President of the School of Pastoral Counseling of Emmanuel University of Oradea (EUO, Romania), founder and Sr Associate of Westfield (NJ) Mental Health Associates, Supervisor and Life Member of the AEI for REBT, Professor of Psychology at the State University of Oradea (Romania), Professor of Psychology and Philosophy at the Emmanuel University of Oradea, and Adjunct Professor in Psychology at The Union Institute Graduate School and Undergraduate School.

Stevan Lars Nielsen earned the PhD in Clinical Psychology from the University of Washington in Seattle, Washington, and practices as a clinical professor at Brigham Young University (BYU) in Provo, Utah. He is an associate fellow of the Albert Ellis Institute for REBT in New York City. In addition to interests in schema theory he has conducted research on client response to day-to-day psychotherapy. He and his clinical psychologist wife enjoy raising four boys, the joint practice of psychology, alpine skiing, and running in tow behind border collies Elvis and Princess.

Nando Pelusi holds a PhD in clinical psychology and is an Adjunct Professor at St John's University. He is a certified supervisor of REBT at the Albert Ellis Institute where he conducts various workshops. He is on the board of advisers for the National Association of Cognitive Behavior Therapists and is in private practice in New York City.

Hank Robb received his PhD in Counseling Psychology from the University of Nebraska, Lincoln in 1978. Dr Robb served as Director of Counseling and Associate Professor of Psychology at Lewis Clark State College, Lewiston, Idaho between 1978 and 1986 and then moved to Lake Oswego,

Oregon where he maintains a private psychology practice. Dr Robb is board certified in both Counseling Psychology and Behavioral Psychology by the American Board of Professional Psychology, Supervisor for the Albert Ellis Institute and immediate Past-President of the American Board of Counseling Psychology, ABPP. He has written papers on a wide variety of psychological issues, and a popular self-help pamphlet titled *How to Stop Driving Yourself Crazy®️ with Help from the Bible*.

Peter Trower, PhD, is Senior Lecturer at Birmingham University and Consultant Clinical Psychologist in South Birmingham, and Associate Fellow of the Albert Ellis Institute, New York. He has written and researched in the areas of cognitive therapy, psychosis (particularly paranoia) and social anxiety, and developed theories regarding self construction processes.

Preface

Rational Emotive Behaviour Therapy was founded in 1955 by Dr Albert Ellis who has been at the forefront of this approach's developments since that date. While usually located in the cognitive-behavioural tradition of psychotherapy, REBT has many diverse influences and like human beings themselves its theoretical underpinnings are constantly in flux. This volume is designed to outline some of the theoretical developments with which its leading practitioners are presently concerned.

As can be seen from the table of contents, the range of topics under consideration is very broad. After my introduction to the ABC theory of REBT, contributors consider developments in REBT theory both from within the theory (e.g. Ellis, Robb and Backx) and from outside the theory (e.g. David, Doyle, Kodish and Kodish, and Pelusi). In two further chapters Nielsen outlines what he calls 'rationally evaluative schema theory' and shows how this may help the integration of REBT with other schema-focused therapies, while McMahon considers the concepts of self and values from a philosophical perspective. The final chapter by Trower details how the developing field of cognitive behaviour therapy (CBT) with schizophrenia has both influenced REBT theory and been shaped by it. This volume is not the last word on theoretical developments in REBT. It does show, however, the exciting work that is currently being done in this area. As such, the book nicely reflects the theme of this series in that it advances theory in REBT.

Windy Dryden

Chapter 1

'The cream cake made me eat it': an introduction to the ABC theory of REBT

Windy Dryden

I remember the moment as if it were yesterday. My client, Mrs Jones, was telling me how hard it was for her to keep to her diabetic diet.

'I know intellectually that I shouldn't eat cakes, but I've got no will power', she said.

'Well', I replied, 'let's see if you're right. Give a recent example where you broke your diet.'

'That's easy', continued Mrs Jones, 'that was this morning.'

'Tell me about it', I urged.

'Well, I was out shopping for kitchenware. I knew exactly what I wanted and where I could go to get it, but blow me if they were all sold out of what I wanted. Well, to cheer myself up I thought I would have a cup of coffee. I know that I have weakness for cakes so I resolved only to buy the coffee. But when I saw that cream cake, perched there with lovely vanilla butter-cream; well, this is going to sound funny, but the cream cake made me eat it.'

While listening to Mrs Jones's account I had a most peculiar image. I pictured in my mind's eye Mrs Jones sitting in the cafe with mouth resolutely closed, but her lips were being prised apart by the cream cake that had levitated itself and flown through the air of its own accord towards the hapless Mrs Jones. Then, having prised Mrs Jones's lips apart, it rammed itself into her mouth and forced itself down her gullet.

'A causes C'

The image of a cream cake making Mrs Jones eat it, while amusing, illustrates a way of looking at psychological events that is widespread in our culture and is part of the way we employ language. Consider the following phrases that you might hear every day:

'He made me so angry.'
'It really depressed me.'
'I hurt her feelings.'

'My mother has the knack of making me guilty.'

'He made me do it.'

And, less frequently,

'The cream cake made me eat it.'

What do all these statements have in common? They all share the idea that another person or life event can directly cause your feelings and behaviour. In Rational Emotive Behaviour Therapy (REBT), the thera-peutic approach upon which this book is based, this is known as the 'A causes C' phenomenon, where 'A' refers to activating events and 'C' refers to our emotional and behavioural responses to these events ('C' actually stands for consequences, for reasons that will become clear).

This can be shown as:

$$A \rightarrow C$$

In contrast, however, REBT theory states that at the core of our emotional and behavioural responses (C) to events lie our beliefs (B) about these events (A). Thus, C arises out of the interaction between A and B.

This can be shown as:

$$A \times B \rightarrow C$$

What does this mean for Mrs Jones? It means that she needs to acknowledge that the cream cake did not make her eat it, but that she ate the cake largely because she held a set of beliefs about the cake that led her to pick up the cake, put it into her mouth and actively chew and swallow it.

In the 'A → C' version of the cake-eating episode, the cake is responsible for Mrs Jones eating it, while in the 'A × B → C' version, Mrs Jones is responsible for eating the cake. This concept of responsibility is central to our understanding of psychological disturbance and health and to our understanding of personal change. Let us now consider the concept of responsibility as it pertains to your thoughts, feelings and behaviour.

Responsibility

The present British Chief Rabbi, Dr Jonathan Sacks, once said that we are responsible for that which falls within our sphere of influence. This, in my view, captures the essence of the concept of responsibility. As it is so important, let me reiterate it:

WE ARE RESPONSIBLE FOR THAT WHICH FALLS WITHIN OUR SPHERE OF INFLUENCE

Returning to the case of Mrs Jones, according to this view, since cream cakes have no power to influence anything or anybody (being inanimate objects they cannot speak or act) they clearly are not responsible for any-thing. Just because Mrs Jones gave the cream cake, in the above example, responsibility over her behaviour, it does not follow that the cream cake actually has this responsibility. You do not become responsible for some-thing that is outside your power of influence because someone assigns you such responsibility.

Clearly then, Mrs Jones is responsible for eating the cream cake since the following actions are within her sphere of influence: buying the cream cake, picking up the cream cake, putting the cream cake into her mouth, chewing the cream cake and swallowing it. Equally clearly, the cream cake has no power over any of these actions. Until we invent cream cakes that do have the power to make us buy them, pick them up, put them into our mouths, chew and swallow them, cream cakes can be said to fall outside the realm of responsibility. To think otherwise is to think magically.

You may be thinking: 'Well, that's fine when it comes to cream cakes, but what about when another person is involved? Surely if someone acts nastily to me and I become angry, then that person is responsible for making me feel angry?'

If you think that other people can make you angry, then you are not alone. I would say that most people would agree with you. Certainly, you will hear phrases like 'What he did made me angry' and 'She made me really mad by what she said', far more frequently then phrases like 'I made myself angry about what he did' and 'I made myself really mad about what she said'. But these two latter statements are more accurate than the previous two statements. In order for you to understand why, I need to explain more about the role of beliefs in psychological functioning.

The legacy of Epictetus

Epictetus was a Roman philosopher who was a representative of what is known as the Stoic school of philosophy. He is perhaps most widely known for the following phrase:

*PEOPLE ARE DISTURBED NOT BY THINGS, BUT BY
THEIR VIEWS OF THINGS*

I will consider the concept of 'views' a little later, but for now these 'views' can broadly encompass such phenomena as thoughts, beliefs, attitudes, philosophies and assumptions. The field of psychology is currently pre-occupied with cognition, which can be broadly understood as the way people think and process information and would include their beliefs, attitudes, philosophies and assumptions. So Epictetus's famous dictum is currently bang up-to-date.

The Rational Emotive Behaviour Therapy (REBT) version of this dictum is as follows:

PEOPLE ARE DISTURBED NOT BY THINGS, BUT BY THEIR IRRATIONAL BELIEFS ABOUT THINGS

Again, I will have more to say about this REBT dictum later, but for now I want you to focus on the idea that our beliefs lie at the core of the way we feel and act. Hence the relation that I introduced to you earlier:

$$A \times B \rightarrow C$$

Stated in words, this means that lying at the core of our emotional and behavioural reactions at C are a set of beliefs (B) that we hold about the events to which we attend (A).

Now, according to REBT theory, if we hold a set of rational beliefs (rB) about a negative event (A) we will experience a set of healthy negative emotions (hne), constructive thoughts (ct) and productive behaviours (pb) at C. This can be shown in the following relation:

$$A \times rB \rightarrow C \text{ (hne + ct + pb)}$$

And if we hold a set of irrational beliefs (iB) about the same event (A) we will experience a set of unhealthy negative emotions (une), biased thoughts (bt) and detrimental behaviours (db) at C. This can be shown in the following relation:

$$A \times iB \rightarrow C \text{ (une + bt + db)}$$

'She made me really mad by what she said'

Let me apply the foregoing analysis to a situation where in response to what his colleague, Mary, said in a meeting, John experienced unhealthy anger towards her, had thoughts of revenge and acted on these thoughts by spreading malicious rumours as a way of getting back at her. What determined his feelings of unhealthy anger, his thoughts of revenge and his spreading malicious rumours against her? Using the relation $A \times iB \rightarrow C$ (une + bt + db) we have the following:

> What Mary said [A] × John's irrational beliefs [iB] →
> Unhealthy anger [C (une)] + Thoughts of revenge [C (bt)] +
> Spreading malicious rumours [C (db)]

Now who is responsible for what here? Clearly, Mary is responsible for what she said in the meeting since this was within her sphere of influence. John, on the other hand, is responsible for his unhealthy beliefs about what she said. He has this responsibility whether or not he assumes such responsibility and whether or not he knows what his unhealthy beliefs are. Just as in law where ignorance is not a legitimate defence, in psychological matters ignorance does not absolve a person from their responsibility.

If John held a healthy set of beliefs about what Mary said, he would have experienced healthy anger, had more constructive thoughts centring on resolving the situation and would have directly asserted himself with her rather than indirectly spreading malicious rumours against her. Using the relation A × rB → C (hne + ct + pb) we have the following:

What Mary said [A] × John's rational beliefs [rB] →
Healthy anger [C (hne)] + Thoughts of resolving situation [C (ct)]
+ Direct assertion [C (pb)]

In this scenario, Mary is again responsible for what she said and John is responsible for his healthy beliefs about what she said.

Drawing upon these two scenarios we can say the following:

(i)   Mary is responsible for her behaviour.
(ii) John is responsible for his beliefs.
(iii) John's beliefs about what Mary said lie at the core of his emotions and behaviours toward Mary. Remember that John can experience healthy anger or unhealthy anger about the same event (what Mary said).
(iv) John is therefore responsible for the way that he feels and the way that he subsequently thinks and acts through the responsibility that he has for his beliefs.
(v)   What Mary says (at A) contributes to, but does not cause the way John feels and acts. This is seen if we take into account two points. First, Mary's verbal behaviour puts John in the arena of anger, but does not determine whether his anger is healthy or unhealthy. Second, if Mary had said something different then John would neither have felt healthy anger nor unhealthy anger.

This analysis is far more complex and, in my view, more accurate than that shown in John's original statement:

'Mary's statement [A] made me mad [C (une)]'

or more formally:

$$A \rightarrow C \text{ (une)}$$

John's heartfelt complaint

When John heard my analysis of the factors that determined his unhealthy anger and destructive behaviour, John voiced a complaint that I have heard thousands of times inside and outside my consulting room.

'But if Mary hadn't said what she did, I wouldn't have got angry. Since she did say it and I got angry, she made me angry.'

What John is doing here and what thousands of REBT clients have done over the years is to mistake a correlation for a cause. John is right about one thing; if Mary hadn't said what she said he wouldn't have become unhealthily angry, but this does not prove that her words caused his unhealthy anger. For, as we have seen, it is John's irrational beliefs about what Mary said that were largely responsible for his feelings. Let me summarize these two positions by using the relevant relations.

John's position (mistaking a correlation for a cause)

1. Mary did not say what she said – I didn't become angry.
    A absent; C absent

2. Mary said what she said – I became angry.
    A present; C present

3. Conclusion: Mary's words made me angry.
    $A \rightarrow C$

REBT's position (clear distinction between cause and correlation)

1. Mary did not say what she said – John didn't become angry.
    A absent; C absent

2. Mary said what she said – John became unhealthily angry.
    A present; C present

3. Conclusion: John's unhealthy anger was determined by something, but not just by Mary's words. Rather, his feelings were determined by the irrational belief that he held about what Mary said.
    $A \times B \rightarrow C$

What is A? The many faces of A

So far in our discussion I have worked on the following assumptions about A:

(a) 'A' stands for an activating event;
(b) When it is critical, A activates the person's belief (rational or irrational) at B that determines his or her emotional, thinking and behavioural responses at C.

However, the concept of 'A' is more complex and in this section I will discuss this complexity. In doing so, I will assume that the person's response is dysfunctional. I now make an important distinction between five different types of A: (i) situational As, (ii) critical actual As, (iii) non-critical actual As, (iv) critical inferential As and (v) non-critical inferential As. I define these as follows:

- *A situational A (SA)* is the situation or context in which an emotional episode occurs (an emotional episode is one in which a person experiences an emotional reaction within a given context). When you accurately describe a situation in which a person disturbed themself this is a situational A. Given that it is descriptive in nature, a situational A is free of inferential meaning. In this context an inference is an interpretation of the situation that goes beyond the data at hand. An inference can be accurate or inaccurate, but is a hunch about reality that needs to be tested against the available data. A situational A is fairly broad and several specific actual and inferential As can be located within it. Situational As can be critical or non-critical. When a situational A is critical it activates the person's belief at B, while when it is non-critical it could potentially activate B, but doesn't. More often than not situational As provide the context in which more specific As activate Bs. When this is the case, it could be argued that situational As should not be called As at all. Rather they should be regarded as situations in which belief-activating and potentially belief-activating events occur.
- *A critical actual A (CrAA)* is the specific actual aspect of the situation about which the person disturbs themself. It is descriptive, but far more specific than a situational A in which several potential specific actual As can exist. What makes an actual A critical is that it triggers the person's belief (at B) that accounts for the emotional–behavioural-thinking response at C.
- *A non-critical actual A (NCrAA)* is another specific actual aspect of the situation about which the person could disturb themself, but doesn't.
- *A critical inferential A (CrIA)* is also a specific aspect of the situation about which the person disturbs themself, but one that is inferential rather than descriptive. Again, what makes an inferential A critical is that it triggers the person's belief (at B) that accounts for the emotional–behavioural-thinking response at C.
- *A non-critical inferential A (NCrIA)* is another inferential aspect of the situation about which the person could disturb themself, but doesn't.

In emotional episodes most critical As are inferential rather than descriptive in nature. Again, they may be true, but they go beyond the data at hand and can only be accepted as true probabilistically.

Let me illustrate the differences between these different types of As with reference to the finger-pointing exercise that I sometimes use in training workshops to teach REBT's ABC model (Dryden et al., 1997). In this exercise, I tell workshop participants to think of a secret. I then tell them that I will walk about the room pointing my finger and when I stop whomever I am pointing at will tell the group their secret. In fact, I never ask anybody to reveal their secret, but instead ask people to share what feelings they experienced during the exercise.

What I discover is that people have a range of different emotions about different aspects of the situation. Here are some of the specific aspects (actual and inferential) that people have feelings about:

- You are going to ask me to tell the group my secret (inferential A)
- Your finger pointing at me (actual A)
- People will think I am strange if I disclose my secret (inferential A)
- The internal sense of discomfort that I am feeling (actual A)
- Feeling anxious (inferential A)
- The group will disapprove of me if I refuse to disclose my secret when asked (inferential A)
- Not knowing if I will be chosen or not (actual A)
- You are abusing your position as a workshop leader (inferential A)
- Remembering what I did when I was 12, which represented me falling far short of my ideal (inferential A).

Now the situation or *situational A* here is as follows: Windy Dryden asks workshop participants to think of a secret. He then tells them that he will walk about the room pointing his finger and that when he stops whoever he is pointing at will tell the group their secret. He then walks round the room pointing his finger at people, but then stops the exercise and asks people what their feelings were during the exercise.

Let's suppose that Anthea, one of the workshop participants, said that she was anxious about not knowing whether or not I would choose her to reveal her secret. 'Not knowing whether or not I would be chosen' would be her *critical actual A* since the state of not knowing this is a descriptive, factual aspect of the situation. For Anthea the *non-critical actual As* would include the other actual As listed above, all of which are specific and descriptive.

Now, let's suppose that Phil, another of the workshop participants, said that he was anxious about the group disapproving of him if he disclosed his secret. 'The group disapproving of me if I disclosed my secret' would be his *critical inferential A* and the *non-critical inferential As* would include the other inferential As listed above, whereas, if Rosie, yet another workshop participant, were angry about my abusing my position as a workshop leader then this would be her *critical inferential A* and the group disapproving of me if I disclosed my secret would be one of the possible *non-critical inferential As*.

Now if we hold a set of rational beliefs (rB) about a negative actual aspect (CrAA) of a situation (SA) we will experience a set of healthy negative emotions (hne), constructive thoughts (ct) and productive behaviours (pb) at C. This can be shown in the following relation:

$$SA \rightarrow CrAA \times rB \rightarrow C \ (hne + ct + pb)$$

And if we hold a set of irrational beliefs about this same aspect we will experience a set of unhealthy negative emotions (une), biased thoughts (bt) and detrimental behaviours (db) at C. This can be shown as follows:

$$SA \rightarrow CrAA \times iB \rightarrow C \ (une + bt + db)$$

The following two relations show similar information where the critical aspect of the situational A is inferential and negative rather than actual and negative. The first demonstrates that if we hold a set of rational beliefs about this critical inferential aspect of the situational A we will experience a set of healthy negative emotions (hne), constructive thoughts (ct) and productive behaviours (pb):

$$SA \rightarrow CrIA \times rB \rightarrow C \ (hne + ct + pb)$$

And if we hold a set of irrational beliefs about this same aspect we will experience a set of unhealthy emotions (une), biased thoughts (bt) and detrimental behaviours (db) at C. This can be shown as follows:

$$SA \rightarrow CrIA \times iB \rightarrow C \ (une + bt + db)$$

What is B?

As is well known in REBT and as discussed above, beliefs in REBT are deemed to be rational or irrational. In this section, I will discuss rational beliefs first and then consider irrational beliefs.

Rational beliefs

Rational beliefs have four characteristics. They are:

1. flexible and/or non-extreme,
2. consistent with reality,
3. logical or sensible, and
4. largely constructive to the person.

There are four types of rational beliefs:

- full preferences (FPREF),
- non-awfulizing beliefs (Non-AWF),
- high frustration tolerance beliefs (HFT), and
- acceptance beliefs (ACC).

Full preferences (FPREF)

Ellis's position is that full preferences are at the very core of healthy responses to adversities at A (e.g. Ellis, 1994). A full preference has two components. The first asserts what the person wants (or does not want) and the second negates the idea that the person has to get what they want (or must not get what they do not want). In this way a full preference is flexible. Here are a few examples of full preferences with spaces between the two components to highlight them.

> 'I would like to pass my driving test . . . but that doesn't mean that I have to do so.'

> 'I want you to treat me fairly . . . but you don't absolutely have to do so.'

> 'It would be really nice if my house did not have subsidence . . . but regretfully it does not have to be subsidence-free.'

Ellis (1994) argues that the three other rational beliefs tend to stem from full preferences, although he does recognize that at times full preferences may stem from one or more of the other rational beliefs. In this discussion I will confine myself to the former position.

Non-awfulizing beliefs (Non-AWF)

A non-awfulizing belief has two components. The first asserts that it is bad in some way that the negative event at A has occurred and the second negates the idea that what is bad is awful or the end of the world. In this way, a non-awfulizing belief is non-extreme.

Here are a few examples of anti-awfulizing beliefs again with spaces between the two components to highlight them.

> 'It would be bad if I did not pass my driving test . . . but it wouldn't be awful.'

> 'It would be very unfortunate if you did not treat me fairly . . . but it wouldn't be the end of the world.'

> 'It would be really inconvenient if my house did have subsidence . . . but it would not be terrible if it did.'

High frustration tolerance beliefs (HFT)

A high frustration tolerance belief has three components. The first asserts that it would be hard to tolerate the negative event at A, the second negates the idea that what is hard to tolerate is intolerable while the third asserts that it is worth it to the individual to tolerate the situation (if indeed it is). In this way, a high frustration tolerance belief is non-extreme.

Here are a few examples of high frustration tolerance beliefs, again with spaces between the components to highlight them.

> 'Not passing my driving test would be hard to bear . . . but I could bear it . . . and it would be worth it to me to bear this.'

> 'If you do not treat me fairly I would struggle to put up with it . . . but I could do so . . . and it would be worth it for me to do because it would help me to think about how to assert myself with you.' (Note that this example shows that a high frustration tolerance belief facilitates constructive action and does not lead to your passively resigning yourself to a situation, as many think it does.)

> 'I would be hard-pressed to put up with my house having subsidence . . . but if it did, I could put up with it . . . and it would be advantageous for me to do so because then I would be patient enough to choose the best company to do the underpinning works.'

Acceptance beliefs (ACC)

An acceptance belief can relate to the self (S-ACC), another person (O-ACC) or life conditions (L-ACC). Taking a self-acceptance belief as an example, we can see that an acceptance belief has three components: an evaluation of an aspect of self or of something that has happened to one, a negation of the idea that the self can be globally rated and an assertion of the idea that the self is fallible, complex and unrateable.

Here are a few examples of acceptance beliefs, once again with spaces between the three components to highlight them.

> 'Not passing my driving test would be bad . . . but it wouldn't prove that I was a failure . . . Rather, it would prove that I was a fallible human being who failed on this occasion.'

> 'If you do not treat me fairly that would be very bad of you . . . but it wouldn't prove that you were a bad person . . . It would prove that you were a complex human being capable of acting well and badly who on this occasion acted badly.'

> 'My house having subsidence would be bad . . . but if it did, it would not prove that the world was a rotten place . . . Rather it would prove that the world was a very complex place where good and bad things happen to people and on this occasion something very bad has happened to me.'

Irrational beliefs

Irrational beliefs also have four characteristics. They are:

1.   Rigid and/or extreme,
2.   Inconsistent with reality,
3.   Illogical or not sensible, and
4.   Largely detrimental to the person.

There are four types of irrational beliefs:

- Demands (DEM),
- Awfulizing beliefs (AWF),
- Low frustration tolerance beliefs (LFT), and
- Depreciation beliefs (DEP).

Demands (DEM)

Ellis's position is that demands are at the very core of unhealthy responses to adversities at A (e.g. Ellis, 1994). A demand is a rigid belief where the person dogmatically insists that certain conditions must or must not exist. Demands can concern oneself, others and the world/life conditions. They are most often based on partial preferences which the person transforms into demands. Here are a few examples of demands. I will present each example twice: once where the partial preference is transformed into a demand (here, I will provide spaces between the two components to highlight them) and the other where only the demand is stated (in italics).

> 'I would like to pass my driving test . . . and therefore I have to do so.'
> *'I must pass my driving test.'*

> 'I want you to treat me fairly . . . and therefore you absolutely have to do so.'
> *'You must treat me fairly.'*

> 'It would be really nice if my house did not have subsidence . . . and hence it absolutely must be subsidence-free.'
> *'My house must not have subsidence.'*

Ellis argues that the other three irrational beliefs tend to stem from demands, although once again he does recognize that at times demands may themselves stem from one or more of these other irrational beliefs. In this discussion, I will again confine myself to the former position.

Awfulizing beliefs (AWF)

An awfulizing belief is an extreme belief that has one or more of the following meanings:

(i)   100% bad or 'nothing can be worse'
(ii) Worse than 100% bad
(iii) No good can possibly come from this situation.

An awfulizing belief tends to stem from the demand 'It must not be as bad as it is' and has two components. The first asserts that it is bad in some way that the negative event at A has occurred. This is known as the partial non-awfulizing belief. The second transforms this idea and asserts the idea that what is bad is awful or the end of the world. In this way, an awfulizing belief is extreme.

Here are a few examples of awfulizing beliefs. I will present each example twice: once where the partial non-awfulizing belief is transformed into an awfulizing belief (here, I will provide spaces between the two components to highlight them) and the other where only the awfulizing belief is stated (in italics).

> 'It would be bad if I did not pass my driving test . . . and therefore it would be awful.'
> *'It would be awful to fail my driving test.'*
>
> 'It would be very unfortunate if you did not treat me fairly . . . and thus it would be the end of the world.'
> *'It would be the end of the world if you treated me unfairly.'*
>
> 'It would be really inconvenient if my house did have subsidence . . . and thus it would be terrible if it did.'
> *'It would be terrible if my house had subsidence.'*

Low frustration tolerance beliefs (LFT)

A low frustration tolerance (LFT) belief asserts that the negative event at A cannot be tolerated and is therefore extreme.

An LFT belief tends to stem from the demand 'This frustration absolutely must not exist' and has two components. The first asserts that it is difficult to tolerate the frustration and is known as the partial high frustration tolerance belief. The second transforms this idea and asserts the idea that what is difficult to bear is unbearable. In this way, a low frustration tolerance belief is extreme.

Here are a few examples of LFT beliefs. I will again present each example twice: once where the partial HFT belief is transformed into an LFT belief (here, I will provide spaces between the two components to highlight them) and the other where only the LFT belief is stated (in italics).

> 'Not passing my driving test would be hard to bear . . . and therefore it would be unbearable.'
> *'Not passing my driving test would be intolerable.'*

> 'If you do not treat me fairly I would struggle to put up with it . . . and I couldn't do so.'
> *'If you do not treat me fairly I couldn't put up with it.'*

> 'I would be hard-pressed to put up with my house having subsidence . . . and, in fact, I couldn't put up with it.'
> *'If my house had subsidence, I couldn't put up with it.'*

Depreciation beliefs (DEP)

A depreciation belief can relate to the self (S-DEP), another person (O-DEP) or life conditions (L-DEP). A depreciation belief tends to stem from the following demand: 'I, you or life must conform to my desires'. Taking a self-depreciation belief as an example, we can see that a depreciation belief has two components: an evaluation of an aspect of self or of something that has happened to one (part evaluation) and a global evaluation of the self (whole evaluation).

Here are a few examples of depreciation beliefs. Once again, I will present each example twice: once where the part evaluation is transformed into a depreciation belief (here, I will again provide spaces between the two components to highlight them) and the other where only the depreciation belief is stated (in italics).

> 'Not passing my driving test would be a failing . . . and would prove that I am a failure.'
> *'I would be a failure for failing my driving test.'*

> 'If you do not treat me fairly that would be very bad of you . . . and would prove that you are a bad person.'
> *'You would be a bad person for treating me unfairly.'*

> 'My house having subsidence would be bad . . . and if it did, it would prove that the world is a rotten place.'
> *'The world is a rotten place for allowing my house to subside.'*

Negative emotions: healthy v. unhealthy

As I have already discussed, REBT distinguishes between rational and irrational beliefs. Actually, when a person faces a negative activating event, they have a choice among three rather different types of beliefs: rational beliefs, irrational beliefs and indifference beliefs. An indifference belief is where a person does not care one way or the other about the occurrence of an event. Thus, many of you would not care if Albion Rovers beat Queen's Park at football the next time they met in the Scottish third division. Your stance would be one of indifference to the outcome of this event. Now, indifference beliefs can be true or feigned. Your indifference towards the outcome of the Albion Rovers v. Queen's Park football match would probably truly reflect your attitude. However, if you demanded that you had to obtain promotion at work and you failed to do so, any attempt on your part to convince yourself and other people that you didn't care about your failure would constitute a feigned indifference belief in that you would be trying to lie to yourself. Feigned indifference beliefs are conceptualized in REBT theory as ultimately unconstructive attempts to deal with the underlying presence of irrational beliefs.

If we therefore rule out indifference beliefs as a plausible way of responding to a negative activating event, we are left with a choice of holding a rational belief or an irrational belief towards this event. REBT theory states that in the face of negative events you have a choice of feeling bad, but undisturbed, about this event or of feeling bad and disturbed about it. Thus, when you hold a rational belief about a negative event you will experience a healthy negative emotion and when you hold an irrational belief about this same event you will experience an unhealthy negative emotion.

In the English language we do not have words that reliably and consensually discriminate between healthy negative emotions and unhealthy negative emotions, so the following list should be viewed as one person's attempt (i.e. mine) to discriminate linguistically between these different emotions. I see the following emotions as unhealthy and negative: anxiety, depression, guilt, shame, hurt, unhealthy anger, unhealthy jealousy and unhealthy envy. By contrast, I see the following emotions as their healthy and negative alternatives: concern, sadness, remorse, disappointment, sorrow, healthy anger, healthy jealousy and healthy envy.

It is often assumed that unhealthy negative emotions are of greater intensity than healthy negative emotions. This may be true, but only at the very intense end of the continuum. For example, intense rage (unhealthy anger) is probably stronger than intense annoyance (healthy anger). However, the point here is that healthy anger can be intense. Therefore, it is psychologically healthy to experience strong healthy negative emotions whenever you face a negative event where one of your more important desires has not been met. This is such an important point that I am going to emphasize it and expand on it.

Whenever something negative happens that means that one of your more important desires has not been met – it is not healthy to have an attitude of indifference towards it and feel nothing. It is also not healthy to hold an irrational belief about it and feel an unhealthy negative emotion. The only healthy option is to hold a rational belief about the event and experience a healthy negative emotion. The greater the importance of your thwarted desire the more intense will be your healthy negative emotion.

With respect to the issue of the intensity of a healthy negative emotion, I have already made the point that an intense healthy negative emotion is healthy by dint of its healthiness. Remember that what determines the healthiness of a negative emotion is the rationality of the belief that underpins it. A major goal of REBT is to help people to feel healthily bad when they do not get their important desires met. Again, let me stress that the more important the thwarted desire is to the person, the more intense the healthy negative emotion will be. Thus, when a person comes to me for therapy because they are experiencing an unhealthy negative emotion about a thwarted desire that is very important to them, I will help that person to feel an appropriate strong healthy negative emotion instead. I will do so by helping that person to give up their irrational belief and hold a rational belief about having their important desire thwarted instead. I will not attempt to help the person by encouraging them to make their desire less important.

Ego v. non-ego disturbance, and their healthy alternatives

REBT theory distinguishes between ego disturbance and non-ego disturbance (e.g. Dryden, 2000). In ego disturbance the person is disturbing himself about himself. While the person may hold all four irrational beliefs listed above, the person's main irrational beliefs are his demands and his self-depreciation beliefs. In non-ego disturbance, the person is disturbing himself about aspects of his phenomenological world that does not impinge on his view of himself. Here the person holds a demand, an awfulizing belief and an LFT belief. Usually in a given instance of non-ego demand the person's main beliefs are a demand and an awfulizing belief or a demand and an LFT belief.

If such a person experiences ego disturbance in a context in which they focused on a negative critical inferential A, for example, it will be very likely that they will experience a set of unhealthy negative emotions, biased thoughts and detrimental behaviours as a result of holding a demand and self-depreciation belief. This can be shown in the following relation:

$$SA \rightarrow CrIA \times iB (DEM + S\text{-}DEP) \rightarrow C (une + bt + db)$$

If the client held a full preference and a self-acceptance belief instead, they would be in a state of ego health which would be manifest in a set of healthy emotions, constructive thoughts and productive behaviours. This can be shown as follows:

$$SA \rightarrow CrIA \times rB \text{ (FPREF + S-ACC)} \rightarrow C \text{ (hne + ct + pb)}$$

If a person experiences non-ego disturbance in a context in which they focused on a negative critical inferential A, for example, it will be very likely that they will experience a set of unhealthy negative emotions, biased thoughts and detrimental behaviours as a result of holding a demand and an awfulizing belief or as a result of holding a demand and an LFT belief. This can be shown in the following two relations:

$$SA \rightarrow CrIA \times iB \text{ (DEM + AWF)} \rightarrow C \text{ (une + bt + db)}$$

$$SA \rightarrow CrIA \times iB \text{ (DEM + LFT)} \rightarrow C \text{ (une + bt + db)}$$

If the client held a full preference and either a non-awfulizing belief or an HFT belief instead, they would be in a state of non-ego health which would be manifest in a set of healthy emotions, constructive thoughts and productive behaviours. This can be shown in the following two relations:

$$SA \rightarrow CrIA \times rB \text{ (FPREF + Non-AWF)} \rightarrow C \text{ (hne + ct + pb)}$$

$$SA \rightarrow CrIA \times rB \text{ (FPREF + HFT)} \rightarrow C \text{ (hne + ct + pb)}$$

REBT theory outlines a number of issues that relate to the ABC model. A number of these issues will be covered by other contributors to this volume. In the remaining sections in this introductory chapter, I will discuss the following three issues: why inferential As become critical, the fact that people can create psychological problems about their psychological problems, and the principle of psychological interactionsim.

Why does an inferential A become critical?

Earlier in this chapter, I mentioned that people most frequently disturb themselves in situations about specific inferences that they make about these situations. When these inferences activate irrational beliefs that account for these disturbed feelings they are known as critical inferential As. But what determines which inferential A of the number that could be made become critical for a person? There are a number of such determining factors at work here, but perhaps the most important are core irrational beliefs.

A core irrational belief is a general irrational belief that the person holds in a number of relevant, personally meaningful situations that accounts for the person's disturbed feelings *across* these situations. A specific irrational belief is often (but not always) a specific example of a core irrational belief and accounts for the person's disturbed feelings *in* a specific situation. For example, Betty holds the following core irrational belief: 'People in authority must not criticize me and if they do it proves that I am stupid'. She is also depressed in a specific situation because she holds the following specific irrational belief: 'My boss absolutely should not have criticized me in the meeting today and I am stupid because he did'. Note that in this specific situation Betty's critical inferential A was 'my boss criticized my work'. What is the relationship between Betty's core irrational belief and her specific critical inferential A?

What I think is going on here is as follows. Betty brings her core irrational belief about being criticized to situations where there is a chance that she may be criticized. Her core irrational belief leads her to focus on this negative inference about her situational A to the exclusion of other possible inferences that could be made about the situation. In this way, her core irrational belief leads to biased thinking (this time about the A) in the same way as a specific irrational belief leads to biased thinking (at C). Once Betty infers critically that she will be or has been criticized, this negative critical inferential A activates her specific irrational belief about being criticized by her boss in the specific situation under consideration. This is demonstrated in the following formula where CiB is a core irrational belief and SiB is a specific irrational belief:

CiB (DEM + S-DEP) → SA → [bt] → CrIA × SiB (DEM + S-DEP) → C (une + bt + db)

Meta-psychological problems

One of the aspects of psychological disturbance that REBT theory highlights is our ability as humans to disturb ourselves about our disturbances. These disturbances are known as meta-psychological problems (literally psychological problems about psychological problems). You will recall that REBT theory states that when a person disturbs themself about a negative critical A, for example, by holding an irrational belief (at B) about this A, then that person experiences three consequences at C – unhealthy negative emotions [C(une)], biased thinking [C(bt)] and detrimental behaviours [C(db)]. When the person then focuses on one of these consequences at C (for example, an unhealthy negative emotion), this C becomes a new A about which the person can disturb themself either about the actual nature of this emotion or about an inferential aspect of the emotion. This process also occurs where the C is a cognition or a behavioural act.

To illustrate this, let's suppose that Eric has made himself anxious (ego anxiety) about the possibility of being rejected by a woman he has planned to ask for a date. He also had attendant biased negative thinking and indecisive behaviour. As before, this can be shown symbolically. Before I present this, I want to make an important point. To distinguish between the psychological problem and the meta-psychological problem in any equation, I will use '1' to denote an A, B and C in the psychological problem and '2' to denote an A, B and C in the meta-psychological problem. Now here is Eric's formula:

$$SA \rightarrow CrIA1 \times SiB1 \ (DEM + S\text{-}DEP) \rightarrow C1 \ (une + bt + db)$$

Let me now consider three examples of different meta-psychological problems that Eric could have. I will present these examples both narratively and symbolically.

1. Eric focuses on his anxious feelings (CrAA2), makes himself feel anxious (non-ego) about them [C2 (une)], thinks that they will increase unless he gets rid of them immediately [C2 (bt)] and has the urge to run away [C2 (db)] from the situation.

    $$SA \rightarrow CrIA1 \times SiB1 \ (DEM + S\text{-}DEP) \rightarrow C1 \ (une + bt + db)$$

    $$CrAA2 \times SiB2 \ (DEM + LFT) \rightarrow C2 \ (une + bt + db)$$

2. Eric focuses on his biased thinking and infers that these thoughts are weird (CrIA2), makes himself feel ashamed about these 'weird' thoughts [C2 (une)], thinks that others in the situation will somehow discover that his thoughts are weird [C2 (bt)], and avoids looking at them [C2 (db)].

    $$SA \rightarrow CrIA1 \times SiB1 \ (DEM + S\text{-}DEP) \rightarrow C1 \ (une + bt + db)$$

    $$CrIA2 \times SiB2 \ (DEM + S\text{-}DEP) \rightarrow C2 \ (une + bt + db)$$

3. Eric focuses on his indecisive behaviour (CrAA2) and feels unhealthily angry with himself for not being more decisive [C2 (une)]. These feelings are accompanied by images [C2 (bt)] and urges [C2 (db)] focused on self-harm.

    $$SA \rightarrow CrIA1 \times SiB1 \ (DEM + S\text{-}DEP) \rightarrow C1 \ (une + bt + db)$$

    $$CrAA2 \times SiB2 \ (DEM + S\text{-}DEP) \rightarrow C2 \ (une + bt + db)$$

Psychological interactionism

Up to now, you may have formed the impression that As, Bs and Cs are separate psychological factors. This is definitely not the case, and REBT theory adheres to the principle of psychological interactionism and has done so from its very inception (Ellis, 1958). This principle holds that inferences, beliefs, emotions and behaviours are interdependent processes and are intrinsically bound up with one another. Thus, in REBT theory we cannot accurately speak of beliefs, emotions and behaviours, for example, as if they are separate processes. Rather, we should more accurately speak of beliefs–emotions–behaviours although to do so consistently would make the language of REBT theory quite unwieldy. Thus, when REBT theorists and therapists write about irrational beliefs, for example, it is important to appreciate that they are implicitly referring to the emotions, inferences and behaviours that tend to be associated with these beliefs. In addition, REBT theory argues that the beliefs that one holds, the emotions that one feels and the behaviours that one enacts not only have an influence over the inferences that one makes about the situations (or situational As) that one faces, but also have an impact on what situations one encounters.

Let me illustrate this latter point. Imagine that George believes that his work must not be criticized and if it is it proves that he is an incompetent person. This irrational belief leads George to overestimate the likelihood that his work would be criticized by others and thus to prevent this from happening he does not show others his work and does not ask for help with any work problems. It leads him to play safe in his work and not volunteer for more interesting projects that could possibly advance his career, but that would increase the chances that he might make mistakes. George would thus create an environment where he would only do work that he was good at, but ultimately finds boring. He also creates an environment where he does not advance his career, has a modest salary and thus has less money to spend on family luxuries like holidays. His irrational belief would also lead him to stay quiet at meetings because he is scared of saying anything that could be viewed as incompetence. As a result, others involve him less and less in these meetings.

I hope you can see from the above how influential an irrational belief can be, not only on how one views the world inferentially or on the emotions that one experiences or even on one's behaviour. I hope you can also see how an irrational belief can influence the situations that one faces by orienting a person towards and away from situations and by influencing how others behave towards one.

Recently, Ellis (e.g. 2001) has argued that it is wrong even to refer to the interdependent 'belief–emotion–behaviour' because these nouns imply that beliefs, emotions and behaviours are static 'things' rather than dynamic processes. Given this, he suggests using verbs rather than nouns (e.g. 'believing–emoting–behaving' rather than 'belief–emotion–behaviour) to reflect the ongoingness and in-flux nature of these processes. It is beyond the scope of this introductory chapter to consider this important new development in depth. I mention it to demonstrate the dynamic-process nature of REBT theory which is continually being refined as evidenced in the chapters that follow.

References

Dryden, W. (2000) *Invitation to Rational Emotive Behvioural Psychology*. London: Whurr.

Dryden, W., Gordon, J. and Neenan, M. (1997) *What Is Rational Emotive Behaviour Therapy? A Personal and Practical Guide*. Loughton, Essex: Gale Centre Publications.

Ellis, A. (1958) Rational psychotherapy, *Journal of General Psychology*, *59*, 35–49.

Ellis, A. (1994) *Reason and Emotion in Psychotherapy* (revised and expanded edn). New York: Birch Lane Press.

Ellis, A. (2001) *Feeling Better, Getting Better, Staying Better: Profound Self-help Therapy for Your Emotions*. Atascadero, CA: Impact.

Chapter 2

Differentiating preferential from exaggerated and musturbatory beliefs in Rational Emotive Behavior Therapy

Albert Ellis

The basic theory of Rational Emotive Behavior Therapy (REBT) holds that people have strong biological and social tendencies to constructively help themselves and also to needlessly defeat themselves (Ellis, 1962, 1976, 1994, 2001a, 2001b). I partly derived this theory from my experiences as a psychotherapist since 1943, and from the writings of scientists and thinkers, including Cudney and Hardy (1991), Eysenck (1967), FitzMaurice (2000), Frazer (1959), Hoffer (1951), Horney (1950), Kahneman et al. (1982), Nisbett and Ross (1980), Piatelli-Palmarini (1994), Rokeach (1960), Seligman (1991), and Watzlawick (1978). I especially learned, from reading Korzybski (1991), that all humans easily render themselves 'unsane', have real difficulty seeing how they do this, and then have trouble making themselves saner and less self-defeating. But, as I have long claimed, they *can* constructively do so by working to change their dysfunctional thinking, feeling, and behaving to more constructive and 'rational' functioning.

Since 1955, I have noted that practically all people *easily* and *naturally* raise their healthy and self-helping desires and preferences into an unhealthy and self-defeating 'tyrrany of the shoulds' (Horney, 1950) and I have shown that they do so in three main ways. First, they insist they that they should perform well, or are worthless individuals. Second, they demand that other people must treat them nicely, or else these people are damnable. Third, they insist that living conditions have to be free from serious hassles, or else they can't be happy *at all*.

In the present chapter, I shall try to show that some of the reasons why they do this is because it is biologically and socially difficult for them to consistently discriminate among four positions:

1. Preferential desires and consequences of their not being met. 'I preferably should perform well at tasks that I and many members of my social group consider important because if I do not do so, I probably will get poor results and be disapproved of by a good many other people.'

2. Preferential desires and exaggerated results of their not being met. 'I preferably should do well at tasks that I and many members of my social group consider important because if I don't, I will get exceptionally bad results and be immensely disapproved by almost all other people.'
3. Musturbatory desires or demands that one's desires absolutely must be met and exaggerated consequences of their not being met. 'I absolutely must do well at projects that I and many members of my social group consider important, because if I don't do as well as I must, I am an incompetent, unlovable person who will always fail and get rejected and who can't be happy at all!'
4. Musturbatory and perfectionistic desires and exaggerated consequences of their not being met. 'I must at least do outstandingly and even perfectly well at tasks that I and many other members of my social group consider important, or else I am an incompetent, unlovable person who will always fail and get rejected and who can't be happy at all!'

If you hold the first of these beliefs about succeeding at important tasks and being accepted by others, that is fairly rational and self-helping because it will usually, in your social group, help you to achieve more desirable results – for example, money, approval, and accomplishment. But not always! For, succeeding at important tasks may result in some people disliking you, and getting people to like you may interfere with some of your performances. You can't win and be approved all the time! But this kind of preferential behavior works pretty well.

If you hold the second belief, you will find it partly accurate, but it also exaggerates the results of your performing badly. Good performances will not get you all the things you want; and sometimes bad performances, while not leading to disaster, may get you some real benefits. However, your exaggerations in this belief may well lead to unrealistic expectations of pleasure and pain, and therefore create needless dangers.

The third belief, as REBT points out, is quite unrealistic because, if you have it, you are certain you always must succeed and be approved by others and that if you fail you will be completely inept forever and will never be approved. Then, out of self-created panic, you will probably perform below your ability and often lose social approval. This belief just won't work. But it overlaps with the first two beliefs because if you could always do well, you would most likely benefit considerably. So it unrealistically may keep you trying – and thereby often succeeding.

The fourth belief is even more unrealistic – since your always doing perfectly well, no matter how competent you basically are, is impossible. You, like all humans, are quite fallible. Too bad! But this belief, again, has *some* truth in it, because if you could be perfectly competent, that would have distinct advantages. The problem, then, is for you to keep a rational and preferential belief, to not exaggerate the grim results of your not achieving your desires, to refuse to make them into absolutistic musts, and to stop yourself from raising them into a perfectionistic demand.

Now this would seem to be relatively simple – especially for those people who learn and practice REBT. Alas, it isn't. Even when they temporarily learn to do so, they often fall back to beliefs 2, 3 and 4. When left to their own devices, they frequently invent or create beliefs 2, 3 and 4 – and then have a hell of a hard time giving them up. Why?

The answer to this question is complicated and still in doubt. All I can say – or guess – at present, is that the following reasons for millions of people's commonly holding self-defeating beliefs 2, 3 and 4 seem to be prevalent.

The three irrational or self-defeating beliefs, as I have stated, importantly overlap with the rational beliefs that people also hold. Therefore, they have to be clearly differentiated from their more functional preferences. But this differentiation, because of the overlapping, has to be worked at.

The dysfunctional beliefs all have some practical sense to them – that is, they sometimes work out. Therefore, you may be temporarily turned to have any or all of them. Thus, take Belief 2, 'I preferably should do well at tasks that I consider important because if I don't I will get exceptionally bad results, and be immensely disapproved by all other people'. No, not necessarily *exceptionally* bad results, but *somewhat* bad ones. No, not *immensely* disapproved by all other people, but *somewhat* disapproved by some of them.

How about Belief 3: 'I absolutely must do well at projects that I and members of my social group consider important, because if I don't do as well as I must, I am an incompetent, unlovable person who can't be happy at all!'? No, I would then be somewhat incompetent, would frequently fail, would often get rejected, but could still be somewhat happy even if I do fail and get rejected.

How about Belief 4: 'I must at least do outstandingly well and do even perfectly well at tasks that I and members of my social group consider important, or else I am an incompetent, unlovable person who can't be happy at all!'? No, I easily could fail to succeed outstandingly well and certainly could fail to do perfectly well at important tasks, but I again would not be totally incompetent and unlovable, could sometimes succeed, would not always be rejected by others, and could often still be *somewhat* happy.

To discriminate among these four overlapping beliefs requires careful thought and experimental practice. You may not be sharp enough to make such discriminations. Or you may have the ability to do so, but your low frustration tolerance and desire for short-range gains may stop you from implementing your ability.

Beliefs 3 and 4 are unrealistic and grandiose, in that they imply that ordinary members of the human race – including you! – *can* perform well at all times and under all conditions. Belief 4 implies that you can be supernatural and perform perfectly well. How ego-raising to believe that crap! But quite tempting.

You, like other people, talk to yourself and to others in language that is often impressionistic and vague – unlike mathematical language. Therefore, you often confuse *some* with *all*, *sometimes* with *always*, and so forth. As Korzybski said, humans are often too general and unspecific – and therefore they easily *over*generalize.

Again, as Korzybski noted, generalization and abstraction are very useful; but overgeneralization, which often seems to be the human condition, leads you astray.

For the above – and, I am sure, even more – reasons, people's difficulty in distinguishing their exaggerated, musturbatory, and perfectionistic beliefs from their more rational ones, leads to all kinds of individual and social difficulties. Here are some of the typical life issues that they importantly effect:

- Achievement beliefs about preferential desires and moderate consequences of their being met. 'It is distinctly preferable for me to succeed at projects that I and my social group consider important.'
- Belief about preferential desires and exaggerated results of their not being met. 'I preferably had better succeed at these projects or I will get exceptionally dire and crippling results.'
- Belief about musturbatory desires and exaggerated consequences of their not being met. 'I must always succeed at these projects or I will continually fail at them and prove myself to be an incompetent, worthless person!'
- Belief about musturbatory desires and exaggerated consequences of their not being met. 'I must succeed perfectly at these projects or else I will completely fail at them and prove myself to be an incompetent, worthless person!'

Beliefs that commonly lead to discomfort disturbance

- Rational or preferential belief: 'It is distinctly preferable for me to succeed at projects that I and my social group consider important or else I will be definitely uncomfortable.'
- Exaggerated belief: 'I had better succeed at these important projects or else I will be exceptionally uncomfortable and miserable.'
- Musturbatory belief: 'I must always succeed at these important projects or else my life will be horrible and absolutely pleasureless!'

- Perfectionistic belief: 'I must always succeed perfectly at these important projects or else my life will be horrible and absolutely pleasureless!'

Beliefs that commonly lead to lack of self-acceptance or conditional self-acceptance

- Rational or preferential belief: 'I distinctly prefer and am determined to work at unconditionally accepting myself, whether or not I perform well at important tasks and whether or not other people approve of me. I will acknowledge and criticize my failings and poor behaviors but I will not damn myself as a person for having them.'
- Exaggerated belief: 'I distinctly prefer to do well and be approved by others, but if I do very *poorly* I get *exceptionally* disappointed, I cannot really accept myself and deserve to be damned by others.'
- Musturbatory belief: 'Since I am responsible for my failings and poor behaviors, as I must not be, I will decidedly damn myself for engaging in them, and will consider myself to be a rotten, incompetant person.'
- Perfectionistic belief: 'Since I am responsible for my failings and my poor behaviors, I absolutely must act perfectly well at all times, or else I will decidedly damn myself and will acknowledge that I am a rotten, incompetent person.'

Beliefs that commonly lead to disturbance about disturbance

- Rational or preferential belief: 'If I make myself disturbed by thinking, feeling, and behaving dysfunctionally when I have a choice not to do so, I can feel healthily disappointed and regretful about disturbing myself when I only wish and prefer that I do so and do not insist that I absolutely must not disturb myself and am an incompetent person for doing so.'
- Exaggerated belief: 'I distinctly prefer that I do not disturb myself about my disturbances but if I foolishly do so really awful things will happen to me and I will disturb myself forever!'
- Musturbatory belief: 'Since I am responsible for creating my disturbance, and I absolutely should not and must not create it, if I do, I am an incompetent person who will always keep disturbing myself.'
- Perfectionistic belief: 'Since I am responsible for creating my disturbance, and create such havoc by doing so, I should never under any circumstances do so, and should be perfectly undisturbable. Or else I am an incompetent, hopeless person.'

If what I have just said is largely correct, people – and particularly clients – had better learn to discriminate their preferential beliefs from their preferential desires and exaggerated beliefs about the consequences of their not fulfilling these desires, as well as from their musturbatory and their musturbatory/perfectionistic beliefs – and then, of course, learn to keep the former and reduce or eliminate the latter. More of this later.

First, let me highlight some other important ways that are common in people's failing to discriminate between effective and self-sabotaging modes of thinking and living. In fact, I find them to be almost ubiquitous. Let me describe a few important – as well as common – lapses in this respect.

- People fail to discriminate between their healthy negative feelings (C) and their unhealthy negative feelings when unfortunate adversities (As) occur in their lives. They do not see that feelings of sorrow, regret, frustration, and annoyance at adversities are distinctly different from feelings of panic, depression, and rage at similar As.
- Similarly, people refuse to discriminate between their dysfunctional and often compulsive behaviors (such as addictions) at point C and their light indulgences in harmful habits like overeating, smoking, drinking, and procrastinating.
- They fail to see that their acknowledging self-destructive behaviors and the thoughts and feelings that go with them is far removed from working hard at changing these behaviors. In fact, acknowledging their destructive behaviors by itself without their giving up their demands that they *must* not be destructive may lead to self-deprecation that blocks people's hope for change.
- People focus so mightily on gratifying themselves with their harmful addictions that they leave no room for focusing on the disadvantages of these compulsions.
- They concentrate so strongly on some of their personal pleasures that they forget about the harm that these may do to their social group. Or, they concentrate so much on pleasing others that they sadly neglect their personal desires and goals.
- People focus so obsessively on their thinking, feeling, and behaving that they fail to see the important interactions among these three main human processes.
- They worry obsessively about the possibility of even slight dangers, instead of taking practical precautions against them; and, doing so, they frequently create more dangers.
- They persist in projects and relationships that they very much want and often refuse to see that they're putting themselves in no-win situations and will most probably never achieve a particular goal that they desire.
- They see the worst things that could occur if they take risks and ignore the pleasures of achieving – or even the challenge of striving for achievement.
- People view words as hurtful – and thereby make themselves exceptionally hurt.

- They fail to discriminate between trying too hard to get what they want and their trying too little. They are impatient or too patient.
- They are often too gullible – and sometimes too skeptical.

As you can see, this list of people failing to discriminate between effective and ineffective behaviors could go on and on. Again, why is *accurate* discrimination so difficult for many people to make? For the reasons listed above and several more that can be added:

- If people discriminate clearly between their 'good' and 'bad' behaviors, they might have to admit their errors – and then damn themselves for these errors. As I noted above, this encourages another lack of clear discrimination!
- People are frequently wish-fulfilling – and thereby deluded and undiscriminating.
- They think that they absolutely *can't stand* looking at the facts – especially if they see them as 'grim'.
- If people more often acknowledge and find 'bad' or 'uncomfortable' incidents, they easily awfulize about them, make them even worse than they are, and therefore avoid facing them.

These reasons, as you would suspect from following REBT, amount to two main ones: First, people put themselves rather their behavior down for doing poorly – and for failing to discriminate amongst their poor behaviors. Second, they have low frustration tolerance (LFT) about taking the effort and trouble to discriminate and, on a secondary level, LFT about the painful emotions they might experience if they indeed faced their delinquency about discriminating. According to REBT, they often avoid recognizing their errors because, if they did recognize them, they would denigrate themselves and motivate themselves to take 'needless' trouble. So they take an 'easy' way out!

If I am reasonably accurate about what I have said so far, what can be done to help clients (and other people) to clearly discriminate among their preferential, exaggerated, musturbatory, and perfectionistic beliefs that they easily construct and have difficulty deconstructing? Here are some REBT-oriented suggestions that therapists can use to help their clients minimize their self-sabotaging neglect.

1. Distinguish between three of the main forms of self-defeating beliefs or irrational thinking: (a) exaggerating negative consequences of adversities; (b) demanding that adversities absolutely must not exist; (c) perfectionistically demanding that if adversities do exist, they must deal with them perfectly and completely solve them.

2. Show clients how common are these dysfunctional thoughts and how they are powerfully and 'normally' abetted by human biology and social learning.
3. Help clients fully acknowledge their creating their dysfunctional philosophies as well as their strong tendencies to fail to distinguish among them and deal effectively with them.
4. Help clients to unconditionally accept themselves (and other people) with their destructive thinking, feeling, and behaving – to accept the sinners while acting to minimize their sins.
5. Help clients work on their low frustration tolerance by taking the trouble to look for, to find, and to dispute their major dysfunctional beliefs – particularly the three that I mention in suggestions number 1.
6. As is usual in REBT, help clients to reveal and dispute their self-defeating beliefs cognitively but also use a number of REBT methods to forcefully and emotionally minimize them and to act against them behaviorally. REBT, as I have said since 1956, sees thinking, emoting, and behaving as 'holistically integrated' and therefore helps clients to learn and to construct many interrelated techniques to help themselves. This is not primarily a therapy paper, so I shall not go into more specific REBT techniques here.

Does this chapter add anything important to REBT theory? Yes, I think it does by making some aspects of this theory more precise. In my original formulations, I stated that there are really two parts to dysfunctional or irrational beliefs, but that they usually seem to be integrated and go together. The first and perhaps the most important part is people's tendency to escalate their strong desires and preferences into musts: especially, 'I absolutely must perform important tasks well at practically all times or I'll bring about dire results!' The second part emphasizes what kind of dire results will follow from people's doing more poorly than they supposedly must do: 'If I don't perform important tasks well at practically all times, as I must, (a) I'll be a worthless, undeserving individual who will not be able to succeed or be lovable; and (b) the results I will get will not merely be bad and inconvenient but be absolutely horrible, and I will not be able to enjoy life at all.'

As has been sometimes pointed out in the REBT literature, the first part of this demand leads to lack of self-acceptance and the second part leads to awfulizing about conditions. Some critics of REBT have pointed out that actually these are irrational sub-thoughts in themselves and that just as musts may lead to awfulizing, awfulizing may also lead to musts (Walen et al., 1992). Thus, 'Since the kind of life I will lead after I don't perform well or be lovable will be horrible, I MUST therefore perform well and be loved by every significant person in my life at all times!' Then, of course, people who tell themselves that because it is terrible that they perform badly and are unloved, they MUST succeed and be loved, circularly tell themselves that they MUST succeed and be loved – or else it is TERRIBLE.

I previously thought that these two irrational beliefs – awfulizing and musturbatory – naturally go together and are one compound – and circular – belief. Now I think I see that they do not HAVE to go together: that some people can first musturbate and then awfulize and some people can first awfulize and then musturbate. I suspect that *usually* musturbation comes first and awfulizing second; but this does not *always* have to be the case. Some people, perhaps, are natural exaggerators, see bad things as totally bad and leading to catastrophic consequences, and therefore may awfulize first and musturbate second. But others may well musturbate first and awfulize second and partly derive their musturbation from their awfulizing. There is no reason why people *have to be* monolithic or consistent in this regard. Moreover, since humans individually differ from each other – for innate and acquired reasons – some people can *largely* awfulize and *then* musturbate and some can *largely* musturbate and then awfulize. The same person, of course, can *sometimes* musturbate first and awfulize second and *at other times* awfulize first and musturbate second.

What I am trying to emphasize in this particular chapter is that humans have two somewhat distinct, but often interrelated, self-disturbing tendencies: (1) to musturbate and then very often awfulize about adversities; and (2) to awfulize and exaggerate the consequences of their acting in certain ways, and then, interrelatedly, to musturbate and insist that they absolutely must not react in a 'bad' manner *because* they will get 'terrible' results. Let me give two common aspects of these two kinds of self-defeating thinking, and see if I am right about suspecting two somewhat different thinking processes instead of one invariable compound process.

Let us suppose that you want to do very well at certain tasks and be thoroughly approved by others for doing so. You then have four major possibilities, the first sensible and rational and the last three not so sensible and self-defeating:

1. 'I want very much to perform well and be approved by significant others but in case I don't, it's too bad and unfortunate but not the end of the world, and I can perform better and be approved by significant others later.' This is a preferential or, in REBT terms, a rational belief.
2. 'I want very much to perform well and be approved by significant others but in case I don't, bad things and indeed *exceptionally* bad things are very likely to happen and that would be *awful*. I couldn't stand such exceptionally bad adversities and be happy at all!' This is still a preferential belief and a rational one – but it exaggerates the likelihood and enormity of bad things happening and therefore starts out as being rational but ends up by being irrational and self-defeating.

3. 'I absolutely must perform well and be approved by significant others but in case I don't do as I must, it is *awful*, I'll *never* succeed at important tasks, and *never* be as approved by others as I have to be!' This is an irrational, musturbatory belief and will most likely make you anxious or depressed in case you fail and are disapproved.

4. 'I absolutely must perform outstandingly or perfectly well and be completely approved by significant others and in case I don't do as I must it is *really awful*, I'll *never* succeed as well as I must and *never* be completely approved by others as I definitely have to be!' This is a perfectionistic irrational belief and will make you more often and more intensely anxious or depressed in case you fail to do perfectly well and are even slightly disapproved by others.

It seems to me that the last three of these beliefs are all self-defeating but not *equally* so. Belief 2 is an exaggerated belief about the consequences of your 'terrible' behavior. Belief 3, even if it doesn't produce extremely bad consequences, is more rigid and likely to cause you much more trouble. Belief 4 is still more rigid and demanding and is likely to cause you still more intense and frequent feelings of anxiety and depression.

Now, as I will say a little later in this chapter, the second preferential belief, has some explicit or implicit musturbatory aspects – because you are really saying that if you don't act as well *as you want* and succeed in winning as much approval *as you must*, not only 'bad' things but *exceptionally bad* things will happen, *as they must not*. But it at least *starts off* with a preference and then adds a must – as perhaps all dysfunctional beliefs to *some* extent do. But it still seems to me that this belief includes, perhaps, less definite *musts* than the third or fourth belief and more awfulizing, in certain respects, than those beliefs include.

Again, one more illustration may make this clear. Let us say that you greatly exaggerate and overemphasize the degree of badness of certain events, such as real inconveniences, that may happen to you. You still may then have Belief 1, which is both preferential and not too self-defeating: 'If bad things happen to me, such as it is raining when I want to play tennis, that's unfortunate but not awful and I can wait till it stops raining and play.'

However, if you really are an exaggerator and awfulizer, you may have Belief 2: 'I would much *prefer* to play tennis today, but it won't kill me if I don't play because it is raining. However, not only will I be deprived of playing – which is most inconvenient – but I will miss practicing tennis, will get worse and worse at playing it, will lose the partner I have arranged to play with, and will be so bad at tennis and so upset about missing this game that I will suffer enormously, will not be able to stand my suffering, and will have innumerable bad things happen to me in regard to tennis and probably everything else!' This belief, again, starts with a preference but still awfulizes about the results you may probably get if your preference is not met. It may, somewhat circularly, therefore make you believe that 'Therefore it *absolutely must not* rain and stop me from playing tennis today'.

Let me say, almost parenthetically, that actually situations, beliefs about them, and emotional–behavioral reactions to them, are much more complicated than a simple ABC theory seems to indicate. For example, when you want to play tennis, it just may rain and stop you from doing so, or a hurricane may occur and stop you from playing tennis and disrupt much of the rest of your life. In this latter case, you are much more likely to awfulize about the hurricane and conclude that it will bring about absolutely awful consequences. From a self-preservative, biological point of view, *really* bad events may have far worse consequences for people than mildly bad ones. As some researchers have shown (David in Chapter 7), emotion focuses on unconscious as well as conscious information processing and involves cortical and subcortical structures. Therefore, humans may awfulize about particularly bad events much more than they will awfulize about mildly unfortunate ones. There are many possible complications in this respect, and I merely point them out instead of discussing them in this chapter. But I want to show that awfulizing has strong biological, as well as socially learned elements, and therefore in some (not all) instances may easily and naturally follow from events that are seen as life-threatening. Again, awfulizing may come first in these instances, and the view that 'awful' events absolutely must not happen, may be in part a derivative of your awfulizing about them.

Let me say again that to some extent the three irrational beliefs I describe in this chapter may all include explicit or tacit *musts*. Thus, the first of the dysfunctional beliefs I have described starts with a preference, 'I preferably should do well at tasks that I and many members of my social group consider important', but then it goes on to state, 'because if I don't, I will get exceptionally bad results, *as I must not get*, and be immensely disapproved of by almost all people, *as I must not be*'. People who hold this belief exaggerate *how bad* will be the results – because they *demand* that things absolutely must not be *as* bad as they are or may be. And they exaggerate *how* disapproved they will be by others and *how* disastrous this disapproval will be by *demanding*, once again, that serious disapproval absolutely *must not* exist, or that, if it does exist, it *must not* be more than slight disapproval. So their exaggeration of the dire results they will suffer stems from their explicit or implicit musturbatory belief that only good results or slightly bad results must exist.

The second dysfunctional belief considered in this chapter is obviously not a preference but includes an absolutistic must: 'I absolutely must do well at tasks that I and many members of my social group consider important, because if I don't do as well as I must, I am an incompetent, unlovable person who will always fail and get rejected and who can't be happy at all!' Clearly an imperative demand!

The third dysfunctional belief considered here not only demands, rather than prefers, that the believers do well but insists that they must do *perfectly well* or all is lost. Where all absolutistic insistences are obviously unrealistic, this perfectionistic one is doubly so!

All three of these dysfunctional beliefs are therefore basically musturbatory convictions. The value, I think, of clearly distinguishing the first one is that it shows that people can easily start with a preference that they do well and that their life goes nicely on and then – by sneaking in a tacit must – insist that it would be awful and terrible, instead of definitely inconvenient, if conditions actually go somewhat badly. So they easily awfulize even about denied preferences – and thereby disturb themselves.

The value of people – and especially of therapists – distinguishing the third dysfunctional belief considered here, is that their doing so emphasizes the arrant perfectionism of some clients. To insist that one has to do well at all times is palpably self-destructive. But to insist that one has to do perfectly well is utterly unrealistic and even more destructive. Not only anxiety and depression but also panic and deep, steady depression will likely ensue from this perfectionistic belief. Real perfectionists are relatively rare. But they are extremely difficult to work with therapeutically, and include a number of people with severe personality disorder. Therapists had better be aware – and, possibly, beware!

Does distinguishing among the three dysfunctional beliefs considered in this chapter have limitations and disadvantages? Yes:

- My position that these beliefs exist and are important to human disturbance still includes the REBT theory that preferences lead people to have healthy negative emotions and behaviors and that their absolutistic musts and demands lead them to have unhealthy emotional and behavioral consequences. A great deal of empirical research seems to support this hypothesis but most of it is backed up by giving subjects paper-and-pencil tests of musturbatory beliefs, and answers to these tests can easily be faked and are therefore unreliable.
- If my hypotheses about three main forms of people's dysfunctional beliefs are partly correct, they may encourage therapists and their clients to look obsessively for these beliefs, to 'find' questionable evidence to support them, and to lead disturbed individuals astray in the process of doing so.

Even if my hypotheses are shown to be correct, my REBT suggestions for having people minimize their three major kinds of self-disturbing beliefs had better be empirically supported by research studies that are carefully done.

In conclusion, I hope that my hypotheses about three major kinds of dysfunctional beliefs will be properly checked to see if they add appreciably to REBT theory and especially to determine if exploring and changing them in therapy leads to better results. Considerable research in this respect would seem to be in order!

References

Cudney, M.R. and Hardy, R.E. (1991) *Self-defeating Behaviors*. San Francisco: Harper San Francisco.

Ellis, A. (1962) *Reason and Emotion in Psychotherapy*. Secaucus, NJ: Citadel.

Ellis, A. (1976) The biological basis of human irrationality, *Journal of Individual Psychology, 32*, 145–168. Reprinted: New York: Albert Ellis Institute.

Ellis, A. (1994) *Reason and Emotion in Psychotherapy*, revised and updated. New York: Kensington.

Ellis, A. (2001a) *Feeling Better, Getting Better, Staying Better*. Atascadero, CA: Impact.

Ellis, A. (2001b) *Overcoming Destructive Beliefs, Feelings, and Behaviors*. Amherst, NY: Prometheus.

Eysenck, H.J. (1967) *The Biological Basis of Personality*. Springfield, IL: Thomas.

FitzMaurice, K.E. (2000) *Planet Earth – Insane Asylum for the Universe*. Omaha, NB: Palm Tree.

Frazer, J.G. (1959) *The Golden Bough*. New York: Macmillan.

Hoffer, E. (1951) *The True Believer*. New York: Harper & Row.

Horney, K. (1950) *Neurosis and Human Growth*. New York: Norton.

Kahneman, D., Slovic, P. and Tversky, A. (eds) (1982) *Judgment Under Uncertainty*. New York: Cambridge University Press.

Korzybski, A. ([1933] 1991) *Science and Sanity*. Concord, CA: International Society of General Semantics.

Nisbett, R.E. and Ross, L. (1980) *Human Inference: Strategies and Shortcomings*. Engelwood Cliffs, NJ: Prentice-Hall.

Piatelli-Palmarini, M. (1994) *Inevitable Illusions: How Mistakes of Reason Rule Our Minds*. New York: Wiley.

Rokeach, M. (1960) *The Open and Closed Mind*. New York: Basic Books.

Seligman, M.E.P. (1991) *Learned Optimism*. New York: Knopf.

Watzlawick, P. (1978) *The Language of Change*. New York: Basic Books.

Chapter 3

REBT: thinking it through once more

Hank Robb

As an Associate Fellow and Supervisor of the Albert Ellis Institute, I once submitted an article criticizing Rational Emotive Behavior Therapy (REBT) from the 'inside out'. I received a letter from the journal editor stating that REBT is simply whatever Albert Ellis says it is. This chapter begins with the premise that REBT is not the 'intellectual property' of any single individual, including its founder. If REBT theory and practice are to move forward, they can only do so with the collective efforts of all those interested in them. Progress will be marked by the actual identification of theoretical and practical problems and the actual solution of those problems rather than pronouncements, or approval, by any individual or doctrinal group.

Classic REBT basics and some problems with them

Classic REBT theorizing offers several concepts:

1. The ABC analysis in which 'activating events' are said to be responded to with 'beliefs' which 'cause' emotional and behavioral 'consequences' is the basic unit of analysis.
2. Some Cs are said to be dysfunctional while others are functional.
3. This occurs because the Bs that produce the dysfunctional Cs are 'irrational', while the Bs that produce functional Cs are 'rational'.
4. Functional Cs are functional precisely because they contribute to an individual's staying alive and being happy while alive. Dysfunctional Cs are dysfunctional precisely because they shorten life and produce unhappiness.
5. While many beliefs may be factually wrong, that is not what makes them 'irrational'. Instead, it is the erroneous evaluation of either facts or interpretations of facts that constitutes irrational beliefs.
6. The chief erroneous evaluation is that I, you or the world absolutely must (or must not) be a certain way.
7. Three additional irrational beliefs are derived from this demandingness. They are declaring some aspect of I, you or the world: (a) awful,

(b) unbearable or (c) proof that otherwise ordinary members of the human race have become sub-humans or super-humans.
8. Effective 'treatment' consists of helping clients recognize irrational beliefs and rational beliefs and to stick more strongly with the latter in order that the clients may have more functional emotional and behavioral consequences more frequently, more intensely and for longer periods of time.
9. This is chiefly done by the therapist actively and forcefully disputing the veracity of the irrational beliefs while also offering more sane and sensible beliefs and teaching the client to do likewise.

Problem 1: The centrality of evaluation

Classical REBT maintains that evaluations, rather than facts or inferences, are its fundamental concern. Thus, in classical REBT, I am not supposed to be so interested in the fact that your lover did not return your phone call or the inference that your lover is going to leave you for another. I want to know your *evaluation* of this fact and inference. 'How bad will that be?', I ask, while expectantly waiting for 'Awful!' from my client.

In seeking the client's evaluation of the facts and/or inferences about the facts, I am seeking something with a good/bad dimension as was clearly specified by Wessler and Wessler (1980), over twenty years ago. Does the client evaluate the situation as merely 'bad', even as 'really bad', or does the client go even further along this good/bad dimension. But suppose the client adds, 'And by the way, I could not stand that'. The client is no longer talking about a good/bad dimension. The client is stating what s/he believes to be a fact, namely that the client literally could not tolerate a certain state of affairs. However, the client is factually wrong, because 'I don't like it' does not equal 'I can't stand it', the latter being a factual, not an evaluative, claim. In truth, the client *is* standing and *will* stand whatever it is the client dislikes until it stops, or the client escapes by death or some other means.

Rating an individual human being's 'personhood' as 'good' or 'bad' also fits with the classical REBT's assertion that it is interested in evaluations rather than facts or inferences. However, demandingness, like frustration intolerance, does not. That I, you and the world absolutely must (or must not) be a certain way has no good/bad dimension to it. Instead, it is simply an emphatic assertion, which, again, is factually wrong. As the classical empirical dispute of this assertion notes, if something, as a matter of fact, absolutely must, or had to be, a certain way, then that is the way it would be. The *fact* that it is not that way proves the assertion wrong. Thus, two of REBT's core irrational beliefs, awfulizing and person-rating, are errors in evaluation. However, frustration tolerance and demandingness are not errors in the evaluation of facts (good/bad dimension) but straightforwardly errors of fact.

Problem 2: 'Derivations' from demandingness

A second problem in classical REBT theory is the assertion that three of the core irrational beliefs are 'derived' from demandingness. There has never been any demonstration of this 'derivation' nor could there be. Logic requires a conclusion be derived by combining a major and a minor premise (e.g. All men have Y chromosomes. This person is a man. Therefore, this person has a Y chromosome). Let us assume the first premise is 'Human beings sometimes assert that I and/or you and/or the world absolutely must go a certain way.' The conclusion we wish to derive is: 'When human beings assert that I and/or you and/or the world must absolutely go a certain way, they may also assert something is awful and/or unbearable and/or proves a change in someone's humanity and will never make these last three assertions without having made the first one.' In point of fact, there is no second premise that, when added to the first premise, would allow one to derive this conclusion. What REBT theory asserts to be derived as a conclusion is, in fact, a second premise. When combined with the first, one is allowed to conclude: 'When human beings are asserting something is awful and/or unbearable and/or proves a change in someone's humanity, they also will be asserting, or will have asserted, that I and/or you and/or the world absolutely must go a certain way.' This conclusion could be empirically tested. However, if the results were consistent with this concluding statement, they would only provide evidence for believing the empirical, not logical, relationship, asserted in the second premise, is correct.

Problem 3: The concept of belief

'Belief' is central to classical REBT because it conceptually precedes and 'causes' the emotional and behavioral 'consequences' signified by C. If one wants to change C, the theory suggests one should go after B. In practice this often works well enough because, from a practical standpoint, the main import of the ABC explanation is to encourage clients to give up their typical theory that in the presence of A they have no choice but to C. By insisting on C being not a function of A but, instead, a function of B, and further insisting that retaining or changing B is under client control, although 'hard work' may be necessary to change certain current Bs, clients are positioned to change Cs whether or not they change As. Since many As cannot be changed, or might only be changed if the client begins acting and emoting differently, giving up the notion that As cause Cs is an important aspect of effective treatment.

However, in practice, B turns out to be several different things. Following classical REBT, I generally tell my clients there are three ways to recognize one's beliefs. First, the client says it out loud or 'thinks' it (has a reportable private experience) to him- or herself. Second, someone else states the belief and the client agrees with the statement. Third, the client acts consistently with a belief. Thus, with regard to this third method, if I were to ask clients how to get out of my consultation room and they pointed to the door and said, 'Through the door', but then attempted to actually leave by walking through the wall, I could explain that their behavior *showed* they did not actually *believe* what they had said. Instead, the 'actual belief' would be the intellectual construction that is consistent with their actual behavior: 'The way out of this room is through the wall.'

Using the first 'way of recognizing' a belief, I can focus on clearly extant aspects of the client's verbal repertoire because, in this method of 'recognizing' a belief, clients have verbal behavior (either overt or covert) on which they can make reports. Using the second 'way', we might say the aspect of interest in the repertoire is 'latent', but can readily be made manifest. Once elicited, the practitioners and clients are in the same spot as when clients initially say their 'belief' out loud or 'think' it privately.

However, the third case is very different. Clients are told that because they engage in certain actions that are consistent with a verbal construction, they also 'have' that verbal construction (presumably inside their heads) but just don't recognize they 'have' it. This is quite different from the second case in which the practitioner elicits the 'latent' belief. In that second case, if you ask clients, 'Do you think the way out of the room is through the wall (or this is awful, intolerable, etc.)?', they answer, 'Yes'. But in the third case, they answer, 'No'. It often takes considerable practitioner effort to get clients to agree that if their behavior is consistent with a verbal construction then they actually 'believe' that verbal construction at the time of their behavior even though they have no sense that they do.

The problem here is that REBT theory is confusing proposed empirical relations with theoretical ones. It is one thing to say that when clients admit to having certain Bs present, they are likely to admit to having certain Cs present, or vice versa. It is quite another thing to say that if clients admit to having certain Cs present then certain Bs also must be present whether clients are aware of them or not. This error is typically then compounded. If the practitioner gets clients to act and emote in more functional ways that are, according to REBT theory, consistent with 'rational beliefs', the improvement is taken as evidence the clients must have 'had' the 'irrational belief' which was 'causing' their previously dysfunctional emoting and behaving. The only conclusion warranted is that when clients act and emote dysfunctionally they can be taught to act and emote more functionally. Additionally, teaching clients that their dysfunctional emoting and behaving is consistent with 'irrational beliefs' and their functional emoting and behaving is consistent with 'rational beliefs' may prove helpful in that process. The fact that such a process 'works' is no more proof that it does so because clients formerly 'had' the irrational belief which was consistent with their former behavior than the fact that aspirin 'works' to remove a headache proves the headache was caused by an aspirin deficiency.

Problem 4: Conceptualizing 'emotion'

In classical REBT, the term 'emotion' sometimes denotes one or more sensations within one's skin (e.g. my chest 'feels' tight, I 'feel jumpy inside', my stomach is 'flip-flopping', my heart is pounding). Alternatively, 'emotion' denotes a quality of overt behavior (e.g. when I speak the flow of my words is broken, the enunciation of my words is not crisp, the ideas expressed in my words lack clarity, I stammer, and my body is held either rigidly or moves about in a jerky, 'nervous' way). Even a knowledgeable practitioner is likely to assert that one of these is simply a reflection of the other. This is far from certain. First, both are likely a reflection of a third factor, namely adrenaline. Second, one can occur without the other. For example, a number of conference presenters will appear 'unanxious' when judged by overt behavior such as their speech patterns and head or chest movement. However, when attempting to use a laser pointer during a slide presentation, the audience my notice the laser dot bouncing all over the screen. Such presenters often have learned to 'feel' anxious, i.e. experience the private bodily sensations we call 'anxiety', but not 'act' anxiously, at least not with regard to speech or head and chest movements.

Alternatively, I have worked with a number of 'anger problem' clients who report acting with no sense of 'angry feelings' prior to or even contemporaneous with their overt behavior. 'I don't know, Doc, I was doing OK and then I just blew up on the guy.' Admittedly, I might eventually teach such clients to recognize sensations that preceded, or are contemporaneous with, their overt behavior. The point is, private sensations and the qualitative aspects of public performance are not the same thing and not always 'just reflections' of each other. A useful theory will not be developed when these distinctions are overlooked.

An alternative theoretical approach

Let me say at the outset that in what follows the ABCs of REBT will become the F_{ABITS} (pronounced like habits) of REBT. By this I mean that, relative to an individual's actual or potential fulfillments (F), any situation will have as its analytic features activating, or attention-getting, aspects ($_A$), behavioral aspects ($_B$), imaginal aspects ($_I$), thought aspects ($_T$), and sensation aspects ($_S$). Some of these terms will undergo considerable refinement below. The opening point is that I recommend REBT abandon the notion that A is responded to with B which, in turn, produces C. Rather, F, A, B, I, T, and S are simultaneously the constituent parts of any moment. Change any one and you have a new F_{ABITS}. However, because you have changed one aspect of a F_{ABITS} does not mean you, *necessarily*, will have changed another; though you may have. Nor is changing one, *necessarily*, the means by which another is changed; though it might be.

Fulfillment

1. I begin by asserting that all human beings seek fulfillment. By fulfillment I do not mean something purely verbal, intellectual or abstract such as a 'goal'. I mean something quite concrete and organic. Verbal, intellectual or abstract activities may be either (i) the means by which fulfillments come to individuals or (ii) the type of thing which individuals find fulfilling. In neither case are they the 'thing' inside an individual human being's skin that I am trying to denote by the word 'fulfillment'. By fulfillment I also do not mean want or desire. Wants or desires, like fulfillments, are concrete and organic rather than verbal, intellectual or abstract. Wants or desires may be fulfilled but they are not fulfillments, unless one desires to have a particular desire. The appropriate 'verbal tag' for a fulfillment, at least an intense one, would be something like 'This *is* way cool', in contrast to '*Wouldn't* it be way cool if . . .', which might more accurately verbally tag a want or desire. Though it is true that fulfillments constitute an actuality while desires constitute only a potentiality, I have chosen to let one symbol represent both cases because I do not think this difference makes any difference from the analytic point of view with which I am interested. Of course I could be wrong and I might have to add W_{ABITS} or D_{ABITS} to go along with F_{ABITS}.

    The concept of fulfillment is open-ended in the same way the concept of activating events is open-ended in classical REBT. So, for example, a person can have the experience verbally characterized as, 'Being the sort of being who has experiences such as "Wouldn't it be way cool if . . ." is, itself, way cool'. A thought, a bodily sensation, a behavior, or anything outside one's skin could all serve as activating events in classical REBT. Similarly, what one experiences as fulfillment is not limited conceptually to any particular type of thing.

2. Fulfillments are very likely to be different for different individuals and may be different for the same individual at different times in that individual's life. I often find fulfillment when fly-fishing. My wife does not. I once found fulfillment playing chess. I no longer do.

    A mid-life crisis is said to be getting to the top of the ladder and finding it is against the wrong wall. We may 'imagine', 'theorize', 'hypothesize', 'guess' or whatever other word one may use to denote an entity which is: (i) a verbal (usually linguistic as opposed to pictorial or musical) instrumentality, i.e. used to guide action toward fulfillment, that (ii) always contains an element of uncertainty. Whatever we call this thing, it remains only a guess. We require the actual concrete experience to find out if this or that intellectually articulated 'goal' actually led us to engage in the right activities under the right circumstances to produce actual fulfillment. The verbal articulation called a 'goal' is not the same as the concrete, organic experience called a 'fulfillment'. Further, what provided fulfillment for a while, may stop doing so. Thus, we do not know if our mid-life crisis is: (i) a function of 'going after the wrong thing' in the first place, (ii) finding that, by the time we got there, the concrete experience symbolized by the goal no longer had the ability to fulfill us, or (iii) finding that what once provided concrete, organic fulfillment, and thus provided fulfillment for a while, no longer does.

3.   As indicated above, fulfillments may be more or less enduring. The Christmas presents of US children are often the epitome of unenduring fulfillments – left idle in the corner after the first month, if not after the first day. Wisdom is pursuing and maintaining what an individual finds to be his, or her, more enduring fulfillments.

4.   The nature of the human and non-human aspects of the world preclude individual humans or groups of humans from experiencing some of the fulfillments they might wish for and also prohibit some simultaneous fulfillments. For example, none of us can go back in time and give ourselves a different history no matter how much we might wish to do so or how fulfilling we would find doing so. It is also not possible to have the fulfillment associated with alcohol intoxication and, at the same time, the fulfillment associated with being sober.

5.   What will bring, or what constitutes, fulfillment for an individual does not usually 'announce' itself to the individual or to anyone else and, typically, must be *discovered* for oneself. A listing of the sorts of things that have proved fulfilling for other humans may be a place to start, but that is all it is.

6.   Sorrow is the inevitable result of being deprived of a fulfillment and its intensity and duration are closely proportionate to the zeal with which we long for the fulfillment.

7.   Some things are fulfillments and some things lead to them. Some things are not fulfillments and some things lead to them. By this I want simply to denote the 'means–ends' distinction. While it is most correct to note, as I learned from the American pragmatist John Dewey (1938), that ends are merely means-funded, it is also true that there is a difference between driving to a place where I can go fishing and actually fishing. It would be nice if I experienced both activities as fulfillments. Indeed, it would be nice if all aspects of my living were experienced as fulfillment, but often they are not.

8.   'Good' is the name for what leads to fulfillment or for fulfillment itself. 'Bad' is the name for the opposite. Thus, to paraphrase Shakespeare

(1954), rather than Epictetus (1890), there is no good or bad for particular human beings independent of the particular human beings' fulfillment. 'Good' always means fulfillment for at least one human being. There is nothing independent of human fulfillment that is 'good', at least for humans, nor anything independent of human fulfillment that is 'bad', at least for humans. There are those who hold the view that when anything (action, object, condition, etc.) is designated 'good' or 'bad', a quality of that thing which is *independent* of its relationship to some human individual's potential, or actual, fulfillment has been designated. In other words, 'good' or 'bad' identifies a quality that inheres in objects rather than in the relationship of objects to the instantiation of human fulfillment. The position taken here is that such a view is not only wrong but constitutes an error so fundamental as to be the source of a great deal of intellectual confusion and human suffering. In simple, if not quite accurate, parlance, 'good' simply means 'I (or we) like it' and 'bad' simply means 'I (or we) do not like it'.

9. Language can help, or hinder, experiencing fulfillments.
10. Maintaining action or action patterns, including language or language patterns as well as emoting and emoting patterns, that produce fulfillment is rational. Maintaining action or action patterns, including language or language patterns as well as emoting and emoting patterns, that deprive us of fulfillment is irrational.

    There are two important aspects to this point. First, the terms 'rational' and 'irrational' denote a relationship between human action patterns and human fulfillment. Without a relationship to human fulfillment, there would be no basis to determine rationality or irrationality. Second, there is a distinction between momentarily making a mistake (e.g. over-drinking on one occasion) and persisting in that mistake over time. The terms 'rational' and 'irrational' are reserved for the more enduring rather than the momentary.
11. Effective *living* for an individual human being, rather than mere survival, consists of discovering and pursuing what, for that individual, constitute enduring fulfillments. Effective treatment means assisting human individuals in such discovery and such pursuit. This includes helping individuals realize when they are acting rationally and irrationally and helping them do more of the former and less of the latter. It also includes helping individuals recognize that they cannot have every fulfillment simultaneously and must choose not only between good and bad, but also between competing goods and competing bads.

Pragmatism as the sole truth test

REBT currently offers four 'truth test' criteria, as can be seen in DiGiuseppe's (1991) disputing grid: logical, empirical, pragmatic and alternative rational (Beal et al., 1996). I propose pragmatism as the thoroughgoing, unambiguous 'truth test' for REBT. Does it lead to your fulfillment? If not, it is irrational. If so, it is rational.

With regard to the empirical truth test, it is certainly true that humans can engage in 'wishful thinking' and 'self-delusion' so what 'feels good or bad', 'seems true or false' or is 'working' *at the moment* is not the criterion I mean to be offering. Enduring fulfillments are, by definition, not momentary. I most emphatically agree that one of our main human problems is indulging momentary fulfillments at the expense of enduring ones. This is plain old classical REBT. What is different about adopting a pragmatic standard for truth is dropping the notion that the 'reason' wishful thinking and self-delusion do not work is because they conflict with something called 'reality'. The fact of their failure to 'work' enduringly becomes the end of the 'explanation chain'. We do not add, 'because they conflict with reality'. Such epistemological theorizing is unnecessary metaphysical baggage (Dewey, 1938). Of course, one is free in ordinary language to talk about 'reality' just as we continue to talk about 'sunrises' and 'sunsets' with the full knowledge that, relative to the earth, it is not the sun that does the moving.

Illogical and anti-empirical thinking, and other behavior, are of interest only because they are markers of approaches to life that have proven unlikely to 'work'. This does not mean that within the verbal game called 'logic' one cannot determine what is logical and what is not. It means that finding something is illogical will not 'carry the day' if it also 'works' in the context of an individual seeking and maintaining enduring fulfillment. The same is true empirically. If the 'facts' show there is a chair right in front of the client but the client reports it is more fulfilling to crash into the chair than walk around it, then the 'empirical facts' will not 'carry the day'.

The alternative rational belief is the positive aspect of the pragmatic criteria for truth. If certain verbal and other practices do not 'work', then let us use verbal and other practices that do. We, as practitioners, offer these verbal and other practices to our clients, and hopefully use them ourselves, for no reason other than they are effective in producing and maintaining enduring fulfillments, i.e. they 'work'. Crucially, they must 'work' for the individual in question. If these verbal and other practices 'work' for five, or five billion, other humans, but not for the one in question, then, for that individual, they are not rational alternatives.

More than sensing, thinking, emoting and behaving beings

At least from *Reason and Emotion in Psychotherapy* (1962) onward, Ellis maintains that human beings are simultaneously sensing, thinking, emoting and behaving organisms. Thus, individuals are never said to be only doing one of these things. Rather, they are said to be momentarily emphasizing one over the others; sensing, *thinking*, emoting and behaving. Though this premise is very helpful and important, the listed categories start our theoretical enterprise with inherent confusions and difficulties:

1. Unless we accept something like Descartes's spaceless, weightless, timeless mind stuff, then 'sensing, thinking and emoting' are also kinds of behavior. That which distinguishes what we mean by 'sensing, thinking and emoting' from what we call 'behavior' is mainly that the latter refers to overt, largely motoric, behavior.
2. 'Sensing' actually goes in two directions: to those things one identifies as being outside one's skin and to those one identifies as being within it.
3. 'Sensing' can mean either 'affects an individual' or 'has an effect reportable by the individual affected'. Thus, there are times I 'sense' things, meaning I am affected by them whether I can make a report about them or not. At other times, I 'sense' things, meaning I can make a report about them, or, strictly speaking, I can make a report about my being affected by them. This is the same distinction as saying I am 'conscious', rather than being comatose, in contrast to being 'conscious of being conscious', meaning I am able to make reports about my consciousness. To illustrate, I am a veteran and ardent fly-fisher. When fishing an underwater fly, I often can say what happened that led me to pull the line swiftly, and simultaneously raise the tip of my rod, in an attempt to hook a fish (i.e. I am conscious of my consciousness). At other times, I 'react' but cannot really say exactly why (i.e. I am conscious but not conscious of my consciousness).
4. As noted at the beginning of this chapter, the term 'emotion' is typically being used in two different ways. Sometimes it refers to bodily sensations (e.g. my chest 'feels' tight, etc.) and sometimes to qualities of overt behavior (e.g. the flow of my words is broken when I speak, etc.). Because these two categories are not 'just reflections' of one another, a reformulated theory should keep the distinctions clear. Thus, in technical contexts, I recommend making reference to bodily sensations and qualities of overt behavior.
5. Another problem comes with the 'thinking' aspect of the formula. Certainly human beings do have private events which are much like 'radio productions' inside their heads (the sounds of talking or music, etc., without any accompanying 'pictures'). We may call these experiences 'thoughts' but they hardly exhaust what it is to think. I have occasionally experienced a 'muse' which 'gives' me words to say or write. I 'listen' and say, write or type that which I have 'received'. This, however, is the great exception when it comes to 'thinking'. Real thinking is a mostly public affair. I write or type things down. I read them over. I cancel some out. I write some more. I consult some text. I talk with other people. I write some more, etc. Real thinking includes

all the activities associated with developing a verbal repertoire which will, in turn, effectively address some aspect of life including other aspects of my, or others', verbal repertoire. Thinking is far more than the privately experienced 'radio production-like' events 'inside our heads', though, certainly, such private experiences are often important in the lives of human beings. However, for practical purposes, I would continue to use the label 'thoughts' to designate those 'privately experienced "radio productions" inside our heads'.

6. The world of private events is not exhausted by the kinds of bodily sensations described in 4 above or the 'radio productions' we often call 'thought'. Visual imagery is a prominent part of the private world of which only we can make reports. Gustatory and olfactory imagery are also theoretical possibilities, but, in my experience, far less important than the 'still pictures', 'silent movies' or 'motion pictures with sound' that humans report as occurring 'inside their heads'.

7. The various reportable or unreported, 'internally/externally located' or 'caused' sensations and qualities of overt behavior described above have a couple of other important dimensions. One is controllability. The other is intensity. Many clients seek treatment precisely because certain thoughts, images or bodily sensations arrive unbidden and 'refuse to leave'. Additionally, the intensity may seem to vary from highly intense to near zero intensity. Oddly enough, individuals may accurately describe themselves as intensely or infinitesimally anxious, or intensely or infinitesimally relaxed. Being less anxious is not the same as being relaxed, nor is being less relaxed the same as being anxious. While it is taken as axiomatic that one cannot be relaxed and anxious, it is also true that, in some sense, one can be 'relaxed *about* being anxious'.

The full complexity

With these concepts in hand, we can begin to get a handle on our problem. Humans are doing much more than simultaneously sensing, thinking, emoting and behaving. Rather, they, more or less, simultaneously have (1) auditory, (2) visual, (3) bodily, (4) gustatory and (5) olfactory sensations which they experience as: (6) more or less intense, (7) more or less voluntary, (8) coming from, or being located, outside or inside themselves. Some of these they (9) can, at least in a current moment, make reports about and some of them they cannot. They also have (10) differing qualities of overt, largely motoric, behavior, as well as (11) seeking fulfillment and (12) experiencing, or not experiencing, fulfillment with greater or lesser (13) frequency, (14) intensity and (15) duration. This seeking and experiencing fulfillment can (16) sometimes be usefully subjected to a means–ends analysis.

How is REBT changed?

I believe the points put forward above have much in common with classical REBT. However, they contrast with it in several important ways.

1. The proposed approach requires a great deal more specificity than 'stay alive and be happy' for guidance in what will count as enduring fulfillments for any particular individual. 'What do you really care about most?' becomes a driving treatment question because it is only in light of answers to this question that what is rational and irrational can be determined. Because classical REBT has quickly answered the 'What's it all about anyway' question with 'Be happy and stay alive', little attention has been devoted to developing techniques to help individuals who hardly sense what they most deeply care about to find those things. That will have to change. In common with classical REBT, I agree that a great delusion is to answer this question not with what one actually cares about most, but with what one *should* care about most. The latter answer puts one's life off course in a most fundamental way. However, avoiding that error is not the same as obtaining the sense of those pursuits to which individuals will make their deepest commitments.

2. *Disturbance is frustration intolerance.* In this analysis, almost all problems of human 'disturbance' become frustration tolerance problems. They are not frustration tolerance problems in the classical REBT 'I can't stand it – itis' meaning of the term, but in the sense that all human beings most likely will find they are deprived of fulfillments, to a greater or lesser extent, at some particular moment or for many moments. They quite literally are stuck tolerating this deprivation. At least one thing classical REBT aims to do is help individuals tolerate deprivation well.

    It seems quite likely that if they begin the process by declaring, 'I cannot stand it', individuals will do less well. However, they also may do less well by demanding fulfillment, awfulizing about not having it or declaring themselves or others 'no good' because they don't have it. I hypothesize they will also do less well if they declare they are entitled to that which they are not currently receiving (Robb, 1992). Alternatively, whether they make such statements or not, if their hearts pound, their mouths become dry, they have difficulty focusing, their 'insides tremble' or they experience any number of other bodily sensations, these also would likely count as not tolerating deprivation well. The point is that while there are a great number of ways to tolerate deprivation poorly, even if individuals tolerate it well, they are still, at that moment, deprived (i.e. not fulfilled).

3. *Disturbance verses irrationality.* 'Disturbance' is not, in and of itself, evidence of 'irrationality'. This is because 'irrationality' is defined as

persistently acting in ways counter to fulfillment. Disturbance, rather, is not tolerating deprivation well. Suppose I want to convince someone of my point of view but do not do so quickly and easily. Suppose I next experience certain thoughts, bodily sensations and qualities of overt behavior that fit the label 'being angry at myself', or 'getting anxious', rather than the label 'remaining calm'. I would be disturbed, i.e. not tolerating my deprivation well. For irrationality, we must calculate the extent to which tolerating certain deprivations poorly contributes to my not achieving particular fulfillments. The answer could be 'a great deal', but it could be 'not much'. First, I might persist with my argument even though I am 'angry at myself' or 'anxious' and still convince the person of my point of view. Second, my 'anger' or 'anxiety' might so disrupt my performance that I fail to achieve my fulfillment. A third possibility is that when disturbance is present, I give up my efforts altogether; though if I had persisted, even with the anger, anxiety, etc. present, I might have succeeded. Whatever the outcome, it is an empirical, rather than a theoretical, matter. Stated in the reverse, what evidence is there that tolerating deprivation well leads to fulfillment? Perhaps it does, but that, too, is an empirical matter. Agreeably, if the fulfillment sought is tolerating deprivation well, then the answer, tautologically, must be that tolerating deprivation in a disturbed manner is irrational. But this is simply because the fulfillment in question is that of tolerating deprivation well. There is no necessary reason that tolerating deprivation badly will always prove irrational or that tolerating it well will always prove rational.

These theoretical distinctions between fulfillment and the toleration of deprivations are obscured by classical REBT's answer to the 'What's it all about anyway?' question, which it answers with 'Staying alive and being happy'. The word 'happy' is covering both the non-disturbed toleration of deprivation as well as achieving fulfillment. This, in part, is because classical REBT draws no distinction between private bodily sensations and qualities of overt behavior. Thus, 'feeling anxious' and 'acting anxiously' are conflated. Further, when these two types of disturbed Cs exist, they are assumed to be preventing the individual from pursuing fulfillment. That assumption is rarely, if ever, challenged and tested with the particular client in question.

Let us consider 'white-knuckle' flyers versus those who refuse to fly. Members of the latter group usually act as they do because they accurately predict that if they fly they will experience certain bodily sensations and qualities of overt behavior, i.e. 'feel anxious' and 'act anxiously'. The 'white-knuckle' flyers make the same accurate predictions but fly anyway. Classical REBT has to handle this by giving a two-layer analysis. The 'white-knuckle' flyers have overcome the secondary problem of claiming that it is 'awful' to experience these sensations and qualities of overt behavior as evidenced by the fact that they fly. The non-flyers have both the primary problem of 'anxiety' and the secondary problem of refusing to fly because experiencing anxiety would be 'awful', 'must not occur', etc.

On the analysis offered here, only one level of analysis is necessary. Both the flyers and non-flyers seek (1) to be at the other end of their flight and (2) avoid disturbance while doing so (i.e. not experience certain bodily sensations and qualities of overt behavior while getting there). For those who fly, the first is achieved while the second is not. On the theory offered here, this is possible because the attention-getting events (A), overt behaviors (B), images (I), thoughts (T) and sensations (S) of F_{ABITS} do not, necessarily, cause one another, though they may correlate. Thus, because sensations and possibly thoughts are as they are does not necessarily determine what behavior will be. In classical REBT, 'emotional and behavioral Cs' are conflated. Thus, it is hard to see how one can have certain sensations and qualities of overt behavior and still act even with those sensations and qualities of overt behavior. Additionally, emotional and behavioral Cs are definitionally a function of 'beliefs'. Thus, by definition, one cannot have different bodily sensations and different actions or qualities of actions while having the same private thoughts or public speech. Of course such events do happen. For example, some people continue to think it is 'awful' to experience certain bodily sensations and qualities of overt behavior but fly anyway when previously they did not fly. In short, they start acting more 'bravely'. Classical REBT can only account for them by asserting that somewhere, unbeknownst to anyone, a B must have existed and been changed because, by definition, emotional and behavioral Cs are always a function of beliefs.

4. *A new fundamental theorem.* As I have already indicated, the ABCs of REBT become the F_{ABITS} of REBT. Its fundamental theorem would change from 'Beliefs cause emotional and behavioral consequences' to 'Because in the context of seeking or experiencing any fulfillment some particular attention-getting event did, or does, occur, no particular thoughts or images and only very few sensations and behaviors must accompany it in the future.' For example, if the attention-getting event is 'pinching a person hard' then, given normal neurological functioning, the person will have sensations of 'pain', but no necessary thoughts or images. Similar examples hold for attention-getting events, which cause reflexive behavior such as eye blinks in response to puffs of air directed at an open eye. In short, this approach does not teach that 'As never "cause" Cs', but, rather, 'As cause less than you think'. The F_{ABITS} of any human being are a function of genetic and individual history. REBT interventions add 'psycho-behaviorally' (rather than pharmacologically, etc.) to the individual's history. Using the language of

classical REBT, we retain the notion that A does not, necessarily, 'cause' C, but drop the notion that B and only B, of necessity, causes C. If one wants to change what classical REBT calls 'emotional and behavioral consequences', one may theoretically try to do so directly and without hypothesizing the necessity of changing Bs because Bs are, of necessity, the means by which Cs are 'caused'. If changing Bs is found to change Cs, as indeed they have been, that is an interesting *empirical* finding. Conversely, if changing Cs is found to change Bs, as also has been found throughout the behavioral activation literature (Jacobson et al., 1996; Martell et al., 2001) that, too, is an interesting empirical finding. Neither affects the theory of REBT, which, under the theory offered here, no longer asserts a *necessary* 'causal chain' between classical REBT's Bs and Cs. Indeed, the theory here proposed is consistent with both sets of facts.

5. Under this alternative approach, REBT would continue to hypothesize and confirm that certain verbal constructions when said out loud, experienced as private 'thoughts', or readily elicited by therapist inter-action are, or are not, associated with poor toleration of deprivation (i.e. disturbance) and/or interfere with the pursuit of an individual's fulfillment (i.e. are irrational). For example, when people say they 'cannot stand' being deprived of a particular fulfillment, they may tolerate the deprivation less than well and also may stop pursuing the fulfillment in question.

6. Under this alternative approach, REBT would continue to hypothesize and confirm that certain of these verbal constructions are more 'fundamental' than others when it comes to tolerating deprivation well and continuing to pursue fulfillment. For example, saying out loud or thinking to one's self some version of 'The world absolutely must go my way' may be hypothesized and demonstrated to be associated with more problems than 'My mother doesn't love me as much as, or in the way, I wish she would'.

7. Under this alternative approach, REBT should look to see if any additional fundamentally disturbance-associated verbal constructions can be identified. For example, do statements such as 'I deserve to get X' contribute to disturbance and failure to pursue fulfillment over and above the four 'irrational beliefs' of classic REBT, i.e. awfulizing, frustration intolerance, person-rating and demandingness?

8. Under this alternative approach, REBT should examine the relation-ship between fundamental disturbance-associated verbal constructions to determine the likelihood that if one is present others will be, or that if one is not present others will not be. For example, is person-rating never present unless demandingness is present? However, under the theory offered here, such a finding would be regarded as a matter of empirical, rather than theoretical, significance.

9. Because, under this alternative approach, REBT stops hypothesizing beliefs 'cause' emotional and behavioral consequences, researchers would stop efforts to show that when certain 'emotions' and 'behaviors' are present, certain 'beliefs' must be present whether the individual in question is able to acknowledge them or not.

Potential errors or problems

1. In my view, it would be an error to hold that because beliefs do not *necessarily* cause private sensations or overt behavior, there is no longer reason to try to change private thoughts and overt speech. This would be wrong on two counts. First, there is considerable practical and scientifically generated evidence to show that sensations and behavior can be changed by getting people to change the way they talk and think. Thus, intervention strategies based on classical REBT disputes are not to be abandoned because of the approach offered here. Second, REBT's greatest contribution to the treatment field, in my opinion, has been its effort to provide a positive and directive philosophy for actively *living* rather than merely surviving. I believe it would be a mistake to abandon this effort on the notion that since private thoughts or public speech are no longer hypothesized to be the necessary cause of other private experiences and overt behavior, then such an effort is a waste of time. The point put forward here is not that talk and thought are unable to affect private sensations and overt behavior but that they are not the *only* way to affect them. Losing a philosophy that unabashedly encourages and supports individual human beings to find what *they* care about most in life and actively pursue it in contrast to one that tells them to do as they *should*, would truly be an enormous loss to the liberation of human beings from so many forms of social tyranny.

2. A related point is the question of continuing to search for verbal constructions which are fundamentally related to disturbance and irrationality. I am convinced that the classic four: demandingness, person-rating, frustration intolerance and awfulizing are more fundamentally related to disturbance than innumerable other possible verbal constructions. Yes, the alternative posed here insists that, in the language of classical REBT, 'not all Cs are a function of Bs'. This alternative should not be taken to mean that every B is as much or as little related to disturbed Cs as any other. Neither should it be taken to mean Bs are simply irrelevant to Cs.

3. Another mistake would be to hold that because this approach can sometimes handle problems at one level that requires two in classical REBT, there is no reason to continue the multiple level examination of problems. In the case offered above, whether the individual is a white-

knuckle flyer or a non-flyer, that individual could become depressed *over* the unpleasant sensations experienced when attempting to fly. As with classical REBT, the approach offered here would use a multi-layer analysis in which the attention-getting event of the second-layer F_{ABITS} would be the 'anxious sensations' experienced in the first level.

4. The approach here presented argues against the notion that when an individual has either certain private sensations, overt behaviors or particular qualities of overt behavior, we are justified in concluding that that individual holds a 'belief' which is consistent with those events whether the individual 'knows' it or not. However, it would be a mistake to take from this view that it is, therefore, an error to point out to individuals that such events are consistent with certain verbal constructions as part of an attempt to get the individual to have different internal sensations, behaviors or qualities of behavior. One can quite legitimately say, 'Look, I know you don't believe other members of your board of directors absolutely must agree with you. But, your images, sensations and behavioral tendencies are certainly more consistent with that idea than with the notion that, like any other member of the human race, you are allowed by the universe to experience this kind of frustration. So, let's work on bringing your reactions more in line with your beliefs.' This intervention notes an inconsistency between thoughts or talk on the one hand and sensations, images, other overt behaviors or qualities of overt behavior on the other. However, it does not assert the inconsistency is because the individual 'secretly' holds beliefs consistent with the proffered verbal constructions. Rather, it allows for the theoretical possibility that the sensational and behavioral aspects of a F_{ABITS} can be inconsistent with public and private speech but could be brought into consistency with them. The means for doing so will certainly not be cognitive disputing because there are no 'cognitive errors' to dispute. Rather, the means would be what classical REBT calls 'emotional and behavioral' disputes – the very ones REBT practitioners so often fail to use (Robb et al., 1999). In these cases, clients are not being taught a new philosophy. Rather, they are being shown how to put their current philosophy into practice. In the language of pop psychology, they are not getting 'new talk' but are learning how to 'walk the talk' they already possess.

The future

The proposed approach has implications for future REBT research and practice. To begin with, I believe REBT researchers need to take very seriously a new approach to language outlined by Hayes and his associates in *Relational Frame Theory* (2001, p. 141):

> Relational Frame Theory is a behavioral analytic approach to human language and cognition. RFT treats relational responding as a generalized operant, and thus appeals to a history of multiple-exemplar training. Specific types of relational responding, termed relational frames, are defined in terms of the three properties of mutual and combinatorial entailment, and the transformation of functions. Relational frames are arbitrarily applicable, but are typically not necessarily arbitrarily applied in the natural language context.

This book offers a radically behavioral approach to language as language relates to itself and to other behavior. Frankly, I have found it difficult to penetrate this work due to the technically precise language required to explicate the theory. I believe REBT researchers will have to put in considerable time to understand the theory and the data supporting it. However, I also believe it offers a bright and wonderful alternative to the 'computer simulation' model of 'cognitive psychology' commonly accepted today.

RFT attempts to directly address exactly how, for human beings, arbitrary signs come to have a controlling role in both the production of other arbitrary signs and on non-arbitrary life events as well as how that role is maintained. It does this without recourse to mechanisms, which are fundamentally and forever hidden from direct inspection. Early in my REBT training when trainees made claims of worthlessness, they sometimes received a trainer response such as 'Well, I think you are a banana'. Participants always found this assertion silly. The trainer was noting that certain arbitrary signs (e.g. 'I am worthless') had a controlling role in trainees' lives while others (e.g. 'You are a banana') did not. Further, the trainer was holding open the possibility that one might change the function (e.g. unpleasant bodily sensations and performance decrement) of the sign even while the sign itself (e.g. the private thought or overt response, 'I am worthless') remained the same. Thus, in principle, one might still think, say, read or hear others assert one was 'worthless' and react as if one had been called a 'banana'. Rather than take a word out of a sentence or substitute a new word or sentence, one could change the controlling function of the word. In ordinary language, they stopped 'believing' they were 'worthless' whether they made such an assertion themselves or it came from someone else. RFT appears to offer insights on how this occurs and how to measure that it has occurred or is occurring. If correct, it could prove a powerful tool for examining such questions as how 'fundamental' certain language (e.g. awfulizing) is to the poor toleration of deprivation or to the failure to actively identify and pursue what are potentially our deepest fulfillments.

The REBT effort in changing the role of arbitrary signs has mainly been aimed at effective disputes. RFT suggests other ways. More importantly, it suggests ways of testing when this or that set of arbitrary signs actually is functioning in a controlling way. I suggest this approach will prove far superior to trying to correlate sensations, qualities of overt behavior and overt behavior with responses on some sort of 'irrational beliefs' inventory. However, achieving these benefits will only be possible by paying the high price, in time and toil, necessary to thoroughly understand the principles of RFT.

In my office

My practice has already been greatly changed by the alternative presented here. I expect a great deal more change is in the offing for me and for all those who take seriously the ideas presented in this chapter. While I still begin my work by showing clients what I regard as the basic five thinking errors (awfulizing, frustration tolerance, demandingness, person-rating and entitlement) as well as alternatives to these beliefs, I do not teach that Bs cause Cs in the classical REBT formula. Rather, I teach that within a F_{ABITS}, a term which I never bother mentioning to my clients, the presence of a particular A does not, necessarily, determine the presence of any other component. I show them that just as one may often control the presence of events outside one's skin, but that often one cannot; one also often can control the presence of events inside one's skin (e.g. thoughts, images and sensations), but often one cannot. Just as one may for a time banish certain events outside one's skin only to find they have returned, so it is with events inside one's skin. However, the presence or absence of certain thoughts, images and sensations does not necessarily determine one's overt perform-ance in a situation even if it may make it more difficult. This is not fundamentally different from finding that certain events outside one's skin do not determine what one does in the presence of those events, though those events may make it more difficult to act. In short, REBT traditionally has shown us not to be thrown off course in the pursuit of our deepest desires by social obstacles even when we cannot change them. This lesson can be applied to events inside one's skin such as thoughts, images and sensations. Just as events outside one's skin make certain actions difficult but not, necessarily, impossible, so it also is with events inside one's skin. By the same token, there is no more point in putting up with events inside one's skin that one does not want there than there is in putting up with things outside one's skin that one does not want there. No point unless there is a point. That brings me to the last big change that will have to come to practice.

How do individuals first find and continue to track what they most deeply care about? I have shown why the 'Stay alive and be happy' answer to the 'What's it all about anyway?' question is too vague. I tell my clients the process is like putting your foot into cold, murky water, pushing it down into the gooey mud and 'feeling around' for something solid. I remind my clients, 'No one can know when you really hit something solid but you, no matter how much they *say* they can.' As a practical suggestion I encourage individuals to try many different things or think back over the things they have tried, while listening for a resonance inside themselves. As I once heard Al Ellis say, 'It's not just experience, it's also reflecting on experience.' It is not just taking a drink of wine. It is rolling it around in your mouth and breathing in air over the top as well as inhaling with your nose in the wine glass that give the full experience. These are all nice analogies. But, where are the concrete technologies for accomplishing these ends? Not well established, as far as I can see.

References

Beal, D., Kopec, A.M. and DiGiuseppe, R. (1996) Disputing clients' irrational beliefs, *Journal of Rational–Emotive and Cognitive–Behavior Therapy*, *14(4)*, 215–229.

Dewey, J. (1938) *Logic: The Theory of Inquiry*. New York: Holt, Reinhart & Winston.

DiGiuseppe, R. (1991) Comprehensive cognitive disputing in ret, in M. Bernard (ed.) *Using Rational-Emotive Therapy Effectively: A Practitioner's Guide*. New York: Plenum.

Ellis, A. (1962) *Reason and Emotion in Psychotherapy*. Secaucus, NJ: Citadel Press.

Epictetus (1890) *The Collected Works of Epictetus*. Boston: Little, Brown.

Hayes, S.C., Barnes-Holmes, D. and Toche, B. (2001) *Relational Frame Theory: A Post-Skinnerian Account of Human Language and Cognition*. New York: Plenum Press.

Jacobson, N.S., Dobson, K.S., Truax, P.A., Addis, M.E., Koerner, K., Gollan, J.K. and Prince, S.E. (1996) A component analysis of cognitive–behavioral treatment for depression, *Journal of Consulting and Clinical Psychology*, *64*, 295–304.

Martell, C.R., Addis, M.E. and Jacobson, N.S. (2001) *Depression in Context: Strategies for Guided Action*. New York: W.W. Norton.

Robb, H.B. III (1992) Why you don't have a 'perfect right' to anything, *Journal of Rational–Emotive and Cognitive–Behavior Therapy*, *10(4)*, 259–270.

Robb, H.B. III, Backx, W. and Thomas, J. (1999) Use of cognitive, emotive and behavioral interventions in rational emotive behavior therapy when clients lack 'emotional' insight, *Journal of Rational–Emotive and Cognitive–Behavior Therapy*, *17(3)*, 201–209.

Shakespeare, W. (1954) *Hamlet*. In *Mr. William Shakespeare's Comedies, Histories, and Tragedies* (a facsimile, prepared by Helge Kokeritz, of the first folio edition, pp. 742–772). New Haven, CT: Yale University (original work published 1623).

Wessler, R.A. and Wessler, R.L. (1980) *The Principles and Practices of Rational–Emotive Therapy*. San Francisco: Jossey-Bass.

Chapter 4

REBT as an intentional therapy

Wouter Backx

Introduction

In contrast to previous formulations of REBT, the present formulation, which is based on intentionality, identifies certain erroneous strategies used to achieve desires as the aetiology of unhealthy actions or reactions, i.e. emotions, thoughts and behaviours.

By 'intentionality' I mean every mental activity from starting to desire something to achieving the desired goal. In this context, I focus especially on the strategies used to implement the desire. The goal can be anything from obtaining sweets to leading a fulfilling life. Psychological problems arise when somebody is blocked in pursuing a goal and then uses erroneous strategies to cope with the frustration. I see this as a derailment of the intention. Cognitions caused by these strategies contain 'musts', 'oughts' and 'shoulds'.

This chapter makes more explicit what REBT practitioners have been doing implicitly for years: helping people to change their unhealthy strategies into productive ones. By articulating the theoretical background of the REBT practitioner, the practice can be better understood, developed and broadened.

REBT as a cognitive behavioural therapy

REBT is widely considered to be a cognitive behavioural therapy – not only because the founder Albert Ellis sees it that way, but mainly because the entire practice of cognitive behavioural therapies effectively started in 1955 with REBT, which at that time was known as Rational Therapy (RT).

As a matter of fact, Albert Ellis began his career as a cognitive behaviourist. He was deeply interested in people's 'wrong' thinking and was able to find certain patterns or categories in clients' irrational thinking (Ellis, 1962). For decades REBT continued to elaborate on these patterns and thousands of therapists were trained to recognize the different categories of irrational thoughts and to help clients to replace them with more rational ones. Other forms of cognitive behavioural therapy started to develop in the 1960s (Beck, 1967; Mahoney, 1974; Meichenbaum, 1977). Although each emphasized somewhat different aspects of clients' thinking and behaviour, REBT increasingly differentiated itself from other similar therapies.

What makes REBT different from other cognitive behavioural therapies?

One main difference between REBT and the other cognitive behavioural therapies was the kind of irrational thoughts REBT practitioners focused on ('musturbatory' thinking, i.e. thinking in 'musts', 'oughts' and 'shoulds'). Although other forms of dysfunctional thinking were still considered important and worth changing, trying to find the 'musts' and replace them with preferences was seen as the 'elegant solution' (Ellis, 1973; Ellis and Dryden, 1990).

Nowadays, REBT trainees are taught to hear the demanding and commanding connotation in clients' disturbed thinking and to translate it into a pure command or demand by the client. This is then identified as an irrational thought if the client agrees that he or she is holding on to that idea.

The other cognitive behavioural therapies do not go so far, although they do acknowledge that an imperative way of thinking plays a role in irrationality. Rather they believe that faulty perceptions and wrong inferences are the source of unhealthy reactions. They may define a statement that is considered to be insane in some way, but does not necessarily include a 'must' as an irrational thought; for example the inference: 'Nobody in this group really likes me'. REBT practitioners do not view this as an irrational belief, because it may actually be true that nobody really likes the client and it therefore does not explain an unhealthy reaction to what may be a possible state of affairs. Only if the client holds a belief, imperative in character, about the possibility that nobody likes him or her, will it lead to unhealthy feelings and behaviour and a disturbed perception of reality. Merely correcting that perception therefore does not get to the root of the problem. A schema as used by Beck and Young (Young, 1999) in Cognitive Therapy can be considered as a generalization over situations and time of specific inferences. The inference 'Nobody in this group really likes me' will be generalized in a schema into 'I am unlovable to significant others if exposed'. REBT disputes the specific incidents rather than the generalization and focuses on the imperative cognitions that lead to the possibly wrong inference.

In REBT you do not dispute inferences but imperative cognitions

You might say that this is a discussion about what belongs to the activating event A and what to the belief B. It is nevertheless fundamental: even if there are people in the group who do like the client, the thought 'nobody likes me', which is then not in accordance with reality, is in REBT neither irrational nor rational. It will therefore not be disputed. It is simply a wrong inference somebody makes about reality, an inference that is wrong this time, but might be correct on another occasion. At least it is a possible outcome. For some reason, the client made an error of judgement in this case. REBT is very much concerned with the question as to whether such an error was made at all.

It is not so much each individual error that we would like to change, but whatever it is that underlies such errors. We want to change the structure that is the root cause of all these errors. That structure is seen as an imperative way of thinking about what one really wants, i.e. that people in the group will like me. The imperative way of thinking and therefore the root cause of the problems is 'people in the group must absolutely like me'.

Some practitioners of other cognitive behaviour therapies will agree here. They believe, as REBT practitioners do, that there is some kind of thought that disturbs the person's assessment of reality in this case or determines the inferences made.

Another difference compared with other cognitive behaviour therapies is that REBT is a much more dynamic approach. Showing clients' errors in inferences is more like correcting arithmetical errors at school; correcting imperative thought processes is like a lawyer pleading their client's case in front of a jury. This makes the REBT therapist more dynamic, i.e. directive and confrontational, rather than a mere schoolteacher.

Irrational thoughts are imperative cognitions or 'musts'

Over the years many irrational thoughts have been identified. Originally Ellis started with eleven (Walen et al., 1980); he then kept adding thoughts and finally ended up with some fifty. Then he reduced them to three essential ones: I *must* do well, you *must* do well, and the world *must* give me what I want to have – all clearly imperative cognitions. All irrational beliefs can be reduced to one or a combination of these three.

Even human worth rating can be considered as a 'must'

When searching for an underlying, irrational way of thinking REBT practitioners look for demanding and commanding forms of thinking. Although it is not strictly necessary to find a literal 'must' or 'should', most other forms of disturbed *thinking* are seen as derivatives of a 'must'. The type of thinking that elicits most discussion amongst REBT theorists and practitioners is thoughts that involve an evaluation of human worth. Some REBT practitioners think there is a demanding kind of thinking underlying such evaluation; others think it is a category in itself. If someone were to say,

'I'm a worthless person because I didn't pass that exam', this would be an irrational thought for some REBT therapists, while others (like e.g. Ellis) would say that underlying this statement is a demand: 'I absolutely should have been able to pass this exam and, because I didn't, I'm worthless.' I agree with Ellis and consider his idea a support of the 'must'.

There has been a lack of consensus in the REBT community about the role of and relationship between evaluations and thoughts consisting of a 'must', 'ought' or 'should'. Richard Wessler, who greatly influenced the first edition of the *Practitioner's Guide*, strongly believes that it is the evaluative part of our thinking that gets us into trouble (Wessler and Wessler, 1980; Walen et al., 1980). He found himself so much at variance with other practitioners that he eventually left the REBT community and started his own form of psychotherapy, which is known as Cognitive Appraisal Therapy (CAT). I consider evaluations being strongly influenced by the imperative or non-imperative attitude of the person most of the time, but not necessarily. Somebody could evaluate an event as the worst thing that can happen to a human being, while at the same time having an attitude of accepting that fact.

Not irrational, but impractical, thoughts

So why does REBT restrict itself to a very specific type of irrational thinking? We can hardly say that this kind of thinking is typical of what people in general would consider irrational. We can ask ourselves: what is so irrational about demanding and commanding? It does not seem to be very irrational in itself. The way in which people hold beliefs can be considered irrational if it is 'absolutistic' (Rorer, 1989). The thoughts themselves are not typically irrational. We can say that they apparently do not often lead to what people expect. Fortunately for the practice of REBT, we have a good explanation of why this type of thoughts gets people into trouble. Simply stated, people cannot in reality put themselves in the position of commanding or ruling the universe. An REBT therapist can almost always make it clear to the client that this is an insane way of approaching reality and thus encourage the client to change his or her attitude. The question as to what precisely is irrational in the thinking process or what error of thinking is made has yet to be answered. However, we can show that this idea will not work and that it is contradicted by reality.

A different, underlying process

Other cognitive behavioural therapies consider a wrong way of thinking (e.g. a wrong conclusion, an over-generalization, or 'black and white' thinking) to be an error of thinking and therefore an irrational thought.

This is on the basis of the content of the thoughts. According to REBT, these irrational thoughts are all derivatives of imperative cognitions (containing a 'must') if they lead to unhealthy reactions. This 'musturbatory' type of thinking is highly intentional, i.e. directed towards a goal. It is not so much the content of the thoughts, but more the way they are held on to, or the way they define actions and tendencies that causes the problems.

What is somebody doing and how is that act so harmful for the individual, when he or she demands things from the universe? Why is somebody turning a desire into a must? First of all, REBT has always claimed that we start, even before there is an activating event, with a goal. With something that we would like to achieve. We call that an intention. The activating event is explicitly stated in this case as something that is between the person and his or her goal, something that is blocking the attainment of that goal. Let us assume, as REBT does, that somewhere in the process of coping with the blockage people start demanding and commanding by using 'musts' in their approach to this part of reality. REBT states that alongside this commanding attitude, with its unhealthy results, a person almost always has a striving, healthy attitude, which is manifest in effectively working towards attaining the goal. This last part would be considered to be the rational part of their reaction. The two parts can have ratios of varying strength. Depending on how strong the irrational part is compared to the rational one, the outcome will be more or less successful. I will focus only on the unproductive part.

The 'best friend' technique shows the underlying process

Let us now examine what happens when somebody is going to make a demand and a command when facing a barrier to their goals. For instance, they might say: 'I should absolutely have been able to pass that exam and I'm worthless for not doing so.' This may be a way of thinking that some people carry with them all their lives without being aware of its harmful effects. However, there is something very strange about it, which becomes clear when we follow the usual REBT procedure in helping such a person.

A REBT therapist would ask: 'And how would you judge your best friend, if she were to fail this exam? Would you also see her as worthless, because she didn't do what she should have been able to do?' Most clients will answer: 'No, it's different for her!' As an REBT therapist, we would then ask: 'But what makes you so different from your best friend? What makes you worthless, but not her? Why is it that she needn't pass the exam, while you feel you have to?' This is a very powerful technique, because it shows the client that something essential is wrong in his or her thinking and can therefore be changed. It's abundantly clear that holding on to the thoughts (1) 'I should have absolutely passed' and (2) 'Now I'm worthless' is psychologically harmful. Both the thoughts are intentional, i.e. they lead to action. The first one is a resolution about the exam, the second one a way of dealing with oneself (I do not deserve good things from life, I should not be loved or approved of, and so on).

So far this is routine REBT, but it shows us something important: the individual does not hold on to a wrong idea about the world, for instance the idea that the sun rotates around the earth. The individual does not have the wrong information. No, there are two incompatible thought patterns working at the same time, about the same subject, but pertaining to different areas of the personal life of the individual: their own life and that of the others.

I think differently when I strive for something

It is very difficult to defend the idea that somebody has a wrong way of thinking when the two patterns are about exactly the same subject (not passing an exam). It is more realistic to say that the individual concerned really does know that not passing an exam does not make you a worthless person. But this involves applying a different rule for oneself than for others. The most articulate way of stating this is: 'This doesn't hold for everybody else, just for me.' It looks as if the discriminating factor in thinking rationally (as the person does about others) and irrationally (about him- or herself) is connected to the process of striving for a goal. This is what I would call intentionality. The process of trying to implement an intention disturbs the thinking process. Not only the thinking process, but the total holistic cluster of thinking, behaving and emoting.

It is not the thinking that is wrong, but the striving

Here we see that it is very difficult to maintain that the basic problem is somebody's wrong thinking. Why would somebody think in one situation that five plus seven equals twelve, while in another situation it equals eleven? And when asked about the validity of five plus seven equals eleven, admit: 'Yeah, in fact you're right, it is twelve, but to me it feels like eleven'? What makes thinking in my case different from thinking in general? How come that when it is about my own world there is a different logic from the one that applies to the world in general? Or can we say: I use another type of logic when it's about *my* desires?

If we examine this more closely, we will see that the essential difference is that the other person (or every other person) is not trying to achieve my goal. That's what makes the difference. The fact that I have not achieved what I want is the point. When the other is trying to achieve my goal and does not succeed, he or she is seen as bad and inferior in my eyes too. It's about me achieving my particular goal and not so much what I think of someone not achieving some general goal. It is about me achieving my goal.

REBT therefore does not so much examine my wrong ways of thinking, but more my wrong ways of trying to achieve my goal.

Trying to achieve a goal starts with certain intentions. When our intentions contain flaws (or rather, when the strategies to implement them contain flaws), they are not suited for a confrontation with reality. In that case, the implementation of our intentions will derail and we find ourselves frustrating our original goal.

How do errors of intending create errors in thinking, behaving and emoting?

We can ask the question: what is the connection between wrong intentions and wrong thoughts? The answer is: wrong intentions cause wrong ways of thinking, feeling and behaving. The new focus is on the strategies for implementing the intention. In fact, a lot of the irrational thinking, and along with it unhealthy feeling and behaving, has to do with not accepting reality, especially that part of reality which we try to influence and change to our benefit. So we could say that in the example above the problem is finding it difficult to accept oneself as a person that failed the exam. Not accepting reality is part of a strategy that is designed to enforce reality to provide what is very much wanted.

What does intentionality contribute to REBT?

Up to now intentionality has been sadly neglected in the REBT community and in psychotherapy in general. Although REBT of all psychotherapies is the most intention-oriented, intentionality has not yet been well articulated. In short, the main tenet of this chapter is that REBT does not focus so much on errors in thinking, but more on intentional errors. REBT therapists have not been explicitly trained to focus on intentional errors. The result is that some people get confused and REBT has been misinterpreted many times by therapists as well as by laymen. Errors in thinking are part of and caused by errors of intention, just like errors in behaviour and errors of emotion are caused by errors of intention. So far correcting errors in thinking has proved a very powerful tool to help people change their unproductive ways of coping with adversity. The intentional approach can also use the irrational thoughts as a starting point, but it can go beyond them.

The difference between intentionality and classical REBT

The most important thing about looking at intentionality, compared with classical REBT, is the notion that people indeed make cognitive, behavioural and emotional errors, but that these are all derivatives of an error of intending. People make all kinds of mistakes, especially in their thinking, which they can correct with the help of logic, realistic thinking and by realizing what the effects of their thinking and emoting and behaving are. Nevertheless, when there is an underlying process or a more basic process, then it will certainly be worthwhile paying attention to this underlying process as well.

Why should there be an underlying process?

What reasons are there to assume there is another process at work? Why would unproductive thinking, emoting and behaving be derivatives of another process – the process of intentionality? In what way will it benefit REBT to take this idea into account?

First of all, in the context of other cognitive behavioural therapies, it is clear that the kind of beliefs that REBT considers to be irrational are, in their purest form at least, special ones. Irrational beliefs in REBT include a 'must', 'ought' or 'absolutely should'. These thoughts are statements of a demanding and commanding nature. These types of thoughts are described theoretically as imperative cognitions. We can wonder what is irrational about them; what is so irrational in commanding and demanding? As already stated, it is not so much the content that makes the belief irrational, but the rigidity with which it is held and the profound conviction about its general validity. Holding on to these beliefs is not really a thinking process, but rather part of an action tendency and strategy to reach a goal.

Secondly, when we try to understand the process behind this imperative thinking, we see people who, when they are commanding others or demanding things from the world, are in fact trying to exclude the possibility that what they would like to happen and are striving for will not happen. They go out of their way to exclude any possibility of failing in what they so very much want. But they do this by using the 'wrong' (i.e. unproductive) means. More importantly, they do it in ways that actually harm them; they target their energy in the wrong direction, in a self-destructive way. In fact they are working against their own best interests, while trying very hard to achieve their goal. Thinking merely serves the process of excluding the unwanted, but it is not the essential thing here.

Now we can ask the question: why do people strive so hard to achieve their goals in the wrong way? We might say that is because they are not aware that it is the wrong way. This is indeed the position most cognitive behaviourists take. They think that people do not know what they are thinking wrongly and they aim to teach them the 'right thoughts'.

Immediate versus postponed gratification

Partly this is what REBT practitioners do too, but they say that people do know that, for instance, procrastination will not yield good results.

Alcoholics do know that continued drinking will get them into more trouble. So what do these people lack that prevents them from using this knowledge to stop acting against their own interests? The REBT understanding is that people more or less deliberately choose short-term gratification over long-term results, disregarding the long-term disadvantages, i.e. suffering. It is hard to defend the position that they are just making an error of thinking. The point is that they very often do not want to think sensibly at all at the crucial moment. As a matter of fact, both procrastinators and alcoholics take the following attitude: 'I want my pleasure now and the hell with the consequences.' This is not an error in thinking. This is not information that is wrongly processed or wrong information that is rightly processed. This is deluding oneself in order to achieve a certain goal, namely attaining immediate pleasure or avoiding immediate discomfort.

Not errors in thinking, but the derailment of intentions

Again, it is very difficult to maintain the position that demanding immediate gratification is an error in thinking. People strive for pleasure and think about how to get it. However, when their striving is wrong, it does not follow that it is wrong thinking that is causing it. A classical REBT approach to this process is to describe it as a hedonistic calculation that is made wrongly, and most people know that the calculation is wrong.

Take someone who is striving to achieve something. Let us again use the example of wanting to pass an exam. The goal is clear, but not the way to the goal. There is uncertainty about how to do it and about whether it is feasible or not. When this person gets blocked, they are likely to try other approaches and to try harder. When they still do not come any closer to their goal, they might embark on a faulty way of intending, i.e. bring in the 'must': 'I *must* pass that exam.' This is a very special mental activity that a person creates and it is the result of a derailment of a very strong desire or wish. As Ellis would put it, 'to turn a desire into a must'. Their strategy is to reach their goal by mentally excluding the possibilty of failing. It means that the person is not prepared to consider even the slightest chance of not succeeding in implementing the intention. To think in 'musts' serves the attempt to exclude failing and is therefore the consequence of a strategy of excluding failing.

The process of intentionality or how we plan

What I will describe here is not necessarily exactly how things happen in reality; to keep it simple, I will describe the events serially, whereas in reality things may happen in parallel. We start to intend something by developing a desire and setting a goal. Once the goal is set, we try to find ways of achieving it and examine what we need in the process. This all happens in our mind and has no effect, so far, on reality. Once we have a plan, we are going to use our power to influence the environment according to our will: will power. We intend to employ our energy in a certain way. Such a plan is more or less equipped for the possibility of being frustrated. When things appear not to succeed at a certain stage, then the person will first take this step differently or more persistently. Nevertheless, the person may not succeed. What will happen next depends on how well the plan is designed for blockages.

We have to realize that as long as the goal has not been attained, there is a tension created by the will power applied to unsuccessfully attempting to get rid of a blockage. Some people cannot stand this tension for long and give up. Others go on and put more energy into the enterprise and the tension increases. Let us assume they still do not get what they want. Going back to the original plan, the person tries to exclude what is actually happening: total or partial failure. But how can you avoid failure? One way – as already stated – is to try harder or differently, or over and over again.

When we cannot fail in our mind we cannot fail in reality

Another way of avoiding failure is to construct in the mind the impossibility of failing. This is almost the same as an attitude of not accepting failure. We go back to the drawing board, i.e. to the planning stage. Part of planning is to create something new in our minds: a desired change in the environment. We now try to create another perception of our *influence* on that environment. We falsely try to create a world in which we cannot fail in what we want to achieve. We can call this meta-planning (planning about planning). So we use our energy in the planning stage to create a world without the possibility of failing and thus remove uncertainty. Although we know this is not possible, it is very tempting to pretend in order to reduce the tension that we might fail. The advantage of this strategy is: as long as I don't accept that it will fail, it will not fail. Or as long as I don't accept failure, I'll keep working on succeeding and keep alive my belief that I will succeed.

Take an incident at Amsterdam airport: an American wants to check in 15 pieces of luggage. We have to wait in line behind him for 40 minutes, because the person at the check-in counter doesn't know how to handle it. After half an hour of waiting the person in front of me says to the American in Dutch: 'Hey, you, hurry up!' I ask him: 'Do you think that will help?' And he answers: 'No, but it makes me feel better.' Here we can see a process taking place in the mind: saying 'hurry up' in a language the other doesn't understand provides some relief for the tension he is experiencing at that moment. In reality it doesn't change anything. But the Dutchman feels he is doing something about a frustrating situation. And that helps, for a short while, even though he is deluding himself!

Short-term gain

Intending on the basis of excluding the possibility of failure helps for a while, but only for a very short while, because all this mental activity does not help to attain the goal. The mind is relieved for a while, because the person is exerting a lot of energy, but without the desired results. This is exactly like the alcoholic who knows that drinking will not solve their problems and the man at Amsterdam airport who knows that his interjection will not speed up the process and thus help him to attain his goal. It is nevertheless a short-term solution for a very strong feeling of tension that the person cannot or is not willing to cope with, like when somebody is told that a loved one has died. Such a person may say: 'It's not true, this *cannot* be true.' For a while, it seems as if the one who has passed away is not dead, because we don't allow it to happen.

Another example: if I accept the fact that my parents and brother treat me badly, I have to live with that fact. As long as I refuse to accept it, I can create a world in which I think I have a good relationship with them. 'OK, so there are rows all the time, but that's merely incidental. Basically, we have a good relationship.' This manoeuvre requires a lot of energy and it doesn't help at all, but I use it to avoid facing the unpleasant reality.

These manoeuvres of the mind are highly addictive and are viewed as coming from outside

In the long run such reactions become more or less automatic or, to put it another way, people get addicted to these kinds of mechanisms, because of the rapid relief they provide. A whole variety of derived reactions will be caused by this basic reaction, which is designed to cope with the frustration of not succeeding in getting what one wants and avoiding what one does not want. Or, as in this case, losing what one does not want to lose.

It is important to realize that the thoughts created by such a manoeuvre become self-deceptive 'truths', as in the example above: 'I'm no good now that I've failed this exam.' After a very short period of relief, the person starts believing a trick of thinking that was originally designed to deal with the tension created by an uncomfortable situation. If we would give up that thought we would immediately have to face the grim reality: the tension comes back, so we continue to think it.

An error in intending: two examples

When we look at intentionality from the point of view of a strategy, it looks like a short cut to getting what one wants as an alternative to a more time-consuming approach to achieving the desired goal. An important error of this kind of intention is that the amount of discomfort is fixed in the mind of the actor. In order to do X, the maximum amount of discomfort the person is willing to endure is so much. That will immediately lead to the thought 'I can't stand more discomfort than . . .'. This thought serves the erroneous strategy. (The intention 'I don't want more discomfort than' becomes the strategy 'I must not have more discomfort than . . .'.) It should be clear that we are talking here about a way of trying to achieve one's goals, rather than mere thinking processes. Again, this is what intentionality is all about.

The second example is the one about failing, which we've already discussed above. In fact, it is rather obvious that the attitude of not accepting the possibility of failure leads to the thought 'I must succeed'. And from 'I must succeed' follows the thought 'otherwise I'm worthless'. Here too the thought serves the wrong strategy.

Dysfunctional emotions in the light of intentionality

We can show how we can reduce irrational thinking, unhealthy emoting and dysfunctional behaviour due to errors of intention. Only then does the concept of intentionality make sense. So far we have seen how the general process works and that people change their original healthy way of intending or striving to achieve a goal into an unhealthy one. I now want to elaborate on this mechanism in a number of areas. I will do this for the basic unhealthy emotions: anger, anxiety, feelings of inferiority (depression), and guilt or shame.

Anger

Anger is the most obvious emotion that can be seen in relation to not getting what one wants or getting what one does not want. The intention is the total mental activity that is involved in directing energy to the goal. The problem is how one uses the energy prescribed by the plan (= intention). The energy of the rage is directed towards the person or thing that is in between the goal and the person who wants to achieve the goal. It is clearly designed to eliminate the blockage. The kinds of irrational beliefs that are involved are:

(1) 'You must help me or give me what I want.'
(2) 'I must be able to achieve what I want.'
(3) 'The world must (immediately) give me what I want.'

We can compare these irrational beliefs with their rational counterparts:

(1) 'You don't have to help me or give me what I want at all, although I would very much like you to help me or to give me what I want and

I will try to persuade you, but if you don't give me what I want or help me, then I can live with it.'

(2) 'I don't have to be able to achieve all that I want, although I would very much like to be able to achieve what I want and will work hard for it, but if I fail, then I fail, and I'm willing to live with that failure.'

(3) 'The world doesn't have to give me anything at all, although I very much like it when the world does, but if it doesn't, so be it – I can live with it.'

There is no doubt that these two different ways of thinking express different ways of trying to achieve the same goal. The irrational one is an attempt to get to the goal in a very undirected way, with a lot of pressure, almost an energy explosion. You could describe the attempt as a short cut. It resembles the way young children stamp their feet when they want a cookie 'right now'. Here too we can see that in fact the child tries to get his or her way immediately without any delay. In such a case we teach children to have patience. We, as adults, know that trying to attain a goal the way a child does will usually not be successful. We would not say that the problem in this case is just wrong thinking. The problem lies in not being willing to wait for the result. And indeed in that not being willing to wait and to accept the apparent reality, we also show a way of thinking that contains a 'must': 'I must get what I want right now, because I want it so much.' But that comes after and as a result of the incorrect attitude or strategy. Together with helping them to accept reality and preparing children to be willing to postpone gratification, we can help them to change their strategy by changing their thinking processes.

Almost the same holds true for adults, except that, as adults, we often have to deal with longer delays and with things that are sometimes not feasible at all. In all of these cases, the mental activity is an attempt to get the frustrating factor out of the way. One of these attempts is to try to think the person or object away. There are many ways in which that can be accomplished. One is that you can 'disqualify' the other person and ask others for help to confirm this disqualification (an extreme case of this occurs in warfare, when the enemy is dehumanized).

Trying to remove the blockage

In fact, what happens in all these examples is an attempt to get rid of what keeps us from our goal, from implementing our intention. But we use the wrong means and therefore do not achieve our goal. It does not help us to be impatient and it usually does not help to become angry. We can consider the thinking process that is part of the anger as one aspect of it. The emotion and behaviour are others. Together they form the holistic triangle of the anger reaction. They are brought into action because the whole is a way of coping with the frustration of not attaining the goal. But why do people rely on this wrong strategy? What is the advantage for them?

Short-term gratification – the advantage of being angry

Very briefly, they get rid of the feeling of frustration by acting against the blockage as if that would have an effect in the real world. Nevertheless the only effect it has is on the mind of the individual concerned: he or she gets angry. For a very short while there's no need to feel frustrated, because it feels like something is being done by not giving in to reality. So for a very short while the person does not have to accept that he or she cannot in fact change reality. This is a form of delusion, combined with a strong explosion of energy.

Anxiety

The next emotion we want to look at is anxiety. At first sight it is not clear how in the case of anxiety a person does not succeed in implementing an intention. The mental activity is one that is active but in an immediate self-destructive way. It can even lead to paralysis and therefore look very passive. Irrational thoughts may be:

(1) 'I must absolutely not get into situation X, because that would be the end of the world or totally unbearable.'
(2) 'I simply must be able to pass that exam or else that would be terrible.'
(3) 'I must be absolutely sure that I will win this verbal fight or otherwise I'm a total loser.'

The corresponding rational beliefs could be:

(1) 'I may find myself in situation X and, although I would very much like this not to happen and will work very hard to avoid it, if it happens, then it happens and I'm willing to put up with it.'
(2) 'I don't have to be able to pass the exam; I may fail and, although I would very much like to pass and will work hard to pass, if I fail, I fail and that would be very bad, but not the end of the world.'
(3) 'I don't have to win this fight; I may fail and, although I would very much like to win and will work very hard to do so, if I nevertheless fail, then I fail and I will not see myself as a total loser.'

Excluding the unavoidable

All these rational beliefs clearly show the intention that is involved. The difference between the rational and irrational belief is that with the former there is willingness to accept any outcome, while the irrational belief is not open to this possibility. The way the person tries to implement the intention is what causes the problem. By trying to totally exclude the undesired outcome (i.e. the strategy for the intention), the person gets anxious. There are a few ways in which the process of striving gets disturbed by not being open to undesired outcomes. First, he or she tries to exaggerate the negative part of the undesired outcome. Like a lawyer pleading their client's case in front of a jury, the person tries to convince other people that this should absolutely not happen to the client. (As a child this strategy may have been partly effective.) This can be seen as a mental activity to preclude the undesired outcome. Making the disadvantages bigger does not help at all; it is not an effective strategy. But, according to REBT theory, it is not damaging either. It makes the A, the activating event, more negative than it actually is. Exaggerations do not create problems in and of themselves, but aiming to exclude negative outcomes does. When exaggeration does not provide the desired results, the next step will be more exaggeration. If the person had only made an error of judgement, which would have resulted in the exaggeration, the process would stop here. The only difference then would be that the degree of negativity surrounding the A (the activating event) is greater. But the exaggeration serves the strategy of exclusion. That's why it gets bigger and bigger. It's not the static mistake in the thinking, perceiving or judging process that is causing the problems, but the dynamic process of continuing to demand harder – against all the odds – to avoid what cannot be fully excluded.

The intention derailed

After the initial exaggeration, there's a second exaggeration and a third, because they are not effective in excluding the unwanted outcome of reality. He or she is using all their energy for one task: excluding the undesired outcome. And when it is not sufficient, more energy is employed. And so on. It is, in effect, a derailment of the planning stage (working out how to avoid that particular situation). All energy is directed to make the world into one in which the unwanted situation simply cannot exist, but this is only imaginary, because all the mental activity has no effect on reality. The effect is a real crisis of the mind.

A second way in which the process of pursuing is disturbed is by being mentally overactive. All systems are put on red alert. It's like being at the dentist and tensing your muscles in anticipation of the pain that may come. We know that tensing muscles almost always results in more pain. Nevertheless we continue to do it. The same thing happens when people get anxious in general. This strategy also comes from not being prepared to undergo what cannot be avoided. Doing many things that seem to us to help, but in fact do not, gives us the false idea we are working on warding off danger and we do not have to cope with the discomfort of enduring the unwanted situation. Both are examples of a derailment of the original intention.

Feelings of inferiority/depression

Depression can be seen as a state of mind in which feelings of inferiority (a negative self image) play an important role. In the depressive state a negative view of the past, the present and the future prevail, especially concerning the role of the person him- or herself.

Feelings of inferiority can also be considered to be intentional rather than mere cognitive distortions. When somebody generates inferiority feelings, because he or she does not achieve what they want to achieve, the person does not just make an error in thinking. When a person is unable to achieve an intended goal, they will try to achieve it by trying harder and/or by trying in different ways. When that does not help, they may rely on the demanding and commanding approach to reality. This dramatically increases the tension experienced. The effect of this mental activity will only be counterproductive. Most people will try to make the tension even higher by commanding and demanding more strongly. (Instead of trying another strategy, they try the same one, only harder.) As we saw before, this is part of a strategy that tries to exclude the unwanted. Eventually the person cannot stand the tension any longer. One way to break out of this force field is to give up the goal. If people do this, they end up as low achievers. Another way to break out of the tension is to undervalue oneself by saying: 'I'm not able to achieve this goal, which makes me less of a person; so how can an inferior person like me ever achieve this goal?' And the answer is: it's impossible because I have defined myself as inferior. But, if I can thus convince myself of the impossibility, then I don't have to try any longer and I will experience immediate relief from the tension. But, like alcohol abuse, the advantage of using this method is short-lived, because I have to live with my inferiority, which means not accepting myself. So we started to exclude failing and ended up designing failure.

Feelings of inferiority as an addiction

As this strategy provides relief so fast, it is very addictive and therefore difficult to break out of. The making of feelings of inferiority is not specifically the effect of wrong thinking, but of the wrong way of trying to achieve intended goals. Of course we can find wrong thoughts caused by the wrong way of intending. That makes it possible to help people to change their counterproductive way of implementing their intentions by tapping in to their thoughts. For example:

(1) 'Because I'm not able to pass this exam, as I absolutely must, I'm worthless.'
(2) 'Now I haven't been able to guide my trainee as well as I was supposed to do, I'm no good as a trainer or even as a person.'

The rational counterparts of these are:

(1) 'I don't have to pass this exam and, although I would very much like to be able to and will work hard to pass it, if I fail, then I fail. I'm willing to live with that and will not become less of a person because of it.'
(2) 'I failed to guide my trainee as well as I was supposed to do and, although I would very much like to do as well as possible and will work hard on it, if I still fail, I fail. I'm willing to live with that and will not feel less of a person because of it.'

We can see how using rational thoughts helps the individual to direct energy in the right direction, i.e. where it can be used effectively and efficiently, and not work against the goal or against the person him- or herself. It's then as if one is willing to leave a negative appraisal for what it is, rather then going through all kinds of contortions trying to change it into something else. I deliberately use the term 'energy' here, because it's another way of addressing the cluster of thinking, behaving and emoting. While these are not exactly the same, the term suits the intentional approach.

From passive victim to active strategist

Hardly any feeling makes people more passive than inferiority feelings. Showing people that they are not the passive victim of some wrong thinking, but that they actively have set up this (emotional) route to comfort themselves, helps them to see their position quite differently. It helps them to give up their unproductive and addictive way of coping with frustration because of the adversities they encounter. This is essentially different from mainly focusing on their thinking processes.

Guilt and shame

Feelings of guilt and shame can more or less be put in the same category as inferiority feelings. Indeed the feeling of guilt means in the first place that the person thinks, rightly or not, that they did something wrong and therefore thinks he or she is no good, less of a person, because of whatever they did wrong. Or, put another way, they cannot accept being the kind of person who made that error. Again we see somebody who wanted to achieve something, yet fails. Thoughts may include:

(1) 'Because I did this wrong thing to my child, I'm no good as a parent and even no good as a person.'
(2) 'Because I didn't speak up well at the meeting, I jeopardized our project and therefore I'm no good as a project leader and, what's more, I'm no good as a person.'

The mental energy used does not help to come any closer to the goal (or to prevent the individual concerned from doing it again), but rather it is turned inwards, resulting in feelings of guilt.

What difference does intentionality make to therapeutic practice?

When we realize that a person is making intentional errors rather than errors in thinking, it gives us the opportunity to pay attention to the more important aspects of the client's dilemma, to find out where things actually go wrong.

We can choose to use intentionality

This does not mean we should always take this route. Many REBT practitioners do not aim for the most elegant solution with all of their clients either. For various reasons, they very often seek pragmatic solutions to clients' emotional problems. Just like when, from time to time, we do Beckian CT when we know in the back of our minds that we have more powerful interventions at hand. Still we decide not to use them at this particular moment.

The client often agrees with us

If we address the intentional part of the disturbed functions of the client, we will very often find the client taking sides with us. It's a natural process to examine the goals that somebody is striving to achieve and to explore the effects of the client's specific inefficient ways of approaching these goals. Because we start explicitly with the goal the client has formulated and look for every flaw in the strategy the client is using, we will find the client working closely with us. If we succeed in explaining why somebody tends to think irrationally, because of a wrong strategy, it will be easier for the client to correct his or her way of thinking (and behaving and emoting). We now align their thoughts directly with their goals. And that makes a lot of sense to them.

Example

We show them a direct link between their striving and their suffering, because of their wrong strategy. Let's take an example to illustrate the difference between a 'classical' and an 'intentional' REBT approach: 'I want very much to give a good sermon, but I get so anxious I almost burst into tears.'

First with 'classical' REBT

What are you most anxious about with respect to giving a good sermon?
'I want so desperately to give a good one; I want my parishioners to approve of me.'
That's not the cause of your anxiety; you probably say something else to yourself too.
'Well, I must do it well and get their approval.'
That's right. And it's the 'must' and not the desire that makes you anxious. Correct?
'Yes.'
But why must you do it well and get their approval?
'Maybe I don't have to do well and get their approval.'
OK, so when you don't have to, and only want to, you don't feel anxious.
'Yes, that's right.'
So what can you say instead of 'I must do it well'?
'I want to do it well.'
And if you don't?
'I still find that difficult.'
But if you convince yourself that you don't have to do it well – that you allow yourself to fail – although of course you would very much like to do it well and keep working on that, but if you fail, you fail and you don't become useless because of that. How would that feel?
[The client will then, most likely, change their attitude.]

Now with 'intentional' REBT

What is your attitude towards giving a sermon that makes you anxious?
'Well, I desperately want to give a good one and I want my parishioners to approve of me.'
That's not the cause of your anxiety. There's probably something else in your attitude that makes you anxious when you try to do it well.
'I simply can't accept doing it less than well.'
Because if you would accept that, that you might do it less than well . . .
'Then I probably wouldn't do it that well.'
[Here it becomes clear how the client is using a strategy.]

Do you see that not accepting the possibility of you doing it less well than you would want to, that's what makes you anxious?

'Yes!'

Are you saying that you do a better job when you are anxious to the point of almost bursting into tears than when you are not anxious?

[Making explicit the wrong strategy.]

'Oh no, of course not!'

Do you realize that you are choosing a strategy that leads to anxiety, when you demand from yourself that you live up to a certain standard? That this strategy works against you?

'Yes!'

So, you see the disadvantages. But now the important question: what do you think is the advantage of choosing this strategy?

'There's no advantage. It's stupid to try to do it this way.'

But then you say you deliberately chose a stupid strategy, assuming this is not the first time you realized how bad this strategy is, right?

'No.'

So there's something else you are trying to achieve by this wrong strategy.

'Well, otherwise I might not deliver such a good sermon.'

That's why you wrongly chose this strategy. But what do you do, when you try to deliver a good sermon by demanding perfection of yourself?

'I try to exclude the possibility of doing it less than well.'

Because you want to . . .

'. . . do it very well.'

Can you see that you are trying to achieve your goal – a sermon that is as good as possible – by excluding the possibility of failure? Actually you work on making failure impossible by adopting an attitude in your mind that does not include failing, don't you? If that would make you give a perfect sermon, that would be great, wouldn't it?

'Yes.'

But you said just a moment ago that this strategy won't work. So what exactly do you try to avoid by mentally excluding failing, apart from failing?

'Before the sermon starts I can't stand the idea that maybe the sermon will turn out not to be so good.'

You cannot stand not being in control?

'Yes, that is it!'

Not being in control means that you can do your best without knowing what exactly will be the outcome. You have to leave it, so to speak, in the hands of God: 'Thy will be done.'

'Yes, but I can't!'

Yes, you can, but you try erroneously to escape this conclusion, because you want so very much to do it well. Do you see that?

'Yes, I see that I delude myself by demanding perfectionism, while I know that not everything is in my hands. But I want it so much to be in my hands!'

And that's OK; there's nothing wrong with that. But you can't make your wish into a demand, because you are not the Ruler of the Universe. So you'd better accept being human and not focus your energy on something that won't work. So save your energy and accept God's will.

'When I do that, I no longer demand of myself that I'm perfect and I also don't think "I have to succeed and win their approval". I can feel this new attitude loosening up my whole body when I think of giving a sermon.'

[At this point we advise formulating a rational belief too, which represents the new productive strategy, as we did in the classical approach quoted above.]

I can think it, but I can't feel it

Many REBT therapists are familiar with the phenomenon that clients see their wrong thinking, but are unable to change their feelings. We can say to them that their irrational thought is stronger than their rational one, so they would do better to give more credence to the rational thought. The elegant side of intentionality is that we can explain to them why they keep feeling and believing unproductively. It's because it looks like a short cut to the goal they so much wanted to achieve.

The drawbacks for REBT theory

When dealing with intentionality REBT practitioners may look less confrontational or softer than when using the old-fashioned classical REBT approach. You do not so much confront the client with his or her stupid thinking, but more with faulty intending. Or, as we saw in the example above about deluding oneself in order to gain the illusion of control, we show that the client is losing emotional stability at the same time.

Nevertheless, one can use irrational thoughts to find out someone's faulty strategies and one can confront clients equally strongly to get them to change these strategies.

This may seem like following a different path from the well-trod way of doing therapy. It may even look like undermining the original insights and theories of REBT. But in fact it does not. It should rather be seen as a broadening of REBT. In fact, most of the time REBT practitioners already take intentionality more or less into account. The main difference may be that it can be done more explicitly if the therapist shows how clients' irrational thoughts serve the wrong way of achieving their strong desires.

Some therapists may think that working from an intentional point of view will distract them from the real work. First of all, we can say that it is not always better to take intentionality into account. In some circumstances the traditional REBT works best. At other times it is better to dispute inferences rather than imperative cognitions. Secondly, what I contend in this chapter is that REBT is essentially intentional, so when you do classical REBT you are using an intentional approach anyway.

Future developments

Research is required to support the tenet that intentionality is at the source of psychological disturbance. Good experiments have yet to be designed. For example, from the intentional point of view one might expect functional or pragmatic disputing to be more effective than a more logical or empirical approach. Experiments could be designed to test whether this is true.

Therapists can also experiment with intentionality in their own practice to see how it works for them. They might find they get new ideas using a system that was in fact part of REBT practice from the very beginning, but has not previously been recognized as such.

References

Beck, A.T. (1967) *Depression: Clinical, Experimental, and Theoretical Aspects*. New York: Harper & Row.

Ellis, A. (1962) *Reason and Emotion in Psychotherapy*. Secaucus, NJ: Lyle Stuart.

Ellis, A. (1973) *Humanistic Psychotherapy*. New York: McGraw-Hill.

Ellis, A. and Dryden, W. (1990) *The Essential Albert Ellis*. New York: Springer.

Mahoney, M. (1974) *Cognition and Behavior Modification*. Cambridge, MA: Ballinger.

Meichenbaum, D. (1977) *Cognitive–Behavior Modification*. New York: Plenum.

Rorer, L.G. (1989) Rational–emotive theory: I. An integrated psychological and philosophical basis, *Cognitive Therapy and Research*, *13*, 477–494.

Walen, S., DiGiuseppe, R. and Wessler, R. (1980) *A Practitioner's Guide to Rational–Emotive Therapy* (1st edn). New York and Oxford: Oxford University Press.

Walen, S., DiGiuseppe, R. and Dryden, W. (1992) *A Practitioner's Guide to Rational–Emotive Therapy* (2nd edn). New York and Oxford: Oxford University Press.

Wessler, R.A. and Wessler, R.L. (1980) *The Principles and Practice of Rational-Emotive Therapy*. San Francisco, CA: Jossey-Bass.

Young, J. (1999) *Cognitive Therapy for Personality Disorders: A Schema-focused Approach*. Sarasota, FL: Professional Resource Press.

Chapter 5

How deep can we go? How deep should we go? Irrational beliefs as schemata

Stevan Lars Nielsen

'Schema' was introduced as a reference term in the American Psychological Association's *Thesaurus of Psychological Index Terms* in 1988 and was defined there as 'a cognitive structure used for comprehension, perception, and interpretation of stimuli' (PsychINFO, 2001b, no page number). Figure 5.1 shows numbers and percentages of publications in *Psychological Abstracts* (*PA*) (PsychINFO, 2001a) with the words schema, schemas, or schemata in titles, abstracts or index lines, arranged by decades: 0.407% of *PA* publications (7147 of 1,757,833 total publications) have schema references. Publications with schema references increased 240% from 0.23% of publications in the 1970s to 0.56% in the 1990s (see Figure 5.1).

Schema terms are cross-referenced with 2611 topics in *PA*. Table 5.1 presents numbers of articles that cross-reference schemata and 62 other index topics, ordered by numbers of publications; 52 of these cross-referenced index topics seem relevant to psychotherapy. More articles indexed to 'Cognitive Therapy' (CT) have cross-references to schema terms than any other psychotherapy-related term (193 articles; 17th most publications; see Table 5.1). Publications indexed to psychoanalysis or psychodynamic models (e.g. psychoanalysis, object relations, fantasy as a defense mechanism, etc.; see Table 5.1) are cross-referenced to schema terms in 441 articles. Twelve articles reference schemata and self-talk or Rational Emotive Therapy.

A brief history of schema models

Marshall (1995) notes that the word schema is a transliteration from the ancient Greek word σχημα (schêma: σ = s, χ = ch or k, η = ê, μ = m, α = a) which appears in the writings of Aristotle, Aristophanes, Euclid, Plato, Xenophon, other ancient Greek authors, and the earliest of New Testament manuscripts (cf. Perseus Digital Library, 2001). Schêma appears to have come from σχησω or schêso, the future tense of the Greek verb ὲχω or ĕcho,[1] meaning to have or to hold.

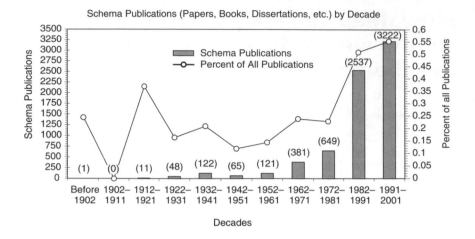

Figure 5.1   Numbers and percentages of publications in *Psychological Abstracts* including references to the words schema, schemas, or schemata in abstracts, titles, or subject lines, by decade of publication.

From its context in ancient texts (cf. Liddell et al., 1968, 1996), schêma is usually translated as form, shape, or figure; that is, geometric form, shape, or figure. Schêma has also been translated to convey more abstract characteristics such as adornment, appearance, attitude, position, conformation, dress, equipment, fashion, or military formation. Schêma sometimes described abstract configurations and has been translated as grammar, law, politics, rhythm, or syllogism. The verb schêso and inflected versions of the noun schêma have sometimes been translated as to adorn, to demean, to make a show, and to construct, including to adorn oneself, to demean oneself, and to make a show of oneself. Schêma also referred to characteristics of thought and has been translated as bearing, expression, gesture, mein, pomp, pretense, and role or character as actors take on roles or characters. Marshall concluded that for Plato it was 'through the schema that we understand what we see' (1995, pp. 6–7).

Kant devoted a chapter in his *Critique of Pure Reason* to 'The schematism of the pure concepts of understanding' ([1781] 1929, p. 180). He proposed that we experience no pure sensory representations of the world, rather,

> the formal and pure condition of sensibility to which the employment of the concept of understanding is restricted, we shall entitle the *schema* of the concept. . . . Indeed it is schemata, not images of objects, which underlie our pure sensible concepts.
>
> (p. 182, italics original to the English translation)

Table 5.1   Numbers of articles in *Psychological Abstracts* with cross-
references to selected index topics and the words 'schema',
'schemas', or 'schemata'

Terms cross-referenced with the words schema, schemas, or schemata	Number of articles so cross-referenced	Rank of the number of cross-referenced articles
Cognitive processes	765	1st
Memory	422	2nd
Models	416	3rd
Theories	376	4th
Self-concept	272	5th
Social perception	268	6th
Recall learning	259	7th
Cognitive development	240	8th
Self-perception	228	9th
Attribution	227	10th (two ties)
Problem solving	227	10th (two ties)
. . .	. . .	. . .
Major depression (the diagnosis)	205	13th
. . .	. . .	. . .
Cognitive therapy	193	17th
. . .	. . .	. . .
Depression (the emotion)	134	26th
. . .	. . .	. . .
Psychotherapeutic processes	125	29th
. . .	. . .	. . .
Psychoanalytic theory	116	33rd
Psychoanalysis	111	34th
. . .	. . .	. . .
Psychotherapy	96	43rd (two ties)
. . .	. . .	. . .
Psychotherapeutic techniques	70	68th
. . .	. . .	. . .
Personality theory	55	90th (four ties)
. . .	. . .	. . .
Self-esteem	54	93rd (five ties)
. . .	. . .	. . .
Family therapy	51	103rd (four ties)
. . .	. . .	. . .
Mental disorders	50	107th (four ties)
. . .	. . .	. . .
Schizophrenia	47	112th (three ties)
. . .	. . .	. . .
Personality disorders	46	115th (seven ties)
Psychodynamics	46	115th (seven ties)
. . .	. . .	. . .
Transactional analysis	39	144th (seven ties)
. . .	. . .	. . .
Psychotherapeutic transference	38	151st (six ties)
. . .	. . .	. . .

continues overleaf

Table 5.1   (continued)

Terms cross-referenced with the words schema, schemas, or schemata	Number of articles so cross-referenced	Rank of the number of cross-referenced articles
Object relations	37	157th (nine ties)
Psychoanalytic interpretation	37	157th (nine ties)
Jean Piaget	32	185th (nine ties)
Group psychotherapy	24	257th (18 ties)
Behavior therapy	19	329th (20 ties)
Defense mechanisms	18	349th (18 ties)
Sigmund Freud	12	491st (32 ties)
Experiential psychotherapy	10	572nd (48 ties)
Self-talk	7	754th (90 ties)
Hypnotherapy	6	844th (118 ties)
Identification (defense mechanism)	6	844th (118 ties)
Behavior modification	5	962nd (123 ties)
Psychoanalytic personality theory	5	962nd (123 ties)
Rational Emotive Therapy	5	962nd (123 ties)
Fantasy (defense mechanism)	4	1085th (169 ties)
Interpersonal psychotherapy	4	1085th (169 ties)
Repression	4	1085th (169 ties)
Projection (defense mechanism)	3	1254th (267 ties)
Analytical psychotherapy	2	1521st (355 ties)
Client centered therapy	2	1521st (355 ties)
Directed reverie therapy	2	1521st (355 ties)
Exposure therapy	2	1521st (355 ties)
Freudian psychoanalytic school	2	1521st (355 ties)
Gestalt therapy	2	1521st (355 ties)

continues

Table 5.1   (continued)

Terms cross-referenced with the words schema, schemas, or schemata	Number of articles so cross-referenced	Rank of the number of cross-referenced articles
. . .	. . .	. . .
Reality therapy	2	1521st (355 ties)
. . .	. . .	. . .
Adlerian therapy	1	1876th (736 ties)
. . .	. . .	. . .
Eclectic psychotherapy	1	1876th (736 ties)
. . .	. . .	. . .
Existential therapy	1	1876th (736 ties)
. . .	. . .	. . .
Expressive psychotherapy	1	1876th (736 ties)
. . .	. . .	. . .
Feminist therapy	1	1876th (736 ties)
. . .	. . .	. . .
Movement therapy	1	1876th (736 ties)
. . .	. . .	. . .
Regression (defense mechanism)	1	1876th (736 ties)
. . .	. . .	. . .
Relaxation therapy	1	1876th (736 ties)
. . .	. . .	. . .
Withdrawal (defense mechanism)	1	1876th (736 ties)

Note. 2611 unique index terms were cross-referenced with the words schema, schemas, or schemata.

The link between sensation and understanding was, in Kant's view, built from mental schemata. Figure 5.2 depicts this transcendental schema model (after Rychlak, 1973).[2]

Plato treated schemata as innate (Marshall, 1995). Kant treated schemata as divinely innate links between the corporeal body's physical senses and the transcendent soul's understanding (Carpenter, 2001).

Bartlett (1932) and Piaget ([1936] 1952) are usually credited with introducing mental schemata to modern psychology (cf. Marshall, 1995; Stein, 1992). Introspectionist psychologists were probably first, however. Titchener (1912) described introspection as the application of mental schemata; at least three other introspectionists identified schemata as the mechanisms by which introspection occurred (O'Brien, 1921; Wheeler and Cutsforth, 1921).

Bartlett (1932) and Piaget ([1936] 1952) demonstrated that schemata both modify and are modified by experience. Piaget described development of mental schemata through accommodation and assimilation from beginnings in reflexes. When, for example, the sucking reflex, nipple, and sensations associated with suckling work well together, a suckling schema is formed; mental associations with subsequent successful suckling will be assimilated, strengthening this schema. When sucking, nipple, and associated sensations

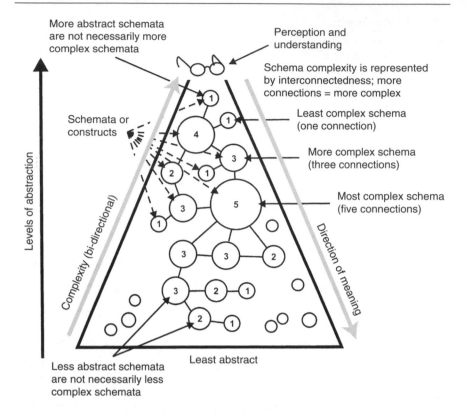

Figure 5.2 The schema model evident in Kant's *Critique of Pure Reason*. Conceptual understanding is based on the mediating effects of schemata. More complex schemata are more richly interconnected. More abstract schemata are closer to conceptual meaning. (Adapted from Rychlak, 1973, Figure 2, p. 11.)

work poorly together, suckling behaviors and linked mental associations will change to accommodate the experience, changing the suckling schema. Schematic mental representations will continue to strengthen through assimilation and change through accommodation, yielding a broader, more flexible, more adaptive suckling schema (Piaget, 1952). Other schemata develop in a similar manner and more complex schemata are formed from connections between simpler schemata. Increasingly complex, interconnected, abstract schemata yield increasingly complex, abstract cognitive development.

In his best-known demonstration of memory schemata, Bartlett (1932) found that British participants were more likely to forget culturally unfamiliar features in a North American tribal story about ghosts than material consistent with British culture. They also erroneously reported –

that is, falsely remembered – elements relevant to British culture that did not appear in the story. Bartlett proposed that culturally contextual, mental schemata interfered with memory for culturally unfamiliar information, facilitated memory for culturally consistent information, and introduced culture-influenced memory distortions.

Bartlett's schema model presented an ultimately successful challenge to then-current models of context- and content-independent memory derived from experiments with nonsense syllables. His book was positively received by British contemporaries, but was largely ignored by behaviorist American psychology and eventually obscured by British behaviorism. The cognitive revolution rehabilitated his theory (cf. Neisser, 1967), to the point that Bartlett's work, *Remembering* (1932), became the second most frequently cited memory publication of the 1980s (Brewer, 2000).

Experiencing a schema in action

Hunt (1999) calls a schema 'a sort of "fill-in-the-blanks" form that is maintained in the mind and that is called up to handle particular situations' (p. 32). The disc depicted in Figure 5.3 is a symbolic representation of a thematic schema with blanks (the white ovals) representing plot, characters, and other story elements. Figure 5.3, based on a demonstration suggested by Gerrig (1988), illustrates schematic processing and offers a demonstration of the effects of a thematic schema on text comprehension. Read the paragraph in the black box in Figure 5.3 (from Dooling and Lachman, 1971). The paragraph is grammatically correct, but nearly incomprehensible. The proposition here is that the thematic schema, when activated, will provide you with blanks for plot, characters, and story elements which, when they become available, render the paragraph comprehensible. For most readers comprehension falls into place when the schema is activated. After you read the paragraph, activate the schema to facilitate comprehension of the text by holding Figure 5.3 up to a mirror and reading the mirror-image cursive script printed on the edge of the disk.[3]

An interesting part of this text comprehension experience is the transparence of the schema facilitation effect. That is, when the schema is activated, comprehension comes without our awareness of how it comes. This reflects the preattentive quality usually evident with schemata. Note, however, that the schema is not unconscious in the sense of being unavailable. Once the schema is activated by the title, it is possible to make the schema explicit by listing a great many details from the story which is the source for the schema. Indeed, once the schema is activated it is possible to go well beyond the data in the paragraph: many readers will know our hero's country or city of birth, for example.

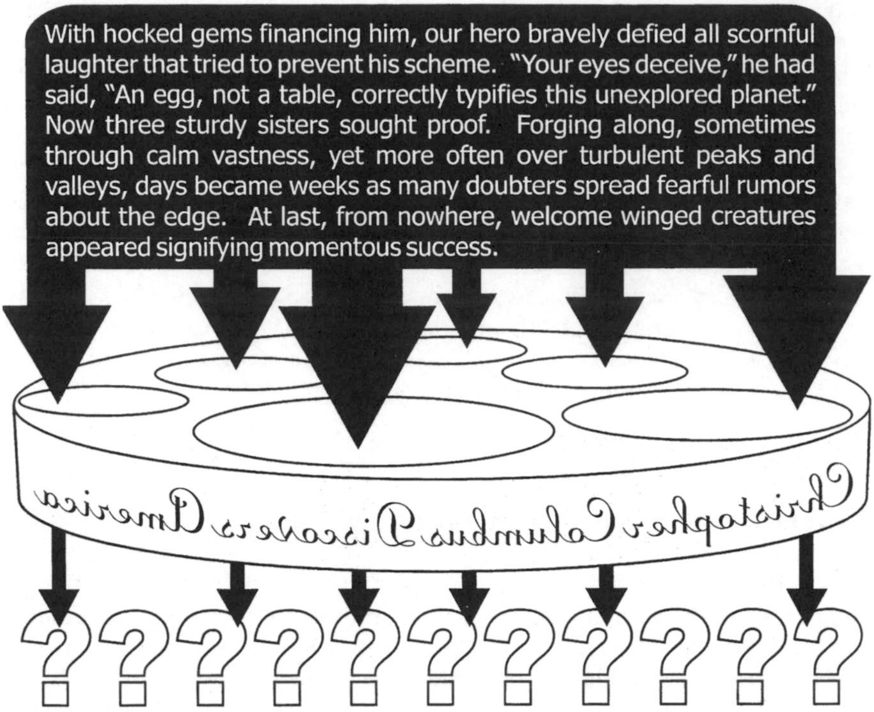

With hocked gems financing him, our hero bravely defied all scornful laughter that tried to prevent his scheme. "Your eyes deceive," he had said, "An egg, not a table, correctly typifies this unexplored planet." Now three sturdy sisters sought proof. Forging along, sometimes through calm vastness, yet more often over turbulent peaks and valleys, days became weeks as many doubters spread fearful rumors about the edge. At last, from nowhere, welcome winged creatures appeared signifying momentous success.

Figure 5.3 To experience the effects of a schema becoming active, read the paragraph in the black field above. The paragraph was written to be grammatical, but nearly incomprehensible. The mirror image of a title for the paragraph, written in cursive script, is printed on the edge of what appears to be a disc. The disc represents the schema that will activate when you read the title. The schema – it is your schema, really – is organized with story elements such as events and characters, represented by oval, blank spaces on the schema-disc, which will make the story become comprehensible. You can activate the schema by reading the reflection of the title in a mirror or by reading the title, one letter at a time, from right to left.

Contemporary schema models

Schemata are fundamental to contemporary cognitive science's connectionist, parallel distributed processing, and neural network models of cognition (cf. Baddeley, 1990; Ceci et al., 1999; Hunt, 1999; Rumelhart et al., 1986; Stinson and Palmer, 1991). There is at least some agreement among schema theorists that mental schemata include some combinations of the following features (cf. D'Andrade, 1995; Hunt, 1999; Marshall, 1995; Norman, 1986;

Rumelhart, 1986; Smith, 1998 – it might interest the reader to see how many of these features would fit the Christopher Columbus thematic schema which operated in the demonstration presented in Figure 5.3):

- Schemata are associations between perceptual and memory information organized according to patterns inherent to experience.
- Patterns in schemata mirror regularities in experience, generalizing from past repetitive patterns to subsequent experience.
- Generalizing creates abstractions based on commonalities in information and experience.
- Schematization occurs for a wide array of cognitive data: events, objects, situations, behaviors, thoughts, and groups of events, behaviors, thoughts, and so on.
- Schemata extend beyond information to the organizing regularity in the information.
- Schemata are predominantly 'top-down' processors; that is, schemata organize information, rather than being organized by events ('bottom-up' processing).
- Some schemata have the bottom-up quality of being activated by specific stimuli.
- Schemata have the bottom-up quality of developing from regularities in experience.
- Schemata have the bottom-up possibility of being modified by experience.
- Because schemata are predisposed to encoding and activation from schema-relevant events, they are selective for these events in perception, memory, and behavior.
- When activated, schemata carry with them most of their organized information.
- Schema activation increases processing capacity and efficiency. For example, an activated memory schema makes all its organized information available, which is quicker and more efficient than matching stimuli with memories detail by detail.
- Because schemata are organized according to regularity in the stimuli from which they are formed, when schemata are activated they fill in for data missing from the activating stimuli with data which tended to have been present when the schema was formed.
- This schematic filling-in of missing elements yields unarticulated theories or predictions about events, perceptions, memories, procedural knowledge, and so forth.
- Because they are based on regularities in an individual's experience, schemata are individualistic, differing from person to person as much as human experience differs or is similar from person to person.
- Schemata encode for and activate other schemata.

- Because schemata activate schemata, they have implicit, interconnected organization.
- Many schemata are hierarchically organized.
- Higher-order relationships among schemata form abstractions between schemata just as schemata abstract raw information.
- Schemata activate and operate in parallel with one another, and as such, tend to be implicit, automatic, effortless, and preattentive, though their operation can be rendered explicit, effortful, and conscious.
- Schemata provide information both to other schemata and to non-schematic processes.
- Schemata are generally passive, waiting to be activated by information, when they then begin to encode information.
- Non-schematic processes, such as comparative reasoning, tend to be active activities, carried out effortfully in awareness, using the products of schemata.
- Schemata may be activated by encoding events or by thoughts about such events.
- Schemata may be flexible in assimilating or accommodating new experience based on quality of fit. This is may a point of controversy between schema theorists. Cognitive scientists lean toward flexibility (e.g. Norman, 1986), while psychotherapists consider schematic inflexibility a major component of psychopathology (e.g. Horowitz, 1988).

In addition to wide acceptance in cognitive science, schema models and related structural views of cognition have demonstrated explanatory usefulness for a wide and still expanding range of psychological phenomena. Schema models are ascendent, if not predominant in theories of social cognition (Fiske and Taylor, 1991; Nisbett and Ross, 1980; Smith, 1998) and have become an important addition to cultural anthropology (e.g. D'Andrade, 1992, 1995; Ridley et al., 2000; Shore, 1996). Schema models have been used to explain cognition in activities as diverse as text comprehension (e.g. Gerrig, 1988; Mandler, 1984), solving of arithmetic story problems (e.g. Marshall, 1995), ability in the visual arts (e.g. Pring and Hermelin, 1993), music appreciation and performance (e.g. Bamberger, 1991; Deliège and Mèlon, 1997; Leman, 1995), response to advertising (e.g. Alden et al., 2000), entrepreneurship (e.g. Mitchell et al., 2000), geographic reasoning (e.g. Williamson and McGuinness, 1990), humor (e.g. Deckers and Avery, 1994; Deckers and Buttram, 1990), political reasoning (e.g. Fiske et al., 1990; Larson, 1994), skilled athletic performance (e.g. Kerr and Boucher, 1992), and tactical problem solving during war (e.g. Marshall et al., 1998; Marshall, pers. comm., 15 November, 2001). Schema models are key elements in modeling expertise and attempting to enhance human cognitive performance (e.g. Dee-Lucas and Larkin, 1988; Druckman and

Bjork, 1994; Hinds et al., 2001; Marméche and Didierjean, 2001; Marshall, 2001; Matthews et al., 2000; Rosenberg, 1997).

Schema-focused therapies

The schematic features described above could economically explain a variety of clinically significant phenomena. So far as is evident from *PA*, the first references both to mental schemata and psychotherapy were made in publications by Harvey, Hunt and Schroder (1961) and by Feibleman (1961a, b, 1962a, b). Harvey and colleagues described a taxonomy of 'categorical schema[ta] . . . through which impinging stimuli are coded, passed, or evaluated' (p. 1). Like Ellis (1962), they cited Korzybski's theory of general semantics (1951) as an example of how semantics modify perception and understanding. They also predicted that inflexible schemata leading to overgeneralizations might contribute to depression. Their suggestions for schema-focused treatment appear to have gone untested.

Feibleman (1961a), professor of philosophy at Tulane University, proposed that a dysfunctional interplay between public and private schemata which he called 'the cultural circuit' (p. 127) might contribute to psychopathology. He proposed three possible treatment methods: (1) following memory disruptions from electroshock therapy patients might be encouraged to test private schemata against public realities (1961b); (2) operant and classical conditioning might reinforce public schemata over idiosyncratic, private schemata (1962b); and (3) rigid schemata might be disputed through careful discussions. Feibleman cited Ellis's first published REBT case study (1959) as inspiration for three sessions of schema-focused disputations from which he published excerpts (1962a).[4] Except for his own foray into talk therapy, there is no evidence that Feibleman's suggestions for treatment were ever tried.

Beck's discussion of 'the activation and dominance of certain idiosyncratic cognitive patterns (schemata), which have a content corresponding to the typical depressive themes in the verbal material' followed during the next two years (1963, p. 332, 1964). Beck cited the previous cognitive structuralism of Piaget's schemata (1948), Postman's categories (1951), Rapaport's conceptual tools (1951), Kelly's personal constructs (1955), Bruner, Goodnow, and Austin's coding systems (1956), Sarbin, Taft, and Bailey's thinking modules (1960), and Harvey, Hunt, and Schroder's schema-concept model (1961). Beck's schema-focused approach then developed into cognitive therapy (Beck et al., 1979). Cognitive-behavioral models of marital difficulties now incorporate models of interpersonal schemata (e.g. Epstein and Baucom, 1993). Cognitive-behavioral models of eating disorders and obesity have incorporated weight-related self-schemas (e.g. Markus et al., 1987; Vitousek and Orimoto, 1993). The most elaborately schema-focused approaches derived from Beck's CT are probably Safran's

Interpersonal Cognitive Therapy (1990) and Young's Schema-Focused Therapy (1999).

The first publication to cross-reference psychoanalysis and mental schemata (as evident in *PA*) appeared in 1975, wherein Sandler described Piaget's schemata as 'structures which function according to childhood laws of cognition and perception' (1975, p. 365). Thereafter disturbed object relations were characterized as dysfunctional schemata (Bauer and Modarressi, 1977) and dysfunctional schemata were described as the mechanisms responsible for the interpersonal disturbances described by Sullivan, Adler, Horney, and Fromm (Knobloch and Knobloch, 1979). Erdelyi (1985) equated the schema-driven omissions and distortions described by Bartlett as synonymous with Freud's unconsciously motivated censorship and revisionistic cognitive processing.

Horowitz (cf. 1988) has probably written the most about the psychodynamic qualities of schemata as organizing mechanisms in personality and interpersonal functioning (46 publications in *PA* which reference schemata). He has also advocated for schema models as an integrative link (1999). For example, he identified Kelly's personal construct theory (1955) as a schema model.

Are irrational beliefs (iBs) schemata?

Muran (1991) and DiGiuseppe (1996) have proposed that Belief in the ABC model of emotion (viz.: A, the Activating event, plus B, Beliefs about A, yields C, emotional Consequences) is too vaguely defined to effectively account for either the complex cognitive elements in emotional distress or the changes that occur during successful treatment. Kwon and Oei (1994) note that the terms assumption, attitude, belief, core cognition, and schemata have been used interchangeably by cognitive–behavioral therapists and theorists, creating confusion about what causes psychopathology, about what changes during treatment, about the nature of cognitions upon which treatments focus, and about the level of cognition at which changes occur. Both DiGiuseppe (1996) and Muran (1991) suggest that evaluative schemata might account for irrationality as it is defined by REBT and help clarify what it is in cognitive behavior therapy that therapists are attempting to change.

These considerations are remarkable for the similarity they bear to deliberations Ellis raised prior to launching REBT. As he worked to reformulate psychoanalysis, Ellis explored the link between evaluative cognition and emotion more than 46 years ago; REBT is really his answer to questions he raised as he examined psychoanalysis:

> An individual *evaluates* (attitudinizes, becomes biased) when he perceives something as being 'good' or 'bad', 'pleasant' or 'unpleasant',

'beneficial' or 'harmful' and when, as a result of his perceptions, he responds positively or negatively to this thing. . . . An individual *emotes* when he evaluates something strongly – when he clearly perceives it as being 'good' or 'bad', 'beneficial' or 'harmful', and strongly responds to it in a negative or positive manner. . . . Evaluatings and emotions are consciously experienced when the individual perceives that he is experiencing them.

(1956, pp. 138–139, italics original)

Muran's (1991) and DiGiuseppe's (1996) proposition that evaluative schemata are probably the best candidates for explaining the irrationality in cognitive processes continues Ellis's 46-year-old line of reasoning. Their considerations could be viewed as a fine-tuning of questions, the therapeutic answers to which Ellis provided when he developed REBT.

Conflicting schemata resolved at the core evaluative level

A difficult session with Ji Hae Park[5] presented a complex situation during which multiple, differentiable, conflicting schemata became evident. The schemata brought into conflict by this situation did not disappear, but the conflict was still resolved. In the conflict and distress she experienced, and in the resolution which followed, a particular kind of schematic processing seemed evident, consistent with Muran's (1991) and DiGiuseppe's (1996) proposals.

Ji Hae, a Korean-American, was a 26-year-old graduate student receiving treatment for anxiety at the Brigham Young University (BYU) Counseling Center when these events occurred. Her parents had immigrated to America from Korea some years before her birth; the family spoke Korean at home, while she and the other children spoke English at school. Though Ji Hae and her family attended a Korean Protestant congregation, she had elected to attend BYU, which is owned and operated by the Church of Jesus Christ of Latter-day Saints, so she could attend classes while working in her family's small business.

During her senior year at BYU, Ji Hae converted to Mormonism. Her parents grudgingly consented because, they told her, she was 'in all other ways a dutiful, obedient daughter'. Though she was an adult, it had never occurred to Ji Hae *not* to ask for her parents' permission. Ji Hae then asked her parents for permission to serve a proselyting mission for the Church. Her parents again grudgingly agreed, saying that her long, dutiful service in the family business had earned her this right. Ji Hae served for 18 months in Seoul, Korea, where her language abilities were very helpful. After returning she continued to live at home and work in her parents' business while attending graduate school at BYU. She had been accepted to graduate programs at three other universities, but felt she owed continued service to her parents because they had given her financial support during her missionary service. Ji Hae sought treatment because she felt quite anxious about participating in seminars, still more anxious about making formal presentations in class, and more anxious still, and depressed, about her prospects for dating and marriage.

We had worked on anxiety reduction exercises in individual sessions and she had tried to practice social skills, speaking skills, assertiveness and flirting during group sessions. Individual sessions included a range of anxiety reduction exercises and tasks, mixed with rational–emotive–behavioral disputation of the demands Ji Hae placed on herself and disputation of her self-downing. Ji Hae and I had met for 33 individual and 15 group sessions when the following incident occurred.

From the intake session on I had, as is my custom, introduced myself as Lars. Whenever Ji Hae addressed me as Dr Nielsen, I repeated this invitation for her to call me Lars. At the beginning of our 34th session, after she had again addressed me as Dr Nielsen, I said, 'Please, call me Lars', emphasizing this with a smile and a sound of mock exasperation. Ji Hae immediately bowed her head and began to sob.

'What is it?', I asked.

'I just can't!', she said between sobs.

Ji Hae reminded me that I was only a little younger than her father and pointed out, with remarkable clarity, that my repeated requests that she call me Lars were challenging long-practiced Confucian principles of filial piety and respect for authority. In schematic terms, my age and social position had encoded for and activated a Confucian schema yielding a pull for respectful address *and* a conflicting pull for respectful compliance.

But this wasn't the only schema that seemed to have been activated. Ji Hae explained that she could often hear an inner voice, her own voice, calling me 'Nielsenpaksanim'. She had never said a word to me in Korean. 'Paksa' is Korean for doctor, doctor of philosophy, actually; 'nim' is an honorific conveying respect. My requests had, it seemed, also activated some part of her Korean language schemata. To her it sounded both grossly ungrammatical and rude to call me Lars. 'Imagine saying, "I *goed*", rather than, "I went", and add *rudeness*', she explained.

Ji Hae told me that she had also seen an image in her head from just a few days before, when one of her classmates had been reprimanded by a professor for addressing the professor by his first name. From her description of the incident it sounded like a very mild correction, but it had made a very strong impression on Ji Hae. My request had apparently encoded for and activated a kind of academic rank schema.

Ji Hae then explained that though the four missionaries who taught her 'the Gospel' were her same age, they had always been careful to address her as Sister Park. They had also always called each other Sister or Elder. During her own missionary service she and other missionaries had been instructed to address new acquaintances as Mr, Mrs, Miss, or by a title such as Dr, and to address members of the Church as Brother or Sister or by titles appropriate to their ecclesiastical position, such as Bishop, President, or Elder. They were also instructed to address each other as Elder and Sister, even after getting to know each other quite well. (Latter-day Saint missionaries work together in pairs of the same gender called 'companionships'. Missionary companions usually remain together between two and six months. Once assigned to work together, companions are to remain together at all times.) She and almost all of the missionaries she knew had followed this instruction. Though she and her companions had always known each others' first names, she had always addressed her companions as Sister, and her companions had always called her Sister Park. This incident had also seemed to activate a religiosity schema developed during her conversion to Mormonism and during her service as a missionary. To call me Lars seemed to her to carry a kind of wrong, immoral sense, she told me.

'I'm sorry', I told her, 'I didn't understand'. And indeed, I had not understood. My own professionally reinforced informality schema had helped me blunder into and activate her several formality schemata. I asked her if she wanted me to call her 'Sister Park', which is how I would have addressed her had we just met at a Church meeting.

She said something like, 'No, I like for you to call me Ji Hae. That's what my family calls me, and it feels quite comfortable.'

The session ended with me telling her something like, 'You know, you can call me whatever you want. What we do here is about what you want. I only hoped you would understand that I don't think you're beneath me.'

A bit more than a week passed and, because Ji Hae had not scheduled another individual session, I worried that the incident had ruined our relationship. I arrived a few minutes late to the next group session and was relieved to find Ji Hae sitting there as I walked in. She smiled and greeted me with, 'Hi, Lars'. This put such a look of shock on my face that several group members laughed. Ji Hae explained to the group what had happened in our previous individual session and then told us all that since our meeting she'd thought a great deal about what had happened and had decided, 'If he doesn't care, I don't have to care.' This had given her the idea of trying to call me Lars right away just to see what would happen. 'It wasn't so bad!', she said.

Ji Hae's explanations revealed several related, but distinct schemata. Her emotional and behavioral responses had changed noticeably, though only one schematic change was clearly evident from her explanations. Figures 5.4 and 5.5 portray the discernible schemata and what seemed to have changed. As in Figure 5.3, schemata are portrayed as discs with blanks or

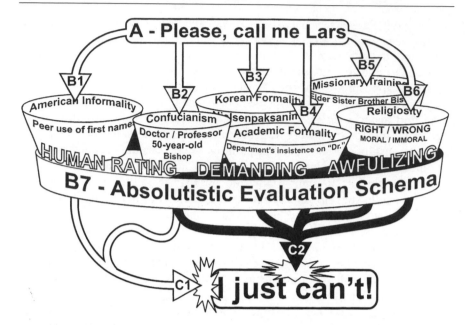

Figure 5.4   A conceptual model of the schematic activity that contributed to Ji Hae's distress. A, the Activating event, was my request that she call me Lars. *B1* through *B7* are Beliefs conceptualized as schemata. *C1* and *C2* are conflicting emotional Consequences arising from combined activation of linguistic, cultural, religious and social schemata *B1* through *B6*, plus *B7*, an absolutistic, evaluative schema; *B7*'s absolutistic quality is depicted as sharp regions of black and white.

slots into which information fits. From schemata comes information as the product of schematic processing. The ABC model of emotion is recast in schematic terms, with Activating events as activating information and Consequent emotions as products of schematic processing.

The request, A, 'Please, call me Lars', Activated seven belief-schemata, *B1* through *B7*. These belief-schemata led to emotionally conflicting Consequences, *C1* and *C2*. Schemata *B1* through *B6* activated academic, cultural, linguistic, social, and even religious schemata linked with formality and informality of address. Schemata *B1* through *B6* had also activated an evaluative schema, *B7*. Figure 5.4 depicts this as a sequential process, but activation of these schemata was likely so rapid as to be nearly simultaneous. Further, it does not necessarily follow that information from all six schemata would necessarily activate the evaluative schema in the same way, though this is how I have depicted the situation. Once *B7* was activated in an absolutistic mode, the information provided by schemata *B1* through *B6* acquired an absolutistic appraisal and a related, extreme emotional quality. The absolutistic quality of *B7* is depicted with distinct

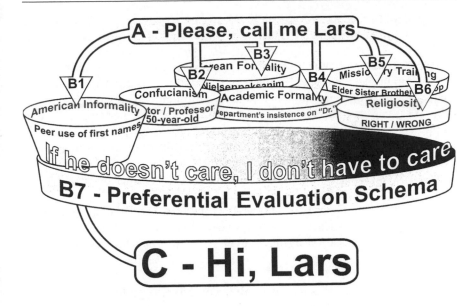

Figure 5.5   A conceptual model of the schematic activity present when Ji Hae's conflict
was resolved. A, the Activating event is relatively unchanged. *B1* through *B6*
remained viable, though *B2* through *B6* were rendered irrelevant by the
change in *B7*. The preferential quality of *B7* is depicted with continuously
varying shades of gray. As a C, Consequence of this shift in *B7*, it was now
comfortable for Ji Hae to address me as Lars.

regions of black and white. *B7* created the sharply conflicting demands that
Ji Hae *should* use an informal form of address, *C1*, and that she *must*
continue to use a formal mode of address, *C2*. To return to Hunt's (1999)
notion of schemata as fill-in-the-blanks forms, inputs from all these
schemata fell into very upsetting places for Ji Hae!

Figure 5.5 portrays what seemed to have changed to resolve Ji Hae's
distress. First, note that Ji Hae's academic, cultural, linguistic, social, and
religious schemata were still viable. Changes in these schemata, if any, were
negligible. She would still quite automatically use appropriate Korean
honorifics if speaking to a Korean, quite automatically call her professors
Dr or Professor so-and-so, and quite automatically continue to call the
leader of her local congregation Bishop so-and-so. She still believed
devoutly in the Mormon Church and in its doctrines and would still likely
experience a lively sense of right and wrong for a host of activities. As she
explained it, what had changed was her evaluation of our therapeutic
situation, so that she didn't 'have to' call me Dr Nielsen. Schema *B7* had
became preferential–relativistic. That is, the appropriateness of addressing
me with familiarity was now appropriate relative to her preferences. This

had rendered schemata *B2* through *B6* largely irrelevant to this situation. The evaluative schema, *B7*, is depicted in shades of gray to portray this shift.

This shift came after many sessions spent disputing the demands Ji Hae placed on herself. We had begun treatment by working to dispute her frequent catastrophizing and her nearly continual self-downing. When I said, 'You can call me whatever you want', it was not, perhaps, a formal disputation, but its patterns had been laid down in previous sessions, including group sessions. I made it clear to Ji Hae that I was not upset with her, and conveyed chagrin at my own insensitivity and ignorance. This supportive reaction to Ji Hae's distress may have helped her believe that she didn't have to use any particular form of address with me.

During the group session Ji Hae told us that she had thought quite a bit about a previous discussion of important religious doctrine. That discussion, which focused on agency, developed into a general disputation of demands:

Lars: Where is it written that you have to go to the Celestial Kingdom?
Group member: Nowhere.
Lars: Then why try to go to Heaven if you don't *have* to?
Group member: Because it's wonderful.
Lars: And *must* you try for something *wonderful?*
Group member: No, but I want to.
Lars: So is the Celestial Kingdom a *must* or a *want?*
Group member: A want, I guess.
Lars: If the ultimate is a want, then doesn't that make *everything else* a want?

The concept of free agency is quite important in doctrines of the Mormon Church. I believed group members, all of whom were members of the Church, would see a contradiction inherent to the demands they placed on themselves given this doctrine of free agency. She reported in group that this dispute had helped her decide she didn't have to call me Dr Nielsen. We turned it into a joke: 'If you don't *have to* go to Heaven, you sure as *Hell* don't have to call me Dr Nielsen!'

Rationally Evaluative Schema Theory (REST)

Muran (1991) suggests that B in the ABC model is a schema which includes perception, inferences about the world, and evaluation of inferences. He noted that this proposed schema's perceptual, inferential, and evaluative functions may subsequently be modified by the information received. DiGiuseppe (1996) agrees, proposing 'that the type of cognitions that Ellis has been defining as irrational beliefs are a type of schema that merges "what is" with "what is desirable, moral, or correct"' (p. 11).

Ji Hae's descriptions suggest that several schemata were activated and contributed to her distress. Her emotions and behavior subsequently changed in profound manner – it seemed profound to her – though all but one of the schemata identifiable from her descriptions were unchanged. Given that Ji Hae's academic, cultural, linguistic, social, and religious schemata did not change, a model that isolates the locus of change is required.

Reisenzein (2001) has recently proposed a promising schematic appraisal model. He proposed that emotions arise as the result of a schema which simultaneously evaluates for congruence with desires and for congruence with beliefs. Desires are organismic values, beliefs are estimates about the probability that desires will be matched by events. Like all schemata, the appraisal schema receives a constant stream of information as other schemata are activated. When information discrepant from desires (one of the evaluative axes) appears unexpectedly (the other evaluative axis) it triggers emotions of surprise. To return to the fill-in-the-blanks analogy established with the Christopher Columbus schema (see Figure 5.3), when a Reisenzein appraisal schema is in a state of high activation, events would fall into place to create a strong emotion and linked thoughts such as 'I can't believe this!'.

Reisenzein's proposition that information is simultaneously evaluated for two qualities is theoretically quite similar to REBT's view of emotions. REBT theorists hold that emotions occur along a gradient from positive to negative associated with matching or mismatching desires. REBT proposes that emotions can also be classified according to their helpfulness versus their self-defeating quality; these qualities of emotion also follow from how events are evaluated (Ellis, 1994; Walen et al., 1992). Reisenzein's model makes explicit a quality of appraisal which is implied in REBT: his proposed appraisal schema evaluates for a match between desires and events *and* evaluates the product of that evaluation.

Using salient emotions to signal the presence of surprisingly important information has obvious survival value. We can probably find evidence of the operation of such an appraisal schema in our day-to-day experience. Such a system fails to account for Ji Hae's strong emotional reaction, however. My invitation that she call me Lars was upsetting, but not because it was unexpected. Some other form of evaluative system is necessary to understand strong emotional reactions like Ji Hae's.

Figure 5.6 portrays the proposed structure for an evaluative schema which could account for the link between irrationality and emotion proposed by REBT. Like Reisenzein's evaluative schema, this schema evaluates the flow of information coming from other schemata along two axes, one matching Reisenzein's desire or valence axis, the other evaluating the

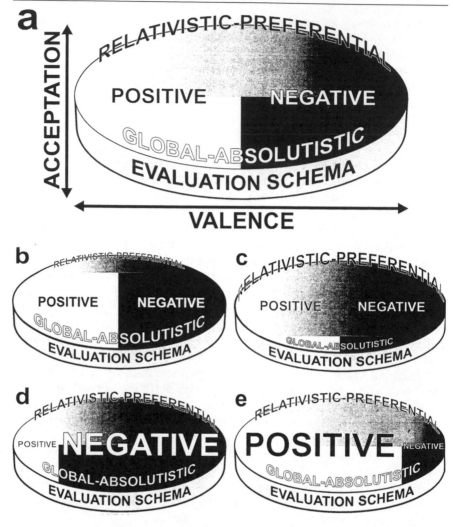

Figure 5.6   Conceptual model of an evaluative schema proposed as the key element in a rationally evaluative schema theory (REST). An evaluative schema (a) would include evaluative processes axes for valence and acceptation, which could also be called desire and belief, respectively. Valence refers to the positive or negative organismic value of information. Acceptation refers to how information is received by the schema, whether with personal–relativistic–preference or global–absolutistism. Evaluative valence is likely to be absolutistic (depicted as black or white) when information is received in global–absolutistic mode (b). Evaluative valence is likely to be continuous (depicted as shades of gray) when information is received preferentially (c). Information may encode for and activate an evaluative schema at any degree of valence, from predominantly negative (d) to predominantly positive (e), independent of the mode of acceptation with which the information is received.

product of the evaluation for valence. Detecting a mismatch between desire and reality (or what we infer to be reality) would create dysphoria. How detection of this mismatch between desire and reality is accepted creates what REBTers call irrationality. Evaluation of the product of evaluation of valence could be called acceptation,[6] conveying that how evaluations are received creates healthy or self-defeating qualities in the resulting emotions. Returning to the fill-in-the-blanks analogy, when this evaluative schema engenders a strongly self-defeating emotion, thoughts linked with the emotion would be something like 'I can't accept this!'.

Returning to Figure 5.6, evaluations will be in the realm of black and white and the resulting emotions will be extreme and of a self-defeating quality when information is received from other schemata in global–absolutistic mode (*b* in Figure 5.6). Thoughts linked with the emotions linked with this kind of schematic activation could well be those described by Ellis in his early formulations of irrational beliefs (e.g. 'It shouldn't be this way', 'This is too much', 'I'm a failure', etc.). Such evaluative statements would be instantiations of this proposed schema system as it is activated in global–absolutistic mode; the quality of the evaluation is global in the sense that the evaluation is applied in a global manner, to the universe, to the whole human, or so forth.

Evaluations will be more graded, in realms of gray, and the resulting emotions will be more moderate and healthy, though perhaps dysphoric, when information received from other schemata is accepted in personal–preferential mode (*c* in Figure 5.6). Information may encode for and activate the evaluative schema at any degree of valence, from predominantly negative (*d* in Figure 5.6) to predominantly positive (*e* in Figure 5.6), independent of the mode of acceptation with which the information is received.

The emotional distress which usually brings clients to treatment may often come from absolutistic reception of predominantly negative information, as with depression or anger. During depression self-schema might activate, yielding information discrepant from the desired view of the self. If this information is received in global–absolutistic mode, the evaluation adheres to the whole self, which is more likely to create depression. If, alternatively, information discrepant from the desired view of the self is generated by the self-schema, but received in preferential mode, the evaluation would more likely adhere to some element of the self, such as a habit or skill, creating an unpleasant, but motivating, emotion such as concern or annoyance. Anger would likely ensue if a schema activated by a situation discrepant with an important rule and information from this schema is received in global–absolutistic mode (rule-processing schemata, called deontic schemata, have been considered by Cheng and Holyoak, 1985 and Holyoak and Cheng, 1995). If discrepancies between events and rule schemata are received in the evaluative schema preferential mode they would yield healthy, if dysphoric emotions. For example, confronted with a child's misbehavior, a religious parent might experience a strong sense that the behavior is morally wrong, but feel only regret, sadness, or annoyance without anger if the misbehavior were received as countering a strong preference.

A few implications of REST

I began to explore schema models to better understand client difficulties with the ABC model. Clients often agree with the rational beliefs (RBs) to which I attempt to lead them, but state that they agree in their heads, not in their hearts. A particular client's experience with this kind of head-versus-heart difficulty was remarkable in this respect. She felt better during sessions, but this lasted only for short periods. Then, all of a sudden, she felt much, much better. She had decided to tell herself 20 times per day for one week that she was no better or worse than anyone else, and no better or worse than the moment she was born, only better *off* or worse *off*. She did this by reading this disputation from a card she kept in her wallet. Part-way through the second day the idea fell into place for her. Her explanation sounds a great deal like schematic facilitation of text comprehension (see Figure 5.3). The similarities between the two experiences offer possibilities for testing how rational–emotive–behavioral interventions have their greatest impact.

While CT has received extensive empirical support (cf. Hollon and Beck, 1994), and while considerable evidence suggests that depressive and anxious thinking are organized schematically (Beck et al., 1983; Dykman et al., 1991; Hammen et al., 1985; Mongrain, 1998; Penland et al., 2000; Shah and Waller, 2000), it is has *not* been demonstrated that focusing therapeutic time and effort on restructuring dysfunctional schemata actually helps clients more than other therapeutic interventions. So far as is evident from *PA*, the only test of schema-focused elements in CT failed to validate the efficacy of these specific interventions: Jacobson and colleagues (1996) recruited therapists with extensive experience in and strong allegiance to CT and had them deliver treatment according to CT's proposed active ingredients: encouragement to behavioral activation, correction of cognitive errors, and restructuring of maladaptive schemata. Clients randomly assigned to behavioral activation, treatment with behavioral activation plus thought correction, or behavioral activation, thought modification, and schema-focused treatment all showed improvement, though clients treated through encouragement to behavioral activation improved as much as clients treated with the full CT package. Schema-focused treatment did not add to the effectiveness of treatment.

The schema models of CT, especially Young's schema-focused version of CT, are considerably more elaborate than the schema model proposed by

REST. REST may be easier to test. As an initial informal test of REST, I have attempted to observe my sessions through a mental template resembling Figure 5.6a. I attempt to observe the valences clients give their situations and how they accept their own evaluations. My first impression is that most – perhaps all – irrational statements can be restated in the form 'X is *UN*acceptable' without losing the emotional meaning evident in more traditional irrational statements. For example, 'It's *UN*acceptable that I did that' has the same self-defeating emotional meaning as 'I shouldn't have done that'. Both statements convey negative evaluation of the result of the situation with absolute non-acceptance of the negativeness of the situation.

My second impression, derived from this first observation, is that it is easier to find the irrational thread in a client's distress when I stop looking so hard for classic indicators of irrationality such as the words 'should', 'must', and so forth. These words are still excellent indicators of irrationality. Further, it still seems likely that the most efficient way to help the largest number of people overcome their self-defeating upsets is to didactically explain how 'shoulds', 'musts', and so on create trouble. It seems, however, less important during therapy sessions to try to get clients to use these particular words in order to demonstrate their irrationality.

My third impression is that while this seems an easier way to find the thread of irrationality, it may be harder to teach, demonstrate, and detect this form of evaluating the irrationality for research purposes. A next step for evaluating REST would be testing of ability to generate agreement between observers about client evaluations and therapeutic interventions in clients' evaluative schemata.

Notes

1 The verb ἔχω or ĕcho is not the source of the English word echo. The English word echo comes from the nearly homonymous, but distinct, Greek noun ←ἠχω or êcho, which meant sound in ancient texts, including a reverberating sound – an echo in English.

2 Rychlak (1973) categorizes theories of personality and psychotherapy according to their fit with either Kant's phenomenological view or Locke's empirical–mechanistic view. Rychlak used 'construct' for schema in his figure, presumably because of George Kelly's influence – he studied with Kelly at Ohio State University and called Kelly's personal construct theory (1955) the epitome of a Kantian approach. Kant used the words schema and schemata in *Kritik der reinen vernunft* ([1781] 1971, p. 199).

3 The title of the paragraph is 'Chistopher Columbus discovering America' (Dooling and Lachman, 1971, p. 217). I apologize if you come from a culture in which the exploration of the North and South American continents was not studied, which might preclude development of a Christopher Columbus schema.

4 It is not clear whether the individual involved was an acquaintance, friend, colleague or client. Feibleman does not seem to have been a trained or licensed therapist or counselor. Ellis never met Feibleman and knew nothing of the

citation to his first published case study (personal communication, 15 December, 2001).
5 Ji Hae Park is not her real name and a number of significant details from her story have been changed to disguise her identity.
6 The most general definition for acceptance in the *Oxford English Dictionary* (2002) is, 'The action of taking, or receiving, what is offered, whether by way of favour, satisfaction, or duty; reception (electronic reference, no page number).

References

Alden, D.L., Mukherjee, A. and Hoyer, W.D. (2000) The effects of incongruity, surprise, and positive moderators on perceived humor in television advertising, *Journal of Advertising, 29*, 1–15.

American Psychological Association (2001a) *Psychological Abstracts.* Washington, DC: American Psychological Association. Retrieved 6 October, 2001, from the PsychINFO database.

American Psychological Association (2001b) *Thesaurus of Psychological Index Terms* (10th edn). Washington, DC: American Psychological Association. Retrieved 6 October, 2001, from the PsychINFO database.

Baddeley, A. (1990) *Human Memory: Theory and Practice.* Mahwah, NJ: Lawrence Erlbaum Associates.

Bamberger, J. (1991) *The Mind Behind the Musical Ear: How Children Develop Musical Intelligence.* Cambridge, MA: Harvard University Press.

Bartlett, F.C. (1932) *Remembering: A Study in Experimental and Social Psychology.* Cambridge: Cambridge University Press.

Bauer, R. and Modarressi, T. (1977) Strategies of therapeutic contact: working with children with severe object relationship disturbance, *American Journal of Psychotherapy, 31*, 605–617.

Beck, A.T. (1963) Thinking and depression: I. Idiosyncratic content and cognitive distortions, *Archives of General Psychiatry, 9*, 324–333.

Beck, A.T. (1964) Thinking and depression: II. Theory and therapy, *Archives of General Psychiatry, 10*, 561–571.

Beck, A.T., Epstein, N. and Harrison, R. (1983) Cognitions, attitudes and personality dimensions in depression, *British Journal of Cognitive Psychotherapy, 1*, 1–16.

Beck, A.T., Rush, A.J., Shaw, B.F. and Emery, G. (1979) *Cognitive Therapy of Depression.* New York: Guilford.

Brewer, W.F. (2000) Bartlett's concept of the schema and its impact on theories of knowledge representation in contemporary cognitive psychology. In A. Saito (ed.) *Bartlett, Culture and Cognition* (pp. 69–89). Cambridge, UK: Psychology Press.

Bruner, J.S., Goodnow, J.J. and Austin, G.A. (1956) *A Study of Thinking.* New York: Wiley.

Carpenter, A. (2001) Kant, Immanuel. In C. Eliasmith (ed.) *Dictionary of Philosophy of Mind.* Retrieved from www.artsci.wustl.edu/~philos/MindDict/kant.html on 20 December, 2001.

Ceci, S.J., Rosenblum, T.B. and DeBruyn, E. (1999) Laboratory versus field approaches to cognition. In R.J. Sternberg (ed.) *The Nature of Cognition*. Cambridge, MA: MIT Press.

Cheng, P.W. and Holyoak, K.J. (1985) Pragmatic reasoning schemas, *Cognitive Psychology*, *17*, 391–416.

D'Andrade, R.G. (1992) Schemas and motivation. In R.G. D'Andrade and C. Strauss (eds) *Human Motives and Cultural Models* (pp. 23–44). New York: Cambridge University Press.

D'Andrade, R.G. (1995) *The Development of Cognitive Anthropology*. New York: Cambridge University Press.

Deckers, L. and Avery, P. (1994) Altered joke endings and a joke structure schema, *Humor: International Journal of Humor Research*, *7*, 313–321.

Deckers, L. and Buttram, R.T. (1990) Humor as a response to incongruities within or between schemata, *Humor: International Journal of Humor Research*, *3*, 53–64.

Dee-Lucas, D. and Larkin, J.H. (1988) Novice rules for assessing importance in scientific texts, *Journal of Memory and Language*, *27*, 288–308.

Deliège, I. and Mèlon, M. (1997) Cue abstraction in the representation of musical form. In I. Deliège and J. Sloboda (eds) *Perception and Cognition of Music* (pp. 387–412). Hove, UK: Psychology Press.

DiGiuseppe, R. (1996) The nature of irrational and rational beliefs: progression in Rational Emotive Behavior Therapy, *Journal of Rational–Emotive and Cognitive–Behavior Therapy*, *14*, 5–28.

Dooling, D.J. and Lachman, R. (1971) Effects of comprehension on retention of prose, *Journal of Experimental Psychology*, *88*, 216–222.

Druckman, D. and Bjork, R.A. (1994) *Learning, Remembering, Believing: Enhancing Human Performance*. Washington, DC: National Academy Press.

Dykman, B.M., Horowitz, L.M., Abramson, L.Y. and Usher, M. (1991) Schematic and situational determinants of depressed and nondepressed students' interpretation of feedback, *Journal of Abnormal Psychology*, *100*, 45–55.

Ellis, A. (1956) An operational reformulation of some of the basic principles of psychoanalysis. In H. Feigl and M. Scriven (eds) *The Foundations of Science and the Concepts of Psychology and Psychoanalysis* (pp. 131–154). Minneapolis, MN: University of Minnesota Press.

Ellis, A. (1959) Rationalism and its therapeutic applications, *Annals of Psychotherapy*, *1*, 55–64.

Ellis, A. (1962) *Reason and Emotion in Psychotherapy*. New York: Lyle Stuart.

Ellis, A. (1994) *Reason and Emotion in Psychotherapy*, revised and updated. New York: Birch Lane Press.

Epstein, N. and Baucom, D.H. (1993) Cognitive factors in marital disturbance. In K.S. Dobson and P.C. Kendall (eds) *Psychopathology and Cognition* (pp. 352–386). New York: Academic Press.

Erdelyi, M.H. (1985) *Psychoanalysis: Freud's Cognitive Psychology*. New York: W.H. Freeman.

Feibleman, J.K. (1961a) The cultural circuit in psychology and psychiatry, *Journal of Nervous and Mental Disease*, *132*, 127–145.

Feibleman, J.K. (1961b) Transfer matching: a new method in psychotherapy, *Journal of Psychology*, *51*, 411–420.

Feibleman, J.K. (1962a) An illustration of retention schemata, *Psychological Record*, *12*, 1–8.

Feibleman, J.K. (1962b) The stressed conditioning of psychotics, *Journal of Psychology*, *53*, 295–299.

Fiske, S.T. and Taylor, S.E. (1991) *Social Cognition* (2nd edn). New York: McGraw-Hill.

Fiske, S.T., Lau, R.R. and Smith, R.A. (1990) On the varieties and utilities of political expertise, *Social Cognition*, *8*, 31–48.

Gerrig, R.J. (1988) Text comprehension. In R.J. Sternberg and E.E. Smith (eds) *The Psychology of Human Thought* (pp. 242–266). New York: Cambridge University Press.

Hammen, C., Marks, T., Mayol, A. and DeMayo, R. (1985) Depressive self-schemas, life stress, and vulnerability to depression, *Journal of Abnormal Psychology*, *94*, 308–319.

Harvey, O.J., Hunt, D.E. and Schroder, H.M. (1961) *Conceptual Systems and Personality Organization*. New York: Wiley.

Hinds, P.J., Patterson, M. and Pfeffer, J. (2001) Bothered by abstraction: the effect of expertise on knowledge transfer and subsequent novice performance, *Journal of Applied Psychology*, *86*, 1232–1243.

Hollon, S.D. and Beck, A.T. (1994) Cognitive and cognitive behavioral therapies. In A.E. Bergin and S.L. Garfield (eds) *Handbook of Psychotherapy and Behavior Change* (4th edn, pp. 428–466). New York: Wiley.

Holyoak, K.J. and Cheng P.W. (1995) Pragmatic reasoning about human voluntary action: evidence from Wason's selection task. In S.E. Newstead and J.S.B.T. Evans (eds) *Perspectives on Thinking and Reasoning: Essays in Honour of Peter Wason* (pp. 67–89). Hillsdale, NJ: Lawrence Erlbaum Associates.

Horowitz, M.J. (1988) *Introduction to Psychodynamics: A New Synthesis*. New York: Basic Books.

Horowitz, M.J. (1991) *Person Schemas and Maladaptive Interpersonal Patterns*. Chicago: University of Chicago Press.

Horowitz, M.J. (1999) Dynamic psychotherapy. In M. Hersen and A.S. Bellack (eds) *Handbook of Comparative Interventions for Adult Disorders* (2nd edn, pp. 417–432). New York: Wiley.

Hunt, E.B. (1999) What is a theory of thought. In R.J. Sternberg (ed.) *The Nature of Cognition* (pp. 3–49). Cambridge, MA: MIT Press.

Jacobson, N.S., Dobson, K.S., Truax, P.A., Addis, M.E., Koerner, K., Gollan, J.K., Gortner, E. and Prince, S. (1996) A component analysis of cognitive-behavioral treatment for depression, *Journal of Consulting and Clinical Psychology*, *64*, 295–304.

Kant, I. ([1781] 1929) *Critique of Pure Reason* (N.K. Smith, translator). New York: Macmillan.

Kant, I. ([1781] 1971) *Kritik der reinen vernunft* [*Critique of Pure Reason*]. Hamburg: Felix Mainer.

Kelly, G.A. (1955) *The Psychology of Personal Constructs*. New York: Norton.

Kerr, R. and Boucher, J.L. (1992) Knowledge and motor performance, *Perceptual and Motor Skills*, *74*, 1195–1202.

Korzybski, A. (1951) The role of language in the perceptual processes. In R.R. Blake and G.V. Ramsey (eds) *Perception: An Approach to Personality* (pp. 170–205). New York: Ronald.

Kwon, S.M. and Oei, T.P.S. (1994) The roles of two levels of cognitions in the development, maintenance, and treatment of depression, *Clinical Psychology Review*, *14*, 331–358.

Larson, D.W. (1994) The role of belief systems and schemas in foreign policy decision-making, *Political Psychology*, *15*, 17–33.

Liddell, H.G., Scott, R., Jones, H.S. and McKenzie, R. (1968) *Greek–English Lexicon*. Oxford: Clarendon Press.

Liddell, H.G., Scott, R., Jones, H.S., McKenzie, R., Glare, P.G.W. and Thompson, A.A. (1996) *Greek–English Lexicon* (Revised Supplement). Oxford: Clarendon Press.

Mandler, J.M. (1984) *Stories, Scripts, and Scenes: Aspects of Schema Theory*. Hillsdale, NJ: Lawrence Erlbaum Associates.

Markus, H., Hamil, R. and Sentis, K.P. (1987) Thinking fat: self-schemas for body weight and the processing of weight relevant information, *Journal of Applied Social Psychology*, *17*, 50–71.

Marméche, E. and Didierjean, A. (2001) Is generalization conservative? A study with novices in chess, *European Journal of Cognitive Psychology*, *13*, 475–491.

Marshall, S.P. (1995) *Schemas in Problem Solving*. New York: Cambridge University Press.

Marshall, S.P. (2001) *TADMUS Program: Decision-Making Schemas in Rapidly Changing Situations*. Retrieved 21 November, 2001 from www.sci.sdsu.edu/cerf/content/grants.html#hybrid.

Marshall, S.P. Wilson, D.M. and Page, K.V. (1998) *Sharing Decision-making Knowledge in Tactical Situations: Extended Analyses*. Technical Report CERF No. 98-02. Cognitive Ergonomics Research Facility, San Diego State University, San Diego, CA. Cited at www.sci.sdsu.edu/cerf/content/tadmus.html.

Matthews, G., Davies, D.R., Westerman, S.J. and Stammers, R.B. (2000) *Human Performance: Cognition, Stress and Individual Differences*. Philadelphia, PA: Psychology Press.

Mitchell, R.K., Smith, B., Seawright, K.W. and Morse, E.A. (2000) Cross-cultural cognitions and the venture creation decision, *Academy of Management Journal*, *43*, 974–993.

Mongrain, M. (1998) Parental representations and support-seeking behaviors related to dependency and self-criticism, *Journal of Personality*, *66*, 151–173.

Muran, J.C. (1991) A reformulation of the ABC model in cognitive psychotherapies: implications for assessment and treatment, *Clinical Psychology Review*, *16*, 399–418.

Neisser, U. (1967) *Cognitive Psychology*. Englewood Cliffs, NJ: Prentice-Hall.

Nisbett, R. and Ross, L. (1980) *Human Inference: Strategies and Shortcomings in Social Judgment*. Englewood Cliffs, NJ: Prentice Hall.

Norman, D.A. (1986) Reflections on cognition and parallel distributed processing. In J.L. McClelland, D.E. Rumelhart and the PDP Research Group (eds) *Parallel Distributed Processing: Explorations in the Microstructure of Cognition, Vol II* (pp. 531–552). Cambridge, MA: MIT Press.

O'Brien, F.J. (1921) A qualitative investigation of the effect of mode of presentation upon the process of learning, *American Journal of Psychology*, *32*, 249–283.

Oxford University Press (2002) *Oxford English Dictionary Online*. Retrieved 25 Janaury, 2002 from http://dictionary.oed.com/cgi/entry/00001166

Penland, E.A., Masten, W.G., Zelhart, P., Fournet, G.P. and Callahan, T.A. (2000)

Possible selves, depression and coping skills in university students, *Personality and Individual Differences*, *29*, 963–969.

Perseus Digital Library (2001) Boston: Tufts University. Retrieved 11 October, 2001 from www.perseus.tufts.edu/cgi-bin/vor?lookup=.

Piaget, J. ([1936] 1952) *The Origins of Intelligence in Children* (M. Cook, trans.). New York: International Unversities Press.

Piaget, J. (1948) *The Moral Judgment of the Child* (M. Gabain, translator). Glencoe, IL: Free Press.

Postman, L. (1951) Toward a general theory of cognition. In J.H. Rohrer and M. Sherif (eds) *Social Psychology at the Crossroads*. New York: Harper & Brothers.

Pring, L. and Hermelin, B. (1993) Bottle, tulip and wineglass: semantic and structural picture processing by savant artists, *Journal of Child Psychology and Psychiatry and Allied Disciplines*, *34*, 1365–1385.

Rapaport, D. (1951) *Organization and Pathology of Thought*. New York: Columbia University Press.

Reisenzein, R. (2001) Appraisal processes conceptualized from a schema-theoretic perspective: contributions to a process analysis of emotions. In K.R. Scherer, A. Schorr and T. Johnstone (eds) *Appraisal Processes in Emotion: Theory, Methods, Research* (pp. 187–204). New York: Oxford University Press.

Ridley, C.R., Chih, D.W. and Olivera, R.J. (2000) Training in cultural schemas: an antidote to unintentional racism in clinical practice, *American Journal of Orthopsychiatry*, *70*, 65–72.

Rosenberg, J.I. (1997) Expertise research and clinical practice: a suicide assessment and intervention training model, *Educational Psychology Review*, *9*, 279–296.

Rumelhart, D.E., McClelland, J.L. and the PDP Research Group (1986) *Parallel Distributed Processing: Explorations in the Microstructure of Cognition*. Cambridge, MA: MIT Press.

Rychlak, J.F. (1973) *Introduction to Personality and Psychotherapy. A Theory-construction Approach*. Boston: Houghton Mifflin.

Safran, J.D. (1990) Towards a refinement of cognitive therapy in light of inter-personal theory: I. Theory, *Clinical Psychology Review*, *10*, 87–105.

Sandler, A.M. (1975) Comments on the significance of Piaget's work for psycho-analysis, *International Review of Psychoanalysis*, *2*, 365–377.

Sarbin, T.R., Taft, R. and Bailey, D.E. (1960) *Clinical Interference and Cognitive Theory*. New York: Holt, Rinehart and Winston.

Shah, R. and Waller, G. (2000) Parental style and vulnerability to depression: the role of core beliefs, *Journal of Nervous and Mental Disease*, *188*, 19–25.

Shore, B. (1996) *Culture in Mind: Cognition, Culture, and the Problem of Meaning*. New York: Oxford University Press.

Smith, E.R. (1998) Mental representation and memory. In D.T. Gilbert, S.T. Fiske and G. Sindzey (eds) *The Handbook of Social Psychology* (4th edn). New York: McGraw-Hill.

Stein, D.J. (1992) Clinical cognitive science: possibilities and limitations. In D.J. Stein and J.E. Young (eds) *Cognitive Science and Clinical Disorders* (pp. 3–17). San Diego, CA: Academic Press.

Stinson, C.H. and Palmer, S.E. (1991) Parallel distributed processing models of person schemas and psychopathologies. In M.J. Horowitz (ed.) *Person Schemas and Maladaptive Interpersonal Patterns* (pp. 339–377). Chicago: University of Chicago Press.

Titchener, E.B. (1912) The schema of introspection, *American Journal of Psychology*, *23*, 485–508.

Vitousek, K.B. and Orimoto, L. (1993) Cognitive–behavioral models of anorexia nervosa, bulimia nervosa, and obesity. In K.S. Dobson and P.C. Kendall (eds) *Psychopathology and Cognition* (pp. 193–245). New York: Academic Press.

Walen, S., DiGiuseppe, R. and Dryden, W. (1992) *A Practitioner's Guide to Rational Emotive Therapy* (2nd edn). New York: Oxford University Press.

Wheeler, R.H. and Cutsforth, T.D. (1921) The role of synaesthesia in learning, *Journal of Experimental Psychology*, *4*, 448–468.

Williamson, J. and McGuinness, C. (1990) The role of schemata in the comprehension of maps. In K.J. Gilhooly, M.T.G. Keane, R.H. Logie and G. Erdos (eds) *Lines of Thinking: Reflections on the Psychology of Thought. Volume 2: Skills, Emotion, Creative Processes, Individual Differences and Teaching Thinking* (pp. 29–40). New York: Wiley.

Young, J.E. (1999) *Cognitive Therapy for Personality Disorders: A Schema-focused Approach* (3rd edn). Sarasota, FL: Professional Resource Exchange, Inc.

Chapter 6

Notes on self and values in REBT

James McMahon

Cartesian dualism: epistemological objects and process

Modern philosophy and the Enlightenment are often dated from Descartes, and they can be further traced back to a break with priestly and other authority during the Dark Ages. The break offered the opportunity to make each person his or her own authority, and with that goal in mind Descartes tried to doubt everything. He thought that most of what he had learned had been proven wrong by the prevailing spirit of the times when he lived. But, Descartes clearly was convinced that he could not doubt his own existence. Since he could not doubt that he doubted, Descartes concluded, 'I think, therefore I am'. Unfortunately, his maxim, in turn, resulted in more doubt while he attempted to place each person as ground or source of his or her own ontology and epistemology with consequent capacity to reason, to observe an objective world, and to seek the truth. Because Descartes argued that thoughts were incorporeal, a thinker could not logically and rationally conclude that his or her body existed. So, the best conclusion Descartes could coherently offer to posterity in his turn to a person as subject was, approximately, 'I think, therefore I think'.

Descartes was aware of the dualism he created, referred to later by Gustav Theodor Fechner, father of psychophysics, and others, as 'psycho-physical parallelism'. Descartes, thereafter, spent effort and time trying to bridge the mind–body gap. He did not succeed. As a result, the road to skepticism was open. One could doubt that one had a body, and so one could adopt *solipsism* – the end result being that the only reality was one's own constructions. Christine Ladd-Franklin, famous for her vision theory, adopted solipsism and opined to William James that she was surprised that more people had not done so. Additionally, *idealism* took hold, especially on the Continent (Leibnitz, Kant, and Hegel), while *empiricism* took hold in the British Isles, and later in North America, beginning with John Locke and continuing through luminaries such as A.J. Ayer, Lord Russell, and the early Ludwig Wittgenstein.

1. *Epistemology*: how we know what we know.
2. *Idealism*: the doctrine arguing that the reality a person understands reflects the workings of his or her mind.
3. *Empiricism*: experience – or what we know through the senses – has primacy.
4. *Ontology*: the way things really are – their state of being.

Ellis and the TFC

In 1956 when Albert Ellis (1994) addressed the American Psychological Association's Annual Meeting in Chicago, he predicted the revolution he was about to launch in psychotherapy. Even then, Ellis insisted that it was difficult, at best, to separate a thought from a feeling. Debates have played out in the psychological literature thereafter between, for example, Robert Zajonc, who argued that feelings precede thoughts, and Richard Lazarus, who argued for the opposite point of view. However inadvertently, Ellis seemingly has succeeded where Descartes failed concerning situating human existence. Based upon his dictum, summarized as thinking generally being one end and feeling generally being the other end of a thinking–feeling process, if one concluded, 'I think–feel, therefore I am', Descartes's dualism will have been overcome. One's personal existence thus can be conceptualized as process. In process epistemology, object epistemological dualism will have been overcome because feeling represents physical sensation that cannot be separated from thinking. They constitute a thinking–feeling–continuum (process) or TFC.

However, upon closer inspection, were TFC left within the paradigm of object epistemology, one could argue that thinking was incorporeal and that feeling was physical. Thus, Descartes's category error would have been repeated by Ellis. Instead, Ellis argued for TFC within a model of psychotherapy and possible personality theory. In turn, McMahon argues that, once a shift has been made to process epistemology, TFC stops infinite regress and permits individual responsibility from location within culture and culture's offspring, language. Descartes argued that there were two substances, one immaterial and the other material, in his mind–body thesis. He clearly intended self-existence to be demonstrably clear and convincing from the perspective of object epistemology as well as grounded ontology or being, while Ellis did not go that way.

From Plato to the American Pragmatists and into the postmodern times in which we live (perhaps with a postmodernism generated by the latter Wittgenstein now giving way to virtual reality, this last argued for eloquently by Beaudrillard, 1995), there are trends in epistemology. Plato argued for pure forms or being objectively outside of and independent of human knowledge, but which humans could know. Augustine argued for an interior 'self', not just for sensation and perception as epistemology. In

Augustine's philosophy, object epistemology and ontology complement each other. Descartes tried to ground self but failed miserably with his legacy of dualism. It was Peirce, James, and Dewey, especially William James, who situated the human being within a stream of consciousness or process in which that human was both active and passive, or both constructionist and constructed. Process epistemology was born while ontology became less important. The latter Wittgenstein, and other postmodern philosophers, situated the human being within culture, relationships, and texts. There was no Archimedean or 'out-there' starting point from which reality could be measured: language games, contexts, cultures, and texts were processes within which human behavior could be studied. Instead of philosophy being the discipline which passed judgment on other disciplines, it became part of various genres to help learn how ideas related, held together, or interacted. Postmodern philosophy joins the mix of other epistemologies and does not set itself up as being superior to or true compared to other paradigms. There is room for all of them to learn from each other. So, scientific psychology can learn from literature, psychoanalysis can learn from experimental psychology, and REBT can learn from solution-focused therapy (Cade and O'Hanlon, 1993).

Freud thought that he had solved the problem of dualism with his concept of *drive*, a place-holder combination of instinct and social experience. However, there seems little to recommend Freud's argument given his multiplication of essences and violation of Ockham's razor, or the principle of parsimony. Freud sought a solution to dualism but instead multiplied essences (i.e. created a new place-holder rather than make then-available knowledge functional and testable). Ellis did not go that way, and for good reason. Had he, Ellis would have made a category error similar to the one Freud made when the latter tried to combine the physical–animal instinct of an individual with outside-of-the-individual social forces within a paradigm of object epistemology with consequent ontology. On closer inspection, Freud's place-holder combination yielded another dualism, and that violated the warrant of simplicity.

Today, there is substantial information from both neurological imaging and neurophysiology (neurobiology) to recommend the continuum of thinking–feeling argued for by Ellis more than forty years ago. Metabolic studies of the brain through fMRI and PET techniques observe the work of the brain when thinking in specific ways, while indications of Alzheimer's disease inferred from cortical atrophy analysis helps to prepare clinicians and families to anticipate and to attempt to manage deficits in memory-behavior and emotional outburst that are sure to follow onset of the disease. Daniel L. Schacter (2001) reminded us in his text that 'hot' memories of so-called emotionally charged incidents are better remembered than are less emotionally charged incidents. Qualitative factors such as 'hot' and 'cold' emotions that are attached to thoughts (memories) are now being studied alongside of and contiguous with events that subjects conclude to be positive and negative. Positively and negatively held emotions have long been a part of the thinking–feeling continuum in REBT (Ellis, 1994, pp. 255ff).

The concept of EQ, or emotional quotient–emotional intelligence, advanced by Daniel Goleman (1997) and now endorsed by Martin Seligman (1998), makes an approach to the thinking–feeling continuum (TFC) with new vocabulary and observations. Regarding the TFC, emotional intelligence could be conceptualized as an elaboration of REBT but with some new labels.

Since we live in language (Chomsky, Kodish, Korzybski, Presby Kodish, Skinner, Whorf, Wittgenstein, Carnap, and Quine, *inter alia*), whether feelings come first or the opposite is the case, one usually but not always accesses the continuum of thinking–feeling (TFC) through and within language. For both John the Evangelist and Albert Ellis, REBT's father and CBT's grandfather, 'In the beginning was the word . . .'. It is pragmatically demonstrable (McMahon, 1996) that TFC be managed within REBT language alone, the result being a theory-less theory or process. Thus, each person him- or herself, or the dyad in individual counseling, or dyad-plus in group counseling – each, both, and all – can use and access the TFC with REBT language techniques alone. Each person, dyad, or group, then, becomes the guardian within language of the usefulness or 'cash value' of praxis and outcomes. Ellis himself said that he operated within a framework of logical positivism until 1976 (as advanced by Carnap, undermined by Quine, and narrated by Mahoney in *Scientist as Subject*, 1976), but that REBT had previously been and was and could legitimately be considered a constructive/postmodern psychotherapy (Mahoney, 1990; Ellis, 1994; Ellis in Dryden, 1990).

Maxie Maultsby (1975) provides a conceptual model on the horizon of cognitive–behavioral psychotherapies which distinguishes 'who' a person is from 'what' they do. 'Who' in his model represents those aspects of the person involving thought, values, character, ability to abstract, memories, plans, and, perhaps, spiritual appraisal. Since 'who' I am in general differs from 'what' I do in some role, 'who' is not vulnerable to physical attack, negative words, or the vicissitudes of time and space. 'Who' can neither be added to nor taken from in terms of behaviors. It can be pictured in the mind's eye as a circle ('O'). Behavioral roles can be pictured as lines coming from the 'O', each line being distinct. The roles receive their meaning or rank in closeness to the 'O' from the choices made by the person. However, it is the person who gives meaning to the roles, and not the reverse.

Using this model, Ellis has referred to 'USA' or unconditional self-acceptance. To distinguish self-acceptance from self-esteem, it has been argued (Chamberlain and Haaga, 2001) that esteem of any kind involves rating and/or evaluation and so must be limited to rating or evaluation of behaviors and not of the person. Their studies have reinforced Ellis's theoretical claim: there was an inverse relationship between persons who accepted themselves and anxiety, narcissism, and criticism from others. Further, writing from their expansionist theory which really delimits other theories and limits gender differences, Barrett and Hyde (2001) argue that the negative effects of stress or failure in one role can be buffered by success and satisfactions in another role. This whole matter would amount to what REBT practitioners call distraction of an emotion by another emotion or behavior. So-called 'buffering' will last so long as the distraction continues. However, according to REBT theory and practice, when the distraction ceases, irrational evaluations again couple with negative stress. The point of REBT is not only to feel better, as in buffering, but to *be* better by

1. unconditional self-acceptance, and
2. replacing irrational with rational thinking.

Given the importance of self within TFC inferred from arguments made by Ellis, indicated not only ontologically but now through neurobiology, language, new concepts (labels) such as EQ, and process in postmodernism and constructive psychotherapy, the next section will present some historical information concerning Ellis's concept of the value of a human being. Some philosophers, Mortimer Adler being one of them, advanced arguments for concepts after first presenting definitions of that concept. For example, Adler (1980) attempted to define the place-holder concept 'God' before attempting to demonstrate God's existence. That same process of definition–demonstration could have been attempted here. However, it was judged by this writer that readers most likely would be more familiar with Ellis and his concept of TFC than with his definitions and arguments describing human beings and their value.

Historical and other issues of value and worth in REBT

Dryden (1990, p. 77) neatly outlined Ellis's major interactions with Robert Hartman. According to Dryden, Ellis and Hartman both concluded that it was unproductive to rate oneself. This aphorism, not to rate oneself, has become a classical saying, even stratagem, in REBT. But, the saying or stratagem would seem contradictory on its face. For one to argue that self rating is unproductive is itself a rating: the saying implicitly denies what it explicitly affirms and so is self-referentially incoherent. For example, one could raise questions about comparisons (unproductive compared to . . .?) regarding the saying. *First*, if one views self as the totality of all experiences in life, it would seem a waste of time to try to rate all such experiences at the same time under the heading 'self', and in that sense it would seem such a rating would be unproductive. Yet, the notion of lack of production in this example would mean that too much time would be spent to achieve any benefit that might be gained. A human being might spend his or her whole life trying to make such a rating (however, maybe God could do it). Consistent with REBT training and practice, then, counselors and therapists are trained to rate roles and behaviors and to think of rating self as a waste of time.

Second, if *self* is used in a limited sense, say, as the owner of roles and behaviors, rating it would make little sense because self in that sense is merely a role, or means of coordination, or a way to stop the infinite regress of roles. It would be a dimension-less point somewhere on the horizon of individual consciousness. While such a rating would not seem to make much sense generally, one could rate the effectiveness of the point or role ownership or coordination, say, compared to norms such as previous performance, previous outcomes, and productivity – assuming role stability over time. The assumption here would be static means of ownership or role management, however, and another waste of time would probably result from the attempt.

Self also can be used, and has been by Ellis, in a *third*, equivocal way, as a given or ontological starting point. From this phenomenological or existential starting point, a person's reality precedes his or her creation of roles or habits of action and thought. Heidegger's self-in-the world and *thrownness* into life try to capture the concept, one adopted by Tillich. Ellis (1973) has credited Tillich as a source of influence. It is in this ontological sense that self can be used in the remainder of this chapter, whether self is spoken of referentially or when referring to another human being. From this starting point, it would make little sense to rate self. Aside from leading to over-generalization (or the logical fallacy of composition), this conception 'self' is a place-holder and to rate such a concept by physical or observable standards would mix apples and oranges (i.e. take us back to Cartesian dualism). Further, if each ontological self is uniquely associated with personal combinations of habits, attitudes, and behaviors compared to all other human beings, that self would still be analogously like them in the sense of language, ability to abstract, capability to plan, and to know that self knows. A convenient way of comparing selves within this analogy might be to conclude, with Jefferson and others (sexist language notwithstanding): *all men are created* equal on the level of their uniqueness but different in terms of market-place worth of their skills, talents, and possessions.[1]

A *fourth* way of dealing with self is to see it as part of a process, embedded in culture, traditions, and learning. This version of self permits unconditional self acceptance and goal-directed thinking while it plays down the gross responsibility of epistemological individualism which begs for certainty (as did Descartes) as foundation. Process epistemology argues against foundationalism. The argument itself is not foundational because it too is subject to change. While the process self is situated within a context, process self differs from relative self which changes as does the proverbial chameleon. A relative self changes values according to goals, so that the end justifies the means. In self as process, goals are combined with pragmatics that are acceptable to and indispensable for the orderly commerce of ideas and other exchanges within and between contexts, cultures, societies, and traditions. Values come before existence in arguments made by Levinas, so that responsibility for another person (society, culture, traditions, one's religion) helps to create and maintain that other person and oneself. Consistent with REBT, absolute evaluations in this model are eschewed while diversity is celebrated. Alvin Plantinga (1984) has conceptualized the new epistemology as more like a pyramid than a pillar sunk into the ground. Whereas the pillar–ground metaphor relies upon rational language to support its foundationalism, the rational language itself resides in a web of language, belief, and culture, so that foundationalism cannot be demonstrated to be what it claims to be. Again, foundationalism as ground is self-referentially incoherent. In the pyramid metaphor, building blocks here and there can be removed while the pyramid is maintained. In the human condition, certain behaviors, beliefs, traditions, and behaviors can be eliminated and/or replaced, yet the shape of the pyramid is recognizable over time – and all other pyramids would be recognized as pyramids over time even though their building blocks can have been removed and/or replaced.

Within what could generously be described as an ontological model of self or person, Ellis and Hartman differed on whether intrinsic value of a person actually existed. Ellis thought it did not, while Hartman, according to Dryden, thought that intrinsic value did exist. My own reading of Ellis (1972) on the value of a human being convinced me that Ellis thought it wise that a person value him- or herself highly. Ellis concluded that problems were sure to follow when a person did not do so. In a most humanistic way, Ellis argued (1972), 'Being alive, I can choose to see myself as valuable – or as worthless. If I choose the former definition, I will most likely get good results. But will I truly be or become more valuable? Only because I say so.' Within his personal philosophy of humanism, then, Ellis held that the value of a person was established by self-definition.

In his correspondence with Hartman, Ellis argued what I think to be a straw man; namely, that value was synonymous with character and that both depended upon self-definition (i.e. the 'because I say so' definition-issue). That view of character would lead, as Ellis argued, to one person asserting that s/he had more character-value than another, and so one would have argued in a circle (*petito principii*) by asserting that his or her definition was more valuable than another person's definition. But are there phenomena such as objective character and value? Can one person show more courage in a situation, greater honesty, lukewarm loyalty, or ambiguous love? Those values can be measured according to some known standards, and that measurement is in addition to the point of total human value. Character virtues can be measured and are not the same as human value. Back to Thomas Jefferson's words about men being created as equals. Jefferson surely intended an equality of something that did not invite rating. For him, the value of each and every human being excluded rating because of equality. If one person had more value than another, they were not equal to the others. The opposite also was true: if a person had less value than another, they were not equal to the others. The value or worth of someone cannot be objectively measured, as, say, can the value of an automobile, a house, or a pile of diamonds. But, the value of a *class* of human beings and each human life objectively can be placed beyond value because there is no standard except the class itself against which to measure the class. The definition is not individual but social and unique. Ellis himself commented about this '*beyond* value' argument in another context when he was asked if he would condemn Hitler as a person or whether he could, as in Christian teaching, hate the sin but love the sinner. On this score, Ellis has been thoroughly 'Christian' because he could not 'hate' Hitler as a person. This example of a 'who/what' distinction made by Ellis implicitly affirmed the value of *each* person as being independent of what they did. Since Ellis has nowhere said that his opinion was subjective or merely a matter of taste, he implicitly affirmed the value of each and all persons as a member of the *class* called human beings.

Concerning character, it would seem that virtues can be rated and so are not the same as the objective value of a person or a class called human beings. For example, it seems that George Washington displayed more loyalty to the Republic than did Benedict Arnold, and that Mother Theresa showed more love for all humans than did Hitler. Character virtues such as these can be objectively measured, as Gordon Allport (1961) in his work with Vernon and Lindzey commented in the survey, *A Study of Values* (this last based on Spranger's late-nineteenth century *Types of Men*). Since there is no yardstick or way to measure a class called human beings, it would seem that that class is beyond rating. The value belongs to each member of the class in this unique way because, like Jefferson, the meaning applies to each person univocally. Human beings, accordingly, have objective value, and the value of each human being is not based upon self-definition. This sense of value would hold either in individual epistemology–ontology, or in process epistemology (see discussion of foundation and pyramid, above) on the discursive plane of knowledge.

Counselor preparation

At a recent meeting at the Albert Ellis Institute in New York, a discussion ensued about professional ethics. If there is a settled nomenclature, Stephen Benke (2001) of the American Psychological Association's Ethics Office has defined *ethics* as 'thinking about reasons in terms of values'. In turn, and as has been argued here, *values* are character virtues or beliefs sometimes combined with actions into which we each invest self worth and which guide each of us over the long haul. Values can be shared in culture, societies, and in religions. Lastly, *morals* refer to a principle or principles of right conduct compared to a known standard.

Generally, it seems that professional ethics have been eclipsed by law when various professions obtain 'licensing' of their professional name and/ or regulation of their professional conduct. Exceptions would exist for licensed clergy, for example. Before licensing laws, voluntary codes of ethics made great sense for professional adherence in order that the public be protected. Licensing, however, made it quickly apparent that several so-called ethical standards were themselves illegal, standards concerning advertising and methods of collecting fees being examples. When such ethical standards came into conflict with the law (e.g. market-place freedom or restraint of trade, and using collection agents or factors), laws obtained and standards contrary to them were found to be not only unethical but illegal. Whereas a murderer would be spared double jeopardy within American standards of justice counselors and psychologists would not.[2] Another example: two decades ago, the American Speech-Language and Hearing Association's ethics forbade audiologists from dispensing hearing aids for profit, much as optometrists dispensed eye glasses and contact lenses for profit. The Federal Trace Commission learned of the so-called ASHA ethical standard and ordered ASHA to change its rule or face a fine until it was changed. The so-called ASHA ethical rule represented a restraint of trade – a 'no-no' in American law.

When an ethics complaint is lodged, a mental health specialist, for example, could be subject to standards–procedures–sanctions by (1) his or her national association, (2) his or her state association independently, (3) the state board of examiners, and (4) within civil procedures (including closed-door insurance company or managed care company decisions to drop a provider without due process). The writer is familiar with a case of a specialist who introduced into the therapy process ambiguous problem solving. The client complained to the state specialty association which invited the specialist to an informal hearing. The specialist made the mistake of believing that the invitation meant what it said and so attended without legal counsel. It was judged at the *informal* meeting which was attended by a majority of the state association's ethics committee that the specialist violated several ethics principles and, in order to maintain mem-bership, had to (1) submit to supervision by another practitioner acceptable to the committee and (2) take added course work in areas of treatment in which the committee judged the specialist to be deficient. The specialist acquiesced but also protested that over the course of twelve years of prac-tice there had been no complaints by other, similar clients who themselves believed they were treated ethically concerning similar circumstances – as did the practitioner. The specialist was censured and was told that her demeanor was defensive. After one year of following through on the committee's demands, the censure was lifted. Then, the client made a second complaint, to the state board of examiners, which board had the force of law. Within court-like procedures, and after extensive investigation by its agents and deliberation by board members, the board found that the specialist had violated no standards of practice, no law, and was not deficient in any way at the time the complaint had been reviewed by and acted upon by the state association. This last decision dissuaded the client from proceeding with civil action (the client had been interviewed by state investigators who found that individual to have been a complainer). With regard to the conflict, the only person who suffered was the specialist. The same state ethics committee had been told several years before to change several of its so-called ethical standards or else it would be found to be in violation of the law. And so it goes! On the level of ethics, with friends like that state association's ethics committee, the specialist did not need enemies.

Values and a case example

In REBT supervision, a Christian pastor recently indicated that he was very conflicted emotionally about leaving his wife. On the one hand, he wished to leave her, while, on the other, he thought that doing so would be sinful. Purportedly, the supervisor was aghast that the minister would have any misgivings about leaving his wife if that is what he wished to do. After all, the supervisor purportedly offered, the minister could be helped to deal with guilt and separation through rational–emotive insight with disputation, and then move on.

Here, all codes of ethics within the helping professions, as well as canons which have the force of law, indicate that a counselor shall respect a client's personal and religious values. In fact, this simple example shows a clash of values in which the supervisor thought his standards of judgment and ethics to be superior to those of the minister. Since the minister was also in training, it could be argued that the counselor was peddling undue influence (power), but let us stay with the marriage example's clash of values.

In the practice of REBT, what Spinoza and Hume called experiential values generally obtain when one speaks of 'calmness' or other personally experienced feelings that are valued. Love, happiness, and joy generally are valued, whereas boredom, confusion, and worry are devalued. Further, REBT is not just Stoical (accepting) in values, but Epicurean or pleasure-seeking. However, both Stoical and Epicurean values are what will be referred to here as subjective and relative *Stage One Values*.[3] Subjective values are those which one personally favors, whereas relative values correspond to this group, that country, or my time of life by saying that all values are equal. Pushed hard and far enough, this line of reasoning could lead to *nihilism*. This last would insist that Mussolini's concept of democracy for Ethiopia was equivalent to what the Allies had in mind for themselves and for Italy after World War II and that neither value system really mattered.

Stage Two Values generally involve *purpose* or *intent*. Activities are valued because they move toward goals. Thus, one might very much enjoy eating and consider it to be good. However, when one goes shopping for food, or when one cooks a meal, the immediate sensation of food is elongated into a process. These values generally subsume or conflate Stage One Values. Yet, they are still subjective and relative.

Stage Three Values involve habits that become traditions over time, while traditions over time can become what Greeley (1996), MacIntyre (1997), and others denote to be *culture*. Such behaviors include loyalty to the tribe, fidelity to a spouse, work for a church, struggle for a community, and charitable works. Stage Three Values subsume the first two; however, they are more objective and are easier to study because of their social and objective nature. One moves in this stage from subjective values to the values of a group or culture. Yet, the values are relative to that group or culture: they are shared. Most codes of ethics, professional regulations, and voluntary association rules or moral standards can be found on this stage of values.

Stage Four Values are more general principles and sometimes can be considered to be permanent or absolute. Trying to access the absolute imports many problems and sets the stage for lively debate. When one says that all men are created equal, that $E = mc^2$, and that light travels at 86,000 miles per second, such statements are not dependent upon what the tribe thinks or what an individual thinks: they are true generally. But here is where the argument begins between those who say that modern ethics cannot at all access the fourth dimension of ethics (which 'at all' itself is absolute) and others who say that ethics can do so.

Some persons might say that all values are relative, but that is contradictory, for the very statement is absolute or foundational. Some postmodern philosophers might say that one cannot explain a fourth dimension because one is confined to one's language, and to explain such a dimension means that one would explain fourth-dimension language with one's own language. In this example, again, there is a contradiction, for the postmodern thinker would be saying that his or her argument is better or more correct than other arguments, and that is an absolute standard. Many postmodern philosophers (e.g. Gergen, 2001) would not advance the language critique in the same way. They would argue that because so-called claimed generalizations and absolutes exist in language, and language is itself a changing phenomenon, most so-called absolutes or generalizations are time-bound – as would be the language of postmodernism. However, many postmodern theorists would not disdain fields of knowledge and would encourage that their argot and procedures continue so long as they contribute to human knowledge, arguments that are not just what Gergen has called a 'march toward obscurity'. A convenient example of this phenomenon of language being time-bound would be Kant's various critiques through which he believed he had found universal principles. Just one decade later, Hegel undermined Kant's project by showing that the progression of ideas in history was itself time- and culture-bound.

In private correspondence, Albert Ellis pointed out to this writer that all science is open to new information (falsification), and that recent evidence had been offered that, for example, the speed of light can sometimes be achieved at lesser speeds than 86,000 miles per second. This caution, however, hardly disproves Einstein's maxim. The new evidence merely indicates that Einstein had not attained the *whole* truth – not that there is no truth value or pragmatic warrantability in the relativity theory/speed of light issue. The same could be said for Newtonian concepts of motion which, at very high speeds, do not hold. At high speeds, Einstein's theory of relativity works better and so is heuristic. Further, as Bernard Williams (1994) has argued in his defense of the analytic tradition (American logical empiricism), if one accepts rationality within certain language configurations, it would be reasonable to argue for the truth of X or Y.

Concerning the *whole* truth issue, consider the Albert Ellis Institute to illustrate Stage Four Values. Suppose someone asks, 'What is the AEI?' If one were to ask the person staffing the front desk, they might proffer, 'It is a place that offers course work to train psychotherapists, and books are sold here.' That is surely one view of the Institute. Were one to ask the Institute's lawyer the same question, they might reply that 'The Institute is a not-for-profit educational corporation organized under the laws of the State of New York.' If one were to ask the clean-up person the same question, they might answer, 'It's a place where folks leave a lot of dirty chalkboards behind, where the volume of scrapped paper is high, and where people leave bits of their lunch in the public rooms.' If a casual visitor to a Friday-night, public session were asked, they might proffer, 'Well, it seems to be a place where people talk about thinking and feeling and where they curse a lot when they talk about how to keep them balanced.' Each of the persons responding has answered the question, but from his or her point of view. After hearing them, one might still ask, 'Yes, but what is the AEI?' It is all of the viewpoints, no one of which has the whole truth but each has a part of it. Having learned these points of view, plus others, one can conclude that no one point of view captures the whole meaning of the AEI. Upon hearing even one answer to the question, it is doubtful that anyone would conclude that the identity of the AEI has been captured. Nor do the multiple viewpoints represent a consensus. Instead, like truth as objective standard in the postmodern sense, objective in the sense that it can be identified as part of a process, it is the mosaic of descriptions that seeks the truth or wholeness-identify called AEI. Like Plantinga's pyramid, each of the descriptions adds something, but no single description captures the pyramid known as AEI. Of course, the truth or wholeness of what makes up the AEI can be arrived at from other points of view (analytic or logical empiricism, phenomenological, and virtual being three convenient examples), but all would go beyond the scope of these notes on Stage Four Values

Examples of values clarification

For this chapter, hopefully, the first three stages of value probably will suffice most of the time for the counselor to be cognizant of the level of a client's values – but there are exceptions! In the example given above, the supervisor was stuck at Stage One Values while the minister was confused between Stage One and Stage Three Values (his feelings for another woman versus his loyalty to his church and beliefs). The supervisor's comments added to the confusion because they failed to make that distinction since she or he themself probably was operating within Stoical/Epicurean, subjective–experiential parameters at Stage One Values. The following cases are composite of cases available to the writer from many sources, none of which is intended to suggest or identify an actual person, living or dead.

Case 1: Anger

A client consulted a psychotherapist concerning anger. The client was especially angered at a woman who had spurned his affection after one problem-loaded date and one aborted date (she ended the date by leaving him in a public place because he was yelling). The client told the therapist that his anger was so great that it would take very little for him to go to the female's home and to harm her. He stated that if she would not go out with him, he would leave and then punch her face into a mess – perhaps kill her – so that no other suitor would want her or be able to go out with her. The client began to yell at the therapist who had worked with him to change his feeling–thinking and threats. From being spurned on the date, the client had concluded that his pride had been wounded, that he had been an absolute failure at a person, and that the woman who spurned him was the cause of his feelings. During the visit, the psychotherapist was wise enough to get some basic information about the identity of the woman. Immediately after the client left the office, the therapist called the police to report the threats. The therapist judged that there was duty to warn the intended victim about what the therapist judged to be an out-of-control client who intended her harm. The woman was warned, a court order was issued to restrain the client from being within one thousand feet of the client at any time, and the client was detained for threatened assault.

In the foregoing example, we see client conflict between Stage One, Stage Two, Stage Three, and Stage Four Values. At Stage One, the client judged that his 'feelings' were hurt, and so he wished to retaliate. He erred at Stage Two because he thought that since he alone demanded there be a relationship so that a process called dating would ensue. He erred at Stage Three because he had no loyalty to cultural norms for dating, norms which generally imply that one can participate or not participate in the Stage Two Values process. The client erred badly when he indicated that the woman's life was not so important as his own 'pride', and so he judged her life to be less valuable than his own (Stage Four Values). Contrarily, the psychotherapist, to that therapist's great credit, judged that legal and ethical considerations combined into a duty to warn the intended victim through the police (the therapist received assurances from the police that he need go no further because they would immediately warn and inform her). The therapist was guided by ethical standards in Stage Three Values as well as Stage Four Values. Beyond Stage Three Values concerning issues of confidentiality, the therapist judged that the woman's life was at stake (Stage Four Values). For the therapist, there was ambivalence at State Three Values, keeping confidential the client's statements alongside the ethical–legal duty to warn an intended victim. When the therapist thought of Stage Four Values, the equality of all human life, the police were called and the client's stated intentions were thwarted. In the state in which the therapist worked, laws obtained which were interpreted by the therapist's malpractice insurance experts to be 'Good Samaritan'. Their application meant that, had the client tried to take civil action against the therapist for a breech of confidential information when the therapist acted to help another person he judged to be in harm's way, the law protected the therapist from legal action by the client. It could be argued that the therapist overreacted, but the client did not pursue a law suit – perhaps because the spurned woman would be a powerful witness about the client's behavior during that second date.

Case 2: Eating disorder

Next is a case which emphasizes low-level value integration. The case involved impulsive eating, or, when it came to food, 'I can't stand it-itis'.

A man who was one hundred pounds overweight had been referred by his internist to a social worker who specialized in eating disorders. The man knew that excess weight was taxing his heart, and he also knew that he had a problem with high levels of fat in his veins and arteries. The social worker, familiar with the four stages of values presented here, zeroed in on Stage One Value sometimes being consistent with LFT (low frustration tolerance) or discomfort anxiety (DA). It was for this particular client. The client was not able to see that eating for most people was part of a process (Stage Two Values). Once the client was able to conceptualize of eating as part of a process, he quickly came to the conclusion that remaining at Stage One Value level sabotaged any chance of creating Stage Two Values and losing weight. While it may be difficult to objectify either or both Stage One and Stage Two Values, this particular client chose eating process as his goal. In turn, the social worker helped the client incorporate Stage One Values into Stage Two Values as process by using Premack's principle (i.e. turning routines into rewards, such as only eating breakfast the next day if the client had allowed three hours of non-eating before he went to bed the night before, or rewarding himself with lunch after he had walked for thirty minutes). Over a two-year period, or at about one pound of weight loss per week, the client reached his goal, namely, to lose one hundred pounds.

Case 3: Values in coaching: death and dying

The following is a case regarding values clarification within what can be called REBC or rational-emotive behavioral coaching. There was no gross pathology presented, merely preferences in lifestyle.

A couple had been living together for more than twenty years when one of them became terminally ill and was given six months to live. Neither had been married, there was a twenty-five-year age difference between them, and they had an exclusive physical and living-together relationship. The older person told the younger one that she would inherit assets of about $1 million when the older partner died. There were no close relatives so there would most likely be no challenges to the older partner's last will and testament. Loyal and unwilling to admit that death was at hand, the younger partner consulted the personal coach. She told the coach that she had visited an attorney and accountant and that the total tax bite on the estate left to her by the older partner would be about $650,000. The younger partner was distraught because she knew that the older partner had worked her whole life to amass and preserve assets, take excellent care of the home they lived in, and support local charities generously. Still, the tax rate was what it was, and there seemed no way to avoid paying what would be due. Here, there was a conflict in values between the law and Stage Three Values (loyalty to civil authority and loyalty to the about-to-be-deceased partner's legacy). The coach asked if he could interview the older partner who now had about six weeks to live. Asked if she viewed the relationship as one similar to family, the older partner said that the younger partner was more family than she had ever known. The older partner was asked if she ever thought of herself as the more experienced in life of the two, and she said yes by virtue of the fact that she had lived longer and had more business experience. With both partners present, they were asked if they would consider legalizing their feelings of family by having the older partner adopt the younger partner. Once done, asset pass-through benefits would mean that the older partner would be leaving her estate to a daughter, and, between national and local laws, most of the estate would be preserved with taxes due at the rate of 40% on just $400,000. Instead of paying an estimated $650,000 in taxes, the surviving partner would pay an estimated $160,000. Thereafter, an attorney who specialized in family law arranged for the adoption procedure, which was completed in about four weeks. The older partner died shortly thereafter knowing that assets she had worked for had been preserved and passed on to a person whom she loved. In turn, the surviving partner had over $850,000 to invest, the yearly investment interest income from which yielded about $50,000 annually.

In the above example, the personal coach's input only came within the process of values clarification, or what the couple wished to achieve. It was not until their feelings for each other were expressed in terms of family that the adoption issues arose. The younger partner was quite willing to obey the law at Stage Three Values, but she was sad for her partner whose work over many years would go to civil authorities. With this loyalty to her partner in mind, much like a spousal or mother–daughter arrangement, clarification at Stage Three Values resulted in both partners and the law having been satisfied.

Case 4: Taking a life

A fourth example involves a charge of murder, or violation of the law and conflict with Stage Four Values – taking of a human life by another person. A woman befriended a professional man in a large city. Due to his work, he had access to proscribed narcotic substances, and he began to use them when he was tired. That use led to a habit of using street drugs. The woman in the relationship used drugs from time to time, until her live-in friend needed help with money. She, in turn, turned to drug sales to enable his habit and, to a lesser extent, her own. At some point in time, the man said that life was no longer worth living, that he felt more dead than alive, and so he suggested that the couple enter into a murder–suicide pact. The woman refused, and asked him to put the idea out of his mind. He insisted that the idea was a good one and then he threatened her. If she left him, he said, he would murder her anyway, but he would make sure that he murdered her innocent sister first who was a college student within a one-day drive of the city. The threat jarred the woman, who dallied with the idea of going to the police.

However, she immediately experienced a desire to protect the life of her sister (Stage Four Values), and she thought that she herself might be arrested because of drug sales. Within a week of his announcement concerning murder–suicide, the male beat the female to the point that her eyes were blackened, her face was swollen purple, and he left finger marks on her throat. After the beating, he showed her two loaded revolvers that he put into a kitchen cabinet drawer. In the dark, early-morning hours of the next day, the female heard the male's car pull into the house garage. As he entered the kitchen from the garage, she heard him saying that it was time to pray and that they would both be dead by sunrise. In fear for her life, the female raced to the kitchen drawer, she removed one of the weapons, and she fired in the direction of the kitchen entry door. The first shot illuminated the kitchen, while a second shot elicited a loud groan from the male before he hit the floor. The second bullet went through the male's head and killed him. Charges ranging from manslaughter to assault with a deadly weapon were dropped against the female over a several-month period, and she entered counseling for feelings of overwhelming guilt and worry about what she had done. Eventually, values were examined with the client and her minister, a person who had some training in pastoral counseling. During a full-afternoon session, the client realized that she had broken the law (Stage Three Values), but that she had protected her sister and herself (both Stage Four Values) while she took the life of a person who intended to kill her (Stage Four Values) – but for good reason. Once the client realized that she had the support of her religious community (Stage Three Values), she was able, with calmness, from that platform to sort out Stage Four Values conflicts. Her minister was in complete accord with the values clarification, as was a judge who refused to sentence her to probation but who did ask her voluntarily to attend pastoral counseling for vocational and personal redirection over a three-year period.

Case 5: Abortion – a family matter

A young woman was accompanied to a psychologist's office by her parents. The young woman (17 years old) said that she was pregnant, that she had had CVS (an early form of testing to help determine the health of a fetus), and that she wished to abort her pregnancy. The young woman's father was in complete agreement with her, while the young woman's mother was against pregnancy termination except in the case that it would save the life of the mother. The young woman knew that there was a 50% chance that, carried to term, the female fetus would be born with a spinal disease. However, she also stated that she became pregnant within a relationship that she thought would lead to marriage, that the young father of the fetus had changed his mind, and that she herself wanted to continue her college education without having the obligation of caring for a child. She was not interested in pursuing pregnancy to term and then putting a potentially handicapped child up for adoption. She seemed to vacillate between Stage One Values and Stage Two Values in her presentation. She also expressed overwhelming feelings of worry, fear for herself, and bouts of depression marked with long periods of withdrawal. Medication use was out of the question because of the pregnancy. When she spoke of the potential handicap that would result from the birth of her child, the young woman seemed to enter into Stage Three Values, but she was not able to sustain that level consistently.

The family said that they attended an Unitarian-Universalist church. They had consulted their minister who thought that whatever decision the young woman and her family made would be acceptable to the God that they worshipped if the decision were made after careful reflection. The mother of the young woman thought that ending a pregnancy was tantamount to murder. The young woman was caught between the opinion of her father that the pregnancy was an inconvenience (Stage One Values) and her mother's loyalty to motherhood (Stage Three Values) and her strongly held belief about the sanctity of human life (Stage Four Values).

During the course of four visits held over a one-week period, the family read, consulted experts, prayed, and consoled each other. An older, married brother of the young woman was invited to participate in this family matter by the family, and he saw his role as one of support for his sister and for his parents. The young woman learned not to avoid her emotions (LFT or DA), she engaged in relaxation exercises, she learned some basic disputation and reformulation of her guiding beliefs, and, on a scale of 0 to 10, with 10 meaning great depression, she was able to function at a level of 5 or 6.

After the one-week period, the father in the family functioned at a Stage Two Values level. He realized that the process of conception within relationship had been denied to his daughter, so he became more concerned for her wishes than for his own. The mother read both from ethics and from legal decisions. She argued that *human* life was present from the moment of conception, but she was not sure after her investigations when a *person* began to exist. The daughter concluded that her two-month-old fetus did not have viability – one of the signs, she thought, that would indicate the beginning communication of a person-as-fetus. The mother said that she could accept this value clarification by her daughter: no person was yet present in this pregnancy, the family concluded. The young woman aborted her fetus in her eighth week of pregnancy. Thereafter, she worked with the psychologist individually for four visits, and there were two more family meetings. Six years later, the young woman consulted her minister for premarriage preparation within her religious tradition. She complained of no emotional distress during that six-year period according to her self-report.

Case 6: Theft by a college student

Four young men shared a suite in a college dormitory. One of them entered a suite-mate's computer, borrowed his term paper notes, and fabricated his own paper without having undertaken any research. He was awarded a 'B' letter grade. The suite-mate took the same course and achieved a 'B' letter grade. However, the professor of the course accused both students of plagiarism since the professor had no idea of the circumstances. One suite-mate was confronted by the other, but the thief insisted that he had undertaken the research on his own. Both students were barred from completing the final exam for the course, meaning that each had paid for the course but could not earn a letter grade. The student who owned the computer took his computer with the original notes to the student court and accused the suite-mate of theft. In turn, the suite-mate had carefully put together hand notes, maintaining that he had independently researched the material in the college library without having checked out any of the books. A review of book availability on the dates in question indicated that several of the books were not reference texts and had been checked out of the library on the dates the thief said they were there. The student court recommended that the student receive an 'F' letter grade in the course. That did not happen. The professor proposed that the thief take the course a second time. The student with the computer was permitted to take the final exam and received a 'B' grade for the course. The thief decided to leave that college and he did not admit the theft.

Several years later, the thief entered counseling because he had been falsely accused of stealing money from his employer. He took and passed a lie detector (polygraph) test and was reinstated on his job. In the course of recovering from the anguish of having been suspended from his job, the thief consulted a psychiatrist for medication and told that practitioner about the college incident. The psychiatrist referred her patient to an area social worker where values clarification became part of the counseling process.

Throughout his college career, the thief functioned at the level of Stage One Values: he spent copious amounts of time drinking, partying, and dating, and he saw a grade as a means to obtain a diploma and not as feedback about what he had learned. When the shoe was on the other foot – when the thief himself was accused of theft – he realized that he had no empathy for his former suite-mate. Once he put himself in that position, he felt both betrayed and angry (Stage Three Values). In the course of counseling, the thief was able to admit to himself that he had a character flaw, suffered from discomfort anxiety, and he worked at both greater honesty and achieving empathy. These character issues came after the client and therapist worked to achieve unconditional self-acceptance regardless of behavior. Other unconditional self-acceptance can be and was in this case a starting point for empathy and for consistent functioning by the young man thereafter at Stage Three Values.

Case 7: Misconduct by a colleague

A psychotherapist learned that one of his colleagues was having sex with a female patient. The therapist confronted the colleague who said that the accusation was true but that it was none of the therapist's business. The therapist said that it was her business due to legal, ethical, and malpractice issues for the group to which they both belonged. Again, the colleague told the therapist to stay out of what he considered to be his personal business. The therapist consulted a professional colleague who advised that the therapist make one last attempt to confront the colleague to turn himself into authorities or that she would report him. The colleague refused and the therapist followed through with her complaint, whereupon an investigation was undertaken by the appropriate licensing board. The board's investigators learned that the colleague was having sex with a client, and the client, in turn, also charged the colleague with having exploited and taken advantage of her. The colleague's license to practice was suspended permanently, and he was sued independently in civil action. His malpractice insurance carrier refused to defend him since the colleague and all practitioners had been notified in advance that such egregious behavior would not be defended. The colleague lost his home which was sold to pay for an out-of-court settlement. The colleague did not apologize or admit guilt, and he subsequently became employed as a restaurant worker and bartender in a resort community in another state.

The colleague in this matter had to attend, as a matter of court order, a group for sex offenders. In that group, his counselor and the group tried to move the colleague from what they thought to be Stage One Values to Stage Three Values. That attempt was unsuccessful. The colleague did not see his behavior as exploitative and based upon power over a confused person – even though he lost his right to practice and had to sell his home to make restitution to the victim. He remained at Stage One Values. The court, however, was satisfied that the colleague had paid great penalties for his behavior.

Ethics and self: Levinas

In order to exit what he judged to be several millennia of thinking dominated by the ontological point of view – certain responsibility of the individual – Levinas (1998) built upon and redirected the work of Martin Buber. Levinas argued that each of us is responsible for the other person, or other, so that ethics precedes individual existence. In turn, the other is responsible ethically for each of his or her interlocutors, so that ethics, or thinking about reasons in terms of values, shapes the other and the other shapes the other(s), and so on. In this sense, process replaces individual as starting point.

The ethical process outlined by Levinas was also a reaction against Heidegger's version of existentialism While he did not 'throw the baby out with the bath water', Levinas rejected individual *thrownness* as too great a price to pay for beings whose existence was social in creation and formation. However, the Levinasian project complements what is called TFC when referring to the enormous contribution of Albert Ellis, and it is in harmony with the stages of values proposed by Kane. Absent ontology, ethics and self blur in Levinas's arguments, and their truth claims (Stage Four Values) seem supported not only by that argument but by the other arguments stated above.

Summary and conclusions

Albert Ellis, as evidenced by celebrity and award, has made a monumental contribution to mental health counseling and theory. His insistence that thinking and feeling exist on a continuum which can be accessed in words moves evaluation beyond artificial intelligence (or AI) which seems to get stuck in syntax. Searle (1996) has pointed out that AI had no capacity to generate semantics and thus it had propagated another dualism. Ellis has not gone that way, and he has written convincingly that TFC can be examined through constructive belief and evaluations expressed in words. To do this, he has helped place each person within language process without dualism (above) in order that they could conclude, 'I think–feel, therefore I am'. Further, he has made the who/what distinction, and that distinction moved the value of the person into Stage Four Values in the outline adopted from Kane.

Therefore, the following conclusions highlight this chapter:

1. The concept of TFC has support from several well-organized disciplines.
2. The concept of self has been used by Ellis equivocally.
3. In self-as-process, the concept of self has been used analogously, tending to support the value of each person and the value of a unique class of beings.
4. It is argued that character is distinct from virtues.
5. Working definitions for ethics, virtues, and morals are stated.
6. Kane's stages of values are outlined regarding counselor training.
7. A comment is made about laws compared to association ethics.
8. Postmodern criticism, viewed pragmatically, is not itself foundational.

9. Case examples are provided from REBT practitioners within Kane's outline.
10. A sketch is presented from Levinas who rejected ontology.

Notes

A shorter version of this paper was presented at an international meeting sponsored by the Albert Ellis Institute (AEI) at Keystone, Colorado in June 2001. The writer is especially grateful to Steve Johnson, Hank Robb, Len Rorer, and John Viterito. Their comments, criticisms, and suggestions were invaluable to me in idea clarification and expansion, and hence in writing this chapter.

1 In the Keystone discussion, McMahon used the term *irreplaceable* when referring to a human being in the univocal sense he intended. Upon reflection, and with great thanks to his interlocutors, a more cogent notion, he has concluded, would be to use the term *unique* in the analogous sense just outlined. In this unique way, one can speak of all men being equal and not being ratable, but having different behaviors which can be rated compared to some standard.
2 In the O.J. Simpson case, Simpson could not be tried again on similar or related peripheral criminal charges after acquittal, for that would have violated the well-established Constitutionally protected prohibition against double jeopardy. However, he could be and was tried again in civil procedures – procedures that would not subject him to criminal penalties.
3 This outline of four stages of values follows that developed by Robert Hilary Kane of the University of Texas, Department of Philosophy, in his text, *Through the Moral Maze* (1996). Prof. Kane provides generous examples of the stages in his text, none of which is used here.

References

Adler, M. (1980) *How to Think about God*. New York: Bantam Books.
Allport, G., Vernon, T. and Lindsey, G. (1961) Manual: A study of values. Boston: Houghton-Mifflin.
Barrett, R. and Hyde, J. (2001) Women, men, work and family: an expansionist theory, *American Psychologist*, October, pp. 781ff.
Beaudrillard, J. (1995) *Simulcara and Simulation*. Pittsburgh: Duquesne University Press.
Behnke, S. (2001) A question of values, *APA Monitor*, October, p. 84.
Cade, B. and O'Hanlon, W. (1993) *A Brief Guide to Brief Therapy*. New York: W.W. Norton.
Chamberlain J. and Haaga, D.A.F. (2001) Unconditional self acceptance and psychological health, *Journal of Rational-Emotive and Cognitive-Behavior Therapy*, 19(3): 177–189, Fall.
Dryden, W. (1990) *Rational–Emotive Counselling in Action*. London: Sage.
Ellis, A. (1972) Psychotherapy and the value of a human being, *Value and Valuation* (ed. J.W. Davis). Knoxville: University of Tennessee Press.
Ellis, A. (1973) *Humanistic Psychotherapy*. New York: McGraw-Hill.
Ellis, A. (1994) *Reason and Emotion in Psychotherapy (Revised and Updated)*. New York: Birch Lane Press.

Ellis, A. and Dryden, W. (1990) *The Essential Albert Ellis*. New York: Springer.

Gergen, K. (2001) Psychological science in a postmodern context, *American Psychologist*, October, pp. 803ff.

Goleman, D. (1997) *Emotional Intelligence*. New York: Bantam Books.

Greeley, A. (1996) *Common Ground: A Priest and a Rabbi Read Scripture Together*. New York: Pilgrim Press.

Kane, R. (1996) *Through the Moral Maze: Search for Absolute Values in a Pluralistic World*. Dallas: North Castle Books.

Levinas, E. (1998) *Otherwise than Being: Of Beyond Essence*. Pittsburgh: Duquesne University Press

MacIntyre, A. (1997) *After Virtue: A Study in Moral Theory*. South Bend, Indiana: Notre Dame University Press.

McMahon, J. (1996) Unpublished Doctoral Dissertation (#2): Details upon Request.

Mahoney, M. (1976) *Scientist as Subject*. Cambridge, MA: Ballinger.

Mahoney, M. (1990) *Human Change Process*. New York: Basic Books.

Maultsby, M. (1975) *Help Yourself to Happiness: Through Rational Self-Counseling* (out of print text: e-mail text available). New York: Albert Ellis Institute.

Plantinga, A. (ed.) (1984) *Faith and Rationality: Reason & Belief in God*. South Bend, IN: Notre Dame University Press.

Searle, J. (1996) *Minds, Brains and Science*. Cambridge, MA: Harvard University Press.

Seligman, M. (1998) *Learned Optimism*. New York: Simon & Schuster.

Schacter, D. (2001) *Seven Sins of Memory*. New York: Houghton-Mifflin.

Spranger, E. (no date) *Types of Men*. Translated from Vth German Edition of *Lebensformen* by P.J.W. Piggors. Halle: Max Niemeyer. (American Agent, Shechert-Hoffnor, Inc. 31 E. 10th St., New York. Found in Columbia University Teachers College Library.)

Williams, B. (1994) *Problems of Self*. Cambridge: Cambridge University Press.

Chapter 7

Rational Emotive Behavior Therapy (REBT): the view of a cognitive psychologist

Daniel David

Introduction

Rational Emotive Behavior Therapy (REBT) is the oldest form of cognitive behavioral therapy (CBT) and was created by Albert Ellis in 1955. The 'ABCDE' model is the cornerstone of REBT (Ellis, 1994). According to the ABCDE model, people experience undesirable activating events (A), about which they have rational and irrational beliefs (B). These beliefs then lead to emotional, behavioral, and cognitive consequences (C). Rational beliefs (rBs) lead to functional consequences, while irrational beliefs (iBs) lead to dysfunctional consequences. Clients who engage in REBT are encouraged to actively dispute (D) their iBs and to assimilate more efficient (E) rBs, which should have a positive impact on their emotional, cognitive, and behavioral responses (Ellis, 1994). Since its creation, hundreds of papers have been published focusing on the theory and practice of REBT. Some studies (e.g. Dryden et al., 1989) have confirmed the main aspects of the original REBT theory (Ellis, 1962), while other studies (e.g. Solomon et al., 1998) have made critical contributions to the evolution of REBT theory (e.g. Solomon and Haaga, 1995). Furthermore, meta-analytic studies have supported the conclusion that REBT is an empirically supported form of CBT (e.g. Engels et al., 1993).

While many of REBT's insights have been assimilated by the psychological mainstream, it remains noticeably less visible than other forms of CBT (e.g. Beck's cognitive therapy) in mainstream psychological research, although it is very popular among practitioners (Still, 2001). In their early work both Albert Ellis (Ellis, 1962) and Aaron Beck (Beck, 1976) presented their contributions as scientific, and published studies designed to test the theory and the efficacy of their proposed techniques. The difference between the two is that only Aaron Beck made explicit reference to growing areas of research in cognitive psychology, which had led to a program of research in the USA and the UK carried out by people with training in experimental psychology (Still, 2001). By taking a similar approach REBT might not only increase its visibility in mainstream psychology, but might also allow its potential to be more fully explored, and hopefully to be more fully realized. It is hoped that by placing REBT more explicitly in the context of contemporary cognitive psychology, this chapter will be a first step toward enhancing and enriching the development of both REBT's theory and its practice.

The basic of cognitive psychology: a brief introduction

Cognitive psychology is concerned with the human mind, how it processes information it receives (input), and how it develops responses (output) (Anderson, 2000). However, cognitive psychology is not only the science of information processing *per se*, but it is also an information processing perspective which can be used in our attempts to understand all of the workings of the human mind including cognitive processes, behaviors, and emotions (Anderson, 2000). In essence, it is assumed that the human mind is a general-purpose system and that two important functions of the human mind are representation and computation. Representation refers to a 'thing', which stands for something else (e.g. the word 'dog' stands for the animal 'dog') or it can refer to the relationship between a representation and what it represents (e.g. the relationship between the word 'dog' and the actual 'dog'). Computation refers to transformation of representations into other representations in a rule-governed manner. On a more general level, cognitive psychology studies the basic mechanisms governing the human mind, and these mechanisms are important in understanding the types of behavior studied by other social sciences. In this sense, cognitive psychology studies the foundation on which all of the other social sciences stand (Anderson, 2000). Thus far, the cognitive approach has proven to be the most productive paradigm in studying the human mind (Robins et al., 1999). Therefore, it makes sense to analyze REBT's development in the context of cognitive psychology.

To understand the approach of cognitive psychology it is helpful to distinguish between the terms paradigm or framework, theory, and models (Eysenck and Keane, 2000). A *paradigm* is a general pool of constructs for understanding a domain, but it is not tightly enough organized to constitute a predictive theory. If we try to tie all these paradigmatic constructs together with additional details we may develop a *predictive theory*. While we cannot evaluate a paradigm according to standard verification logic, it can be used for the evaluation of the theory. We judge a paradigm in terms of the successful theories it generates. If a predictive theory leads to many correct accounts of interesting phenomena the paradigm is considered successful. A *model* is the application of a theory to a specific phenomenon. A successful theory leads to many models, which account for specific phenomena.

In the theoretical foundation of cognitive psychology, it has become commonplace to analyze cognitive structures of our mind on three different levels: computational, algorithmic–representational, and implementational (Marr, 1982; Newell, 1990). The different levels of analysis of our cognitive structures generate different-level theories about the human mind, and will be defined below.

Theory at the *computational* or *knowledge* level describes the goal of a given computation, and the logic of the strategy by which it can be carried out. Basic questions that research at this level addresses are: 'What is the goal of the computation?', 'Is it appropriate?', 'What is the input and what is the output?', 'What knowledge do we need to transform the input into output?', 'How is the general strategy carried out?' and 'What is the interaction between goal and knowledge?' Suppose that we watch someone playing chess. A computational theory about what is happening in the mind of the player will tell us about (1) their input (e.g. the basic starting position in the chess game), output (e.g. a possible chess-board move), and goals (e.g. to play chess and to win), (2) their knowledge (e.g. the rules of chess), and (3) the general strategy the player uses to transform the input into output (e.g. organizing the chess rules in such a way as to help them win).

Theory at the *algorithmic–representational* level specifies in detail the representations and the algorithms defined over them. At this level, we face questions like: 'How are input and output represented?' and 'What is the algorithm for the transformation of input into output?' In the case of the chess game, we may have a theory about how the player represents the pieces of the board game (e.g. each piece represented in its individual position versus one representation for a combination of pieces) and about the specific sequences of rules the player follows during the game. To approach this level we need detailed computational models. Currently two types of computational models are utilized: symbolic and non-symbolic. *Symbolic models* assume that representations are symbols (e.g. verbal) and that computation involves the manipulation of these symbols by rules (e.g. semantic rules). Some well-known symbolic computational models are schema, semantic networks, propositional representations and networks, and scripts (for details, see Eysenck and Keane, 2000). *Non-symbolic models* (i.e. connexionist models, McClelland and Rumelhart, 1986) assume that representation refers to the activation of some cognitive units organized in networks (similar to neural networks) and the computation refers to the modification of the activation according to some rules (e.g. generalized Delta). Some theorists (McClelland and Rumelhart, 1986) prefer to say that non-symbolic models go through transformations, which can conform to rules but are not really caused by rules. In their opinion rules should refer to the transformation of symbols rather than to the transformation of activation level in a connexionist network. Such non-symbolic models can mimic simultaneously both cognitive processes and their brain circuits. The symbolic and non-symbolic models are complementary and together they can account for the heterogeneity (e.g. different cognitive structures) of the human mind architecture (Eysenck and Keane, 2000).

Implementational-level theory answers the problem of how representations and algorithms can be realized physically. For example, what happens in the human brain during a chess game? How are the different strategies used by the player instantiated in the brain? This is a fascinating field that requires interdisciplinary research in what is called cognitive neuroscience. Brain analysis impacts on our psychological theories by constraining our computational and algorithmic representational theories. On the other hand, our computational and algorithmic–representational theories offer a detailed description of information processing which is the starting point for the analysis of the neurobiological substrate of information processing.

The relationships between these three levels of analysis of the human mind are complex. In general we may say that there is a multiple realizability of a higher-level structure by various lower-level structures (McClamrock, 1991). For a specific computational theory there is a large spectrum of representations and for each type of representation there are several possible algorithms to carry out the same process. Along the same line, the same algorithmic–representational theory may be implemented in different physical systems (e.g. biological, computer hardware). In general, this multiple level analysis has proven to be fruitful in cognitive psychology. Higher-level theories allow us to capture generalization and to approach things with different underlying implementational theory. This higher-level explanation allows for reasonable explanations and predictions on the basis of less detailed information about the system (McClamrock, 1991). Among the higher-level explanations the algorithmic–representational theory is typically seen as the central goal of cognitive psychology because it can predict and explain human behavior in its ecological conditions, and can also accommodate human errors. However, a comprehensive understanding of a psychological phenomenon involves all three levels of analysis.

The potential impact of cognitive psychology on the development of REBT

I will begin this section by mentioning some general guidelines and then focusing on the fundamental components of the ABCDE model.

First, it seems that REBT theory has been developed mainly at the computational level. For example, while we know much about the kinds of beliefs that interact with our goals to impact on our responses (Ellis and Dryden, 1997), less is known about how beliefs are represented (e.g. schemata or propositional networks), and about the exact algorithms by which iBs impact on our emotions. Therefore, for example, Ellis's (1962) proposal that cognition, emotions, and behaviors are inseparable and organized together, as a 'whole', might be tested and detailed by elaborating specific computational models, namely semantic networks (Bower, 1981) and/or connexionist models (McClelland and Rumelhart, 1986) in which beliefs and emotions are similarly represented as connected nodes. Such research is necessary to understand how REBT works and to test its hypothesized theory of change. Also, little is known about the implementational level of iBs. Ellis (1994) has argued that iBs have a strong genetic component but there is virtually no research attempting to determine the neurophysiological counterparts of iBs, or how the process of changing iBs during REBT is accompanied by changes in the brain. Such research is needed not only to test REBT's hypothesis about iBs and their genetic predisposition, but also to connect REBT to research in cognitive neuroscience and biological psychiatry. Among CBT's schools, REBT is most in line with current biological research in psychopathology because of its ideas about the biological basis of iBs and rBs (Ellis, 1994), but this advantage has not yet been exploited. If psychotherapy in itself influences the structure and function of the brain (Gabbard, 2000) then it follows that the monitoring of brain changes during REBT would be informative for developing a theory of psychopathology based on both psychological and biological components. Congruent with this idea, current research supports the idea that a combination of REBT and medication is more effective than either REBT or medication alone in various mental disorders (e.g. dysthymic disorder, unipolar depression) (Macaskill and Macaskill, 1996; Wang et al., 1999). By exploring REBT at the implementational level one might better understand how to maximize this effect. A description of REBT theory about beliefs in terms of connexionist models (McClelland and Rumelhart, 1986) might bridge the gap between REBT and neuroscience research because the connexionist models are designed as analogues of both biological and cognitive systems and can mimic simultaneously both cognitive processes and their known brain circuits. In conclusion, I believe that one of the next steps in REBT research should be the development of REBT theory at the algorithmic–representational and implementational levels.

Second, REBT is presented and has been developed mainly in terms of its paradigmatic constructs (e.g. its philosophical assumptions) and its general theory. Unfortunately, it seems to lack specific clinical and experimental models for understanding specific problems (e.g. social phobia v. generalized anxiety). Following the model of cognitive psychology, a future point on the REBT agenda should be a translation of its general paradigmatic and theoretical constructs into specific clinical and experimental models for specific disorders, which would have strong predictive values, and which would provide powerful guidelines (e.g. treatment manuals) for clinical practice.

Third, it might prove fruitful for REBT theory to assimilate experimental paradigms from cognitive psychology to test some of its hypotheses. Many basic aspects of REBT theory have not yet tested rigorously (DiGiuseppe, 1996). For example, the primacy of demandingness (*'must'*) among the iBs and the idea that rBs and iBs mediate emotion formation are still poorly experimentally supported (e.g. Bond and Dryden, 1996). This paucity of research may relate to the fact that REBT seems to lack powerful experimental paradigms to test its basic theory and hypotheses. Cognitive psychology by its experimental tasks could not only offer REBT a rigorous framework for testing some of its hypotheses, but could also extend and reinvigorate REBT theory and research by offering new constructs and research tools.

Fourth, REBT theorists should be aware that human cognitive architecture is heterogeneous and, in consequence, that it is less probable that the causes of our responses can be explained by using only a few cognitive constructs. In REBT, the whole cognitive theory seems to be organized around the concept of iBs and rBs. While rBs and iBs are important components of human functioning (Ellis, 1962) there are also other factors involved. For example, recent research in the neurobiology of memory has identified the role of unconscious information processing in human emotion independent of the effect of beliefs (LeDoux, 2000). I think that it would be prudent for REBT theory to be extended by assimilating new constructs from cognitive psychology to account for the heterogeneity of human cognitive architecture.

In the next sections I will show how these general suggestions could be applied to each component of REBT's basic ABCDE model.

Activating events – A

In REBT, A stands for an activating event, which may be external or internal. REBT assumes that human beings are purposeful and goal-seeking and that they always bring to A general and specific goals (G).

Cognitive psychology has made an important contribution to our basic knowledge about how people represent external activating events (Anderson, 2000), namely, that the representation of information in our cognitive system is the result of both bottom-up (i.e. stimulus-driven) and top-down (i.e. knowledge-driven) analyses. For example, this explains elegantly how one ambiguous stimulus can generate two different perceptual images depending on the expectations or knowledge of people. Although REBT theorists argue that A virtually never exists in a pure form, and that it always interacts with and partially includes people's B and G, in REBT little research exists trying to show if and how exactly B and G impact upon the representation of activating events. Cognitive psychology research in the areas of perception, attention processes, and categorization could offer important information about how people represent activating events, and could suggest how one could most effectively work with clients' reports of those As in therapy. For example, a specific activating event may be categorized at different levels of abstraction (e.g. 'My wife does not understand me' versus 'The other people do not understand me'). Some people seem to prefer a more specific level while others prefer a more abstract level to represent the event. Other people use both representations. What is the best level to discuss in therapy in order to access the relevant iBs?

Another important distinction made by cognitive psychology that could impact upon the analysis of A is the one between implicit (unconscious) and explicit (conscious) perception (for details, see Kihlstrom, 1999). People sometimes report that they are influenced by feelings that they cannot explain. They often speak about these feelings as 'gut feelings'. Many of these 'gut feelings' seem to involve responses to stimuli of which people are not consciously aware (Katkin et al., 2001). A large body of empirical evidence supports this line of research. For example, Ohman and Soares (1994) found that when participants who were fearful of snakes were shown masked images of these animals, they reported more negative affect and larger skin conductance response to the feared than to non-feared animals. Because participants could not tell what they saw, their judgments of the images were not based on conscious perception of the stimuli. Unfortunately, in REBT little research exists (but see Moeller et al., 1993) on how implicit perception may activate iBs.

Some REBT theorists might argue that this kind of research is not important. They might say that in REBT, A is just an opportunity to initiate the process of B discovery and that one does not really need to focus on such detail on A. My point is that if one can prove a meaningful influence of B on A, then by analyzing A one may find something about the relevant B when it is more difficult to access (e.g. because it is automatized or because of the defense mechanisms people use). Furthermore, if one's implicit perception of A may affect or stimulate certain B, one might want to develop subliminal stimulation techniques to use in addition to current REBT treatment. For example, some research (Dixon and Henley, 1991) suggests that patients may benefit most from psychological interventions if they are exposed first to subliminal information that is difficult for them to accommodate consciously, and are only later exposed to the same information presented supraliminally. I think that such a research program is important from both a theoretical and a practical point of view.

Beliefs – B

General considerations

Beliefs (B) in the broad sense involve both a mental representation and a positive assessment of meaningful information (Gilbert, 1991). REBT focuses on a special type of beliefs, namely evaluative beliefs (Ellis, 1962). Ellis (1962) divides evaluative beliefs into two types, rational beliefs (rBs) and irrational beliefs (iBs). rBs are: (a) pragmatic; (b) logical (non-absolutist); (c) reality-based; and/or (d) flexible. Conversely, iBs are: (a) non-pragmatic; (b) illogical, absolutist beliefs; (c) non-reality-based beliefs; and/or (d) rigid. Initially, Ellis (1962) delineated eleven iBs. With time, his theory has evolved, and now stresses four categories of IBs: (1) demand-ingness (DEM/MUST); (2) awfulizing (AWF); (3) low frustration tolerance (LFT); (4) global evaluation of human worth and self-downing (GE and SD) (for details, see Ellis, 1994). Ellis (1962) proposed that demandingness is the core irrational belief and the other three are products of it. Other authors have challenged this thesis with preliminary empirical findings that suggest various relationships exist among iBs and have argued that these relationships require clarification in future studies (DiGiuseppe, 1996).

A great deal of research exists about beliefs and how they are associated with psychopathology and emotions (for details, see Solomon and Haaga, 1995). However, as I said before, this research is mainly at the compu-tational level. Little is known about iBs at algorithmic–representational and implementational levels. For example, iBs may be organized like 'schemata' or 'propositional' networks (for details about these computational models, see Eysenck and Keane, 2000). While 'schema' encodes the information that certain features are typical of a category and others are not (maybe SD: 'I am stupid and not good' is organized like a schema), 'propositions' refer to the meaning that abstracts away from perceptual information about an event or what is significant about an event (maybe AFW and LFT: 'It is awful and I cannot stand it' is a part of a propositional network). The representational theory of cognitive psychology and its experimental para-digms could be an informative framework in which to analyze beliefs. The more recent model of iBs (Walen et al., 1992), which makes the distinction between processes (i.e. DEM, AFW, LFT, and GE–SD) and the content of these processes (i.e. affiliation, achievement, comfort, fairness, and control), is a good step toward an algorithmic–representational theory of beliefs but it should be developed by testing different computational models to better understand iBs. Once we have a detailed computational model of iBs and rBs we can focus on the development of new disputation strategies guided by the algorithmic–representational theory and then to the implementa-tional analysis of the beliefs.

Another general observation related to B is that REBT is founded on an understanding of iBs and rBs as the direct mediators and proximal cause of our emotional experiences (Ellis, 1994). It would be desirable to explore the other types of beliefs recently shown to have a direct impact on our emotions and how they might fit REBT theory (for details, see David and McMahon, 2001). For example, Kirsch (1999) has shown that response expectancies have been proven to directly influence a large spectrum of non-volitional responses. Response expectancies are beliefs about non-volitional outcomes and they (1) are sufficient to cause non-volitional outcomes; (2) are not mediated by other psychological mechanisms; and (3) are self-confirming while seeming automatic (Kirsch, 1999). Even if the primary mechanisms in the development of psychopathology involve iBs, later, symptomatology once generated by iBs may come under the control of and may be maintained by response expectancy sets. A research program designed to include more cognitive constructs under B, in the ABCDE model, might positively impact upon the development of REBT theory.

Beliefs in the context of memory research

EXPLICIT VERSUS IMPLICIT MEMORY RESEARCH

Declarative or explicit memory refers to intentional and/or conscious retrieval of previously learned information (Schacter, 1987). Non-declarative or implicit memory refers to the unconscious and involuntary influence of prior experience on our responses (Schacter, 1987). The distinction between implicit and explicit memory is highly complex and is a fundamental one in cognitive psychology. The distinction may refer to memory systems/representations (Schacter and Tulving, 1994), memory processes (Richardson-Klavehn & Gardiner, 1996), memory tasks (Schacter, 1987), strategies at retrieval (Jacoby, 1991), or memorial awareness (Richardson-Klavehn and Gardiner, 1996). Unconscious information processing (cognitive unconscious) in the form of implicit perception, implicit learning, and implicit memory is one of the most explored topics in current cognitive psychology research (Kihlstrom, 1999). Unfortunately, the psychotherapy community seems to have received this concept in a distorted fashion. For example, Mahoney (1993) wrongly argued that the cognitive unconscious construct has already penetrated the psychotherapy field, and he gave as examples the concepts of Beck's (1976) automatic thoughts and schema. Mahoney (1993) seems to refer to information processing which functions unconsciously, but which can potentially be made conscious. This is a kind of 'functional dissociation' between conscious and unconscious processes, determined by the automatization of some conscious processes and/or by some defense mechanisms (e.g. suppression, Wegner and Smart, 1997). However, modern work in cognitive psychology (e.g. Schacter, 1987; Seger, 1994) argues for a 'structural dissociation' between conscious and unconscious processes. Some information contents and processes, by their characteristics, cannot be made conscious. They are represented in our memory in a format (e.g. non-verbal associations) that is not consciously accessible (Schacter and Tulving, 1994). Few works have assimilated this kind of research in psychotherapy, yet one notable exception is the work of Thomas Dowd (Dowd and Courchaine, 1996). Contrary to Mahoney (1993) and others, I argue that the 'unconscious revolution in cognitive behavior therapy' has not yet taken place seriously, and that in fact it has to start based on a clear understanding of cognitive unconscious construct. I further suggest that incorporating a conceptualization of non-declarative/implicit memory processing into psychotherapy and into REBT theory is essential. These non-declarative/implicit memory processes (structurally separated from consciousness and not consciously accessible) exert a major impact on interpersonal experience, emotions, cognitions, and behavior independently of beliefs, and they need to be analyzed on their own terms (Tobias et al., 1992). They should not be mistakenly viewed as a form of repressed memory or only as an automatization of explicit memory processes (e.g. beliefs). Some Cs are not mediated by beliefs at all, but instead by unconscious information processing structurally separated from consciousness. The assimilation of cognitive unconscious concept could relate REBT theory to recent research in the neurobiology of memory and emotion (e.g. LeDoux, 2000), which could serve to bring REBT further into the mainstream of current psychological research. In addition, it could contribute to a better assimilation of some behaviorist constructs (e.g. associations) into REBT theory. So far, behaviorism is assimilated into REBT at the level of technique rather than at the level of clinical conceptualization. The concept of implicit memory (Schacter, 1987) combined with Rescorla's (1988) work on classic conditioning (Rescorla has proven that classic conditioning can be described in terms of information processing and computation) might contribute to a better assimilation of behaviorist principles into REBT theory. Also, it might stimulate a movement to elaborate new techniques to deal with unconscious information processing which is structurally separated from consciousness.

AUTOBIOGRAPHICAL/EPISODIC VERSUS SEMANTIC MEMORY

Another important distinction made in cognitive psychology is that between autobiographical and semantic memory. According to Tulving (1983), episodic memory is necessary for context-specific recollection of events from one's personal past (e.g. 'Yesterday, I walked on Broadway'), whereas semantic memory subserves the acquisition and retrieval of general knowledge (e.g. 'New York is located in the USA'). Some iBs are contextually loaded and seem to be a part of the autobiographical memory system (e.g. 'Today at the birthday party my wife must obey me') while other iBs are a part of the semantic memory system (e.g. 'The other people must obey me'). While autobiographical memories are more emotionally loaded and easier to distort (e.g. Tsai et al., 2000) they could pose some special problems during disputations. Further studies in this area could help us determine which type of memory content to dispute first, and which kind of memories are more related to the individual's problem.

WORKING MEMORY VERSUS LONG-TERM MEMORY

Working memory seems to be the activated part of the long-term memory (for details, see Anderson, 2000). In order to have an impact on our responses (C), it seems that iBs would have to be activated in working memory during the activating events (A). To do so, iBs should not only be available (i.e. exist in the knowledge base of the participants), but should be accessible (i.e. activated at that time). If during an A, iBs are deactivated and/or are not relevant to the people's goals, they may have no identifiable effect. Most prior research in REBT has not controlled for this factor. For example, researchers often used scales to evaluate iBs (at time T_n) and later they verified how iBs impacted on various dependent variables measured at time T_{n+1}. In my opinion, such research is relatively meaningless because of the confusion between available iBs and accessible iBs. At time T_n, iBs measured by various scales might have been both accessible and available. However, at time T_{n+1} they might be available but not accessible. Therefore the lack of impact of iBs on various dependent variables may be caused by a lack of accessibility of iBs despite their availability. In future studies of REBT theory, the relevant events should not be generic events, as in most previous studies, but rather specific events that signify thwarting of one's fundamental goals and that access the available iBs (Ellis, 1994).

In general, the analysis of beliefs in the context of memory research may impact not only on the algorithmic–representational theory and on the elaboration of various disputation strategies but also on implementational-level theory and on REBT's relationship with biological psychiatry. Different kinds of memories have been proved to have different neural substrates (for details, see Schacter and Tulving, 1994). If one proves that iBs are related with different kinds of memories, then this line of research could be a first step toward joining REBT research to biological research in psychopathology and cognitive neuroscience.

Beliefs and the cognitive development research

Cognitive development is currently a hot topic in cognitive psychology (Anderson, 2000). Cognitive psychologists believe that human beings develop in terms of both basic cognitive processes (e.g. the capacity of working memory) and cognitive contents (e.g. more information). As they develop, children's improvement in various tasks is due to a combination of these two factors (Hatano and Inagaki, 2000). However, the relative contributions of the two are still unclear (Anderson, 2000). As I said before, a more contemporary REBT model of beliefs (Walen et al., 1992) postulates a distinction between processes and contents. However, we know very little about the development of these two components during the ontogenetic stages (but see Vernon, 1997). Some theorists might argue that REBT could even be dangerous for children, because iBs are an important step in their cognitive development. Although the proponents of this idea do not offer any evidence for this hypothesis, their criticism points to the necessity of studying developmental aspects of beliefs experimentally. Another potential line of research is language acquisition (Anderson, 2000) and iBs/rBs, especially since beliefs are usually verbally expressed. It would be important to know information such as 'Is there a relationship between language acquisition and the development of iBs?' and 'Are there non-verbal indicators of iBs?' These are questions for a cognitive developmental research program in REBT.

Emotional consequences – C

C in the ABCDE framework represents emotional, behavioral, and cognitive consequences of iBs and rBs. Of course, the ABCDE model is interactive. C, once generated, often becomes a new A, and so on (Ellis and Dryden, 1997). Since REBT aims to be not only a cognitive model of psychopathology, but also a general theory of emotion, in REBT, C usually refers to our emotional experiences (Ellis and Dryden, 1997). Cs that follow iBs about negative A are called dysfunctional or maladaptive negative emotions (e.g. depression after failing an exam related to the iB 'I *must* pass all exams') and those that follow iBs about positive events are called dysfunctional or maladaptive positive emotions (e.g. elation after learning that your work was praised by all the graders of the exam, which is related to the belief that 'Everyone *must* only say positive things about me and they did'). Cs that follow rBs about negative A are called functional or adaptive negative emotions (e.g. sadness following the idea that 'I would have liked to pass the exam but I did not'), and those that follow rBs about positive A are called functional or adaptive positive emotions (e.g. happiness derived from the idea that 'I would like all of the exam graders to say only positive things about my performance and this time they did'). According to REBT, the adaptiveness of an emotion refers to its quality rather than its intensity. Maladaptive emotions are qualitatively rather than quantitatively different from functional feelings (Ellis, 1994, but see Cramer and Fong, 1991). In REBT, there is a clear distinction between practical problems and emotional problems. While practical problems are strongly related to A, emotional problems are the result of interactions between A and B. Primary emotional problems are the direct consequences of the interaction between iBs and practical problems, and secondary emotional problems refer to the tendency of people to disturb themselves over their disturbance (i.e. C becomes an A: 'I am depressed because I can't stop being anxious'). In this section, I discuss two influential theories of emotion in current cognitive research, and how they could be related to REBT theory and practice.

Appraisal theory of emotions

APPRAISAL THEORY AND REBT: A BRIEF COMPARISON

According to the appraisal theory of emotion formation (Lazarus, 1991) the information processing begins with a transaction that is appraised as harmful, beneficial, threatening, or challenging. Transaction involves both the goals of the person and the representation of the environmental encounters. Although the representation of the environmental encounter contributes to appraisal, only appraisal results directly in emotions. The terms 'appraisal' and 'evaluative' cognitions are used to define how representations of the environmental encounter are processed in terms of their relevance for personal goals and well-being. The primary and secondary appraisal processes generate emotions. Then the appraisal and its attendant emotion influence coping mechanisms, which in turn change person–environment encounter. The altered person–environment encounter is reappraised and the reappraisal leads to a change in emotion quality and intensity. The process is summarized in the left-hand part of Figure 7.1. This model has received strong empirical support and has seriously penetrated the field of emotion and stress research (Folkman and Lazarus, 1988; Lazarus, 1991). On the right-hand side of the figure I present the analogous REBT processes. Let us have a more detailed look at this analogy.

The appraisal component can be described at least at two levels of analysis: a molecular level referring to specific information processing and a molar level referring to core relation themes (Smith et al., 1993).

The molecular level of appraisal description   At a molecular level of analysis, appraisal represents specific information processing components. Six types of appraisal components have been identified so far and have been organized into three types of appraisals: primary appraisal, secondary appraisal, and reappraisal.

Motivational relevance and *motivational congruence* are two components of the *primary appraisal*. While motivational relevance is an evaluation of the extent to which the encounter is relevant to one's personal goals, motivational congruence refers to the extent to which the encounter is consistent with one's goals (Smith et al., 1993). This description is largely overlapping with REBT's description of the person–environment relationship (Ellis, 1962), which incorporates: an individual's goals, the constraints and opportunities in the environment, and how these two components interact. An exploration of the relationship between REBT's constructs and primary appraisal would be fruitful. For example, DEM might be an important contributor to the motivational congruence component of primary appraisal. Therefore, it would be important to evaluate goals formulated in terms of preferences (e.g. 'I would like . . .') versus goals formulated in

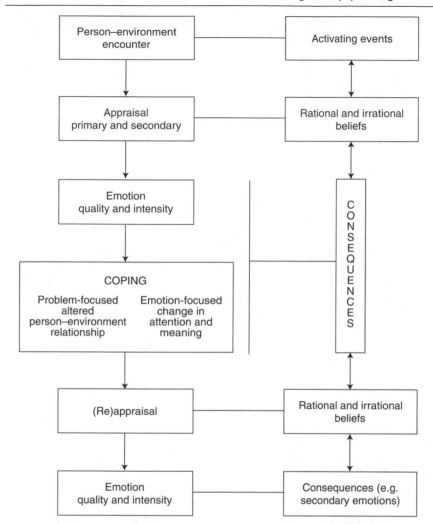

Figure 7.1   An analogy between appraisal theory and REBT theory of emotions formation.

terms of DEM (e.g. 'I *must* . . .'). According to REBT, a motivational incongruence in terms of DEM would generate dysfunctional emotions while a motivational incongruence in terms of preferences would generate functional emotions. I believe that REBT's theory should assimilate the concept of primary appraisal by defining DEM as a maladaptive (or irrational) primary appraisal process involved in motivational congruence. This might be particularly helpful since although many researchers of emotion are unfamiliar with REBT's constructs, most of them are familiar with the construct of primary appraisal.

The four components of *secondary appraisal* are related to one's resources and one's options for coping with a threatening situation (Smith et al., 1993). *Accountability* refers to who and what are to receive credit for the encounter outcome. *Problem-focused coping potential* reflects evaluations of one's ability to act directly on the situation, while *emotion-focused coping potential* refers to one's psychological adjustment to the encounter. The final component of secondary appraisal is *future expectancy*, and it refers to the possibility of making changes in the actual situation. Certain components of REBT can be easy translated into the terminology of appraisal theory (see also, Ziegler, 2001). REBT's derivative iBs (AWF, LFT, and GE–SD) could be seen as maladaptive (or irrational) secondary appraisal processes while their counterpart rBs seem to be adaptive (or rational) secondary appraisal processes. For example, SD seems to be a maladaptive (low) problem-focused coping potential because an SD individual is less likely to engage in problem solving, and therefore will likely fail to act on the situation to bring it in accord with his or her desires. AWF and LFT seem to be maladaptive (low) emotion-focused coping potentials in that they fail to help the individual to adjust psychologically to the encounter by altering his or her interpretations, desires, and/or beliefs. Therefore, they are accompanied by amplification of negative emotional states rather than reduction of them. GE and SD might also be related to the future expectancy component of secondary appraisal. When GE and SD are made frequently, they may lead to expectations about the occurrence of valued outcomes and/or one's ability to change the likelihood of these outcomes. For example, we may expect that a 'stupid' person will display stupid behaviors and low performance. Accountability might be related to REBT's hypothesis that iBs always refer to our own person (self-accountability) and/or other and life conditions (other-accountability).

Reappraisal refers to a changed appraisal based on new information from the environment and/or the person. This concept seems to be useful in understanding REBT's distinction between primary and secondary emotional problems (Ellis, 1994). Reappraisal might be seen as the cognitive mechanism underlying secondary disturbance (see also, Ziegler, 2001).

The molar level of appraisal description   The six components of primary and secondary appraisal combine in different ways to generate a specific emotional experience. This combination can be analyzed at a *molar level* in terms of core relational themes. This refers to the central meaning underlying various emotions. For example, in appraisal theory (Smith et al., 1993), anxiety is believed to result from the combination of the motivational incongruence, motivational relevance, and low emotion-focused coping potential. This combination generates the core relational theme of danger. Similarly, according to REBT's theory (Ellis and Dryden, 1997), anxiety involves the personal relevance of an activating event, incongruence with DEM, and cognitive processes such as AWF or LFT. The core relational theme here too seems to be danger. The analogy seems clear, but it has not yet been highlighted in the writings of influential REBT theorists.

REBT AND APPRAISAL THEORY OF EMOTION: FURTHER ANALYSES AND A HYPOTHESIZED MODEL

An interesting research program would be to study REBT theory in the context of appraisal theory (see Table 7.1). In the left-hand part of the table (i.e. appraisal theory) each emotion is associated with its own core relation theme, and each theme is derived from several appraisal components. In other words, the appraisal associated with each emotion might be described either as a particular pattern across multiple appraisal components or as a single relational theme (Smith et al., 1993). There are many studies providing empirical support for this theory (e.g. Smith et al., 1993). In the right-hand side of the table I present a hypothesized model of emotions based on both appraisal and REBT theory. In comparison with appraisal theory, the proposed model is more complex because it involves the REBT's distinction between functional and dysfunctional emotions, DEM's involvement in primary appraisal, and AWF, LFT, and GE–SD involvement in the secondary appraisal. In comparison with REBT model, it is also more complex because it reveals specific processes associated with each emotion, as specified by appraisal theory (Smith et al., 1993).

Future studies should investigate this model and other related possibilities (see the following comments) using the paradigm of appraisal theory. *A first possibility* is that DEM as a maladaptive primary appraisal process might be followed by AWF, LFT, and/or GE–SD as maladaptive secondary appraisal processes which generate specific dysfunctional emotions. This picture (see Table 7.1, right) would be congruent with Ellis's hypothesis (1962) about the primacy of DEM. A basic question here might be: 'Is the change in primary appraisal (DEM) accompanied by changes in the secondary appraisal?' (e.g. AWF, LFT, GE–SD), or 'Must one intervene in both primary and secondary appraisals?' *A second possibility* is that maladaptive primary appraisal in terms of DEM could be followed by adaptive secondary appraisal involving rational counterparts of AWF, LFT, and/or GE–SD, which would in turn generate more functional emotions. *A third possible scenario* is that a more adaptive primary appraisal (e.g. in terms of preferences) might still be accompanied by maladaptive secondary appraisal involving AWF, LFT, and GE–SD, and thus the individual may still generate and experience dysfunctional emotions. This hypothesis would fit the recent suggestions of DiGiuseppe (1996), who said that AWF, LFT, and GE–SD might contribute to emotional problems independent of DEM. The way in which maladaptive primary appraisal (in terms of DEM) and maladaptive secondary appraisal (in terms of AWF,

Table 7.1 Appraisal theory of emotion formation (left part) and a hypothesized model of emotion formation based on REBT and appraisal theory (right part)

Appraisal theory (Smith et al., 1993)			REBT theory in the appraisal theory's terms: A hypothesized model		
Emotion	Core relational theme	Appraisal components	Emotion: dysfunctional and functional	Core relational theme	Important appraisal components
Anger	Other-blame	Motivationally relevant / Motivationally incongruent / Other accountability	Anger	Other-blame	Motivationally relevant / Motivationally incongruent with DEM / Other-accountability (i.e. the others, life conditions)
			Annoyance		Motivationally relevant / Motivationally incongruent with preferences / Other-accountability (i.e. the others, life conditions)
Guilt	Self-blame	Motivationally relevant / Motivationally incongruent / Self-accountability	Guilt	Self-blame	Motivationally relevant / Motivationally incongruent with DEM / Self-accountability (i.e. myself)
			Remorse		Motivationally relevant / Motivationally incongruent with preferences / Self-accountability (i.e. myself)
Fear–anxiety	Danger–threat	Motivationally relevant / Motivationally incongruent / Low or uncertain emotion-focused potential	Fear–anxiety	Danger-threat	Motivationally relevant / Motivationally incongruent with DEM / Low or uncertain emotion-focused potential (i.e. AWF, LFT)
			Concern		Motivationally relevant / Motivationally incongruent with preferences / Emotion-focused potential (i.e. non-AWF; non-LFT)

Emotion (appraisal)		Outcome emotion	Appraisal details
Sadness Irrevocable loss; helplessness about harm or loss Motivationally relevant Motivationally incongruent Low problem-focused potential Negative future expectations	Irrevocable loss; helplessness about harm or loss	Depression	Motivationally relevant Motivationally incongruent with DEM Low problem-focused coping potential (i.e. SD) Negative future expectations
		Sadness	Motivationally relevant Motivationally incongruent with preferences Problem-focused coping potential (i.e. non-SD) Negative future expectations?
Hope–challenge Effortful optimism; potential for success Motivationally relevant Motivationally incongruent High problem-focused coping potential Positive future expectations	Effortful optimism; potential for success	Dysfunctional hope–challenge	Motivationally relevant Motivationally incongruent with DEM Too optimistic problem-focused coping potential (i.e. global evaluations of human worth) Positive future expectations (e.g. positive global evaluations of human worth)
		Hope–challenge	Motivationally relevant Motivationally incongruent with preferences High problem-focused coping potential (non-global evaluations of human worth) Positive future expectations (e.g. non-global evaluations of human worth)
Happiness Success Motivationally relevant Motivationally congruent	Success	Dysfunctional happiness; elation	Motivationally relevant Motivationally congruent with DEM
		Happiness	Motivationally relevant Motivationally congruent with preferences

LFT, and GE–SD) interact to generate specific emotions has not been definitively answered in REBT, but by using a framework of appraisal theory researchers may find an answer.

In a pilot study (David et al., 2002) we investigated the relationships between appraisal, core relation themes, emotion, and iBs, using a procedure derived from the appraisal theory of emotion (Smith et al., 1993). My findings are in general congruent with the picture presented in Table 7.1 (right) rather than with the other hypotheses advanced. High score of DEM seems to be associated with dysfunctional emotions while a low score on DEM is associated with functional emotions. Also, DEM seems to be associated with primary appraisal while AWF, LFT, and GE–SD seem to be associated with secondary appraisal. However, this study might be criticized on the basis of the following reasons: (1) the study was retrospective rather than prospective; (2) the subjects were psychology students who might have known the theory under investigation; this might explain how some unusually high correlations were found between iBs and various dysfunctional emotions and appraisal components; and (3) most of the measures were not psychometrically elaborated and therefore, maybe were less reliable. Following the same line of supporting evidence, other authors (Harran and Ziegler, 1991; Heppner et al., 1983) have found positive correlations between iBs and appraisal components, confirming the main thesis of the model. However, my results are preliminary and previous studies of this relationship lack specific analyses (e.g. specific iBs related to specific components of appraisal). Therefore, future studies should investigate the complex proposal (see Table 7.1, right) concerning REBT and its appraisal components, using the paradigms of appraisal theory (Lazarus, 1991; Smith et al., 1993).

THE PLACE OF COPING MECHANISMS IN REBT

Several cognitive theorists have suggested that awareness or expression of iBs and other dysfunctional assumptions generates anxiety and distress, from which individuals protect themselves by developing sets of beliefs and coping mechansims that seem to run counter to the content of iBs (Young, 1999). This is already well known in CBT and there are therapeutic strategies to deal with it (Ellis, 1994; Young, 1999). However, as concerning REBT, this finding may impact on its measures of iBs. Most measures of iBs are based on self-report scales, which are sensitive to coping mechanisms. For example, suppression of SD may be an impediment in SD's evaluation by self-report scales. Measures that are not based on the awareness and self-report of iBs are needed. Maybe implicit tasks and priming methodologies could be good tests for an indirect measure of iBs (for details, see Schacter, 1987; Segal and Vella, 1990).

In the following, I want to highlight another issue related to REBT and coping mechanisms. In REBT, coping mechanisms are supposed to be consequences of iBs and rBs. Similarly, in appraisal theory, coping mechanisms are consequences of secondary appraisal. Therefore, future studies might investigate how different iBs involved in maladaptive secondary appraisal generate coping mechanisms and what is the relationship between the type of iBs and the type of coping mechanisms. Although earlier studies (e.g. Denoff, 1991; Heppner et al., 1983) found significant relationship between iBs and various coping mechanisms, these studies lack specific analyses (e.g. specific iBs related to specific coping mechanisms). For example, according to our model (see Table 7.1, right), SD should be accompanied by maladaptive (low) problem-focused coping and AWF and LFT by maladaptive (low) emotion-focused coping. However, as Lazarus (1991) showed, a given coping mechanism may be adaptive in some circumstances, and maladaptive in others, depending on the person using it and on the threatening context. Any act or information processing can have more than one coping function depending on the person–situation interaction. Therefore, SD might be a maladaptive coping potential mechanism because an SD individual is less likely to engage in efficient problem solving, and therefore will fail to act on the situation to bring it in accord with their goals. Yet sometimes SD may be accompanied by adaptive coping mechanisms because it may make the individual more determined to avoid new problematic situations, and in this way it may prevent new distressing emotional states.

To conclude, an integration of appraisal theory into REBT theory could stimulate (see also Ziegler, 2001) a more specific analysis of the relationship between different kinds of iBs and different emotions and a process-oriented approach rather than a more structural approach of the relationship between iBs and emotions (e.g. DEM as maladaptive primary appraisal; AWF, LFT, and GE–SD as maladaptive secondary appraisals and their relationship with corresponding emotions and coping mechanisms). In turn, REBT theory could reinvigorate appraisal theory by adding the iBs as components of the appraisal level and by forcing the research in appraisal theory to examine the hypothesis of the difference between functional and dysfunctional emotions as hypothesized by REBT.

Neurobiology of emotions

Recently LeDoux (2000) and others have argued for another theory of emotion formation. They argue that some emotional problems are subcortically produced (e.g. involving the amygdala), and do not involve appraisal as defined by appraisal theory (Lazarus, 1991). Although many people (e.g. Glenn, 2001), less familiar with basic cognitive psychological research, are tempted to say that these findings are incompatible with the cognitive approach to emotion, that is certainly not the case. Some of the ways in which these two fields are linked are described briefly below (for details, see also Tobias et al., 1992). *First*, these subcortical processes are related to the concept of unconscious information processing. Therefore, these processes preserve the cognitive (computational) component of emotion and connect the theory of emotion to the concept of cognitive unconscious strongly investigated in current cognitive psychology (David, 2000; LeDoux, 2000). *Second*, this subcortical and automatic process can be countered by activating more constructive modes of thinking (Beck and Clark, 1997; Ellis, 1994), and their effects can be controlled by conscious strategies. *Third*, cognitive psychology and CBT do not assume that verbal mediation is the only modality of emotional control. Some very successful exposure methods work specifically on this type of unconscious information processing involved in emotion formation (Ellis, 1962). *Fourth*, an emotion generated by subcortical mechanisms may become an A according to REBT theory, and may then be consciously appraised, thus generating a secondary emotional problem (Ellis, 1994).

Appraisal theory (Lazarus, 1991) and the new developments in the neurobiology of emotions (LeDoux, 2000) can be combined in a cognitive science paradigm to offer us a more comprehensive picture of human emotions. In conclusion, B in the ABCDE model should be expanded to include at least two different basic components: (1) iBs and rBs as parts of explicit memory strongly related to appraisal theory; and (2) unconscious information processing in implicit memory strongly related to research in the cognitive unconscious and the neurobiology of emotions.

Disputation – D and more effective ways of responses – E

Disputation and cognitive–emotive dissonance

The aim of CBT/REBT is to enhance adaptive emotions by enhancing rBs. This is done by disputing iBs (D) and by assimilating new effective (E) rBs. Disputation of iBs and the assimilation of rBs can greatly benefit from cognitive research. As Kristene Doyle will consider in chapter 8 the state of such research in social cognitions and related areas, I will present only brief considerations based on more laboratory-oriented research and will suggest a specific research program.

By the end of cognitive disputation, although patients recognize consciously that their past beliefs are false and/or maladaptive some patients can still feel (cognitive–emotive dissonance) and behave (cognitive–behavioral dissonance) according to their past beliefs (Grieger and Boyd, 1977). Sometimes the habits of maladaptive thinking are so strong and automatic prior to therapy that patients tend to persist in them until new thinking habits become stronger and more generalized through repeated practice.

From a survey of the literature concerning current CBT and REBT practice, the main strategy being used to overcome these types of cognitive dissonance is to strengthen clients' new, adaptive cognitions (Ellis and Grieger, 1977). There are several ways to do so, chief among them being: (1) imagery techniques; (2) educational techniques; and (3) real-life practice (for details, see Ellis and Grieger, 1977). Although these techniques have been proven to some extent successful in dealing with cognitive–emotive–behavioral dissonance, a large part of the clinical population still experiences this phenomenon (Grieger and Boyd, 1977). Therefore, recognizing the merit of prior research and building on its outcomes, I want to suggest another adjunctive possibility to deal with cognitive–emotive–behavioral dissonance. For example, rather than only strengthen the assimilation of adaptive cognitions a patient could simultaneously learn to reduce the unconscious impact of previously held maladaptive cognitions that block the assimilation of new adaptive cognitions. This re-conceptualization of cognitive–emotive and cognitive–behavioral dissonances is made in the context of the phenomenon called *mental contamination* (Wilson and Brekke, 1994).

Mental contamination is defined as the phenomenon whereby a patient has an unwanted judgment, emotion or behavior because of mental processing (e.g. previously held maladaptive cognitions) that is unconscious or uncontrollable (Wilson and Brekke, 1994). By 'unconscious and unwanted' the writers mean that a patient would prefer not to be influenced in the way they are being influenced. According to Wilson and Brekke (1994), the process of mental contamination involves several components organized sequentially. First, there is an activation of unwanted and unconscious information processing (i.e. the content is accessible but not conscious, see Wegner and Smart, 1997). Then, because this processing is unconscious, (a) people are not motivated to correct it, (b) they are not aware of the direction and magnitude of the contamination, and (c) they do not have sufficient control over their cognitions to control the process of mental contamination. This process of mental contamination has been proven experimentally to be involved in cognitive–emotive–behavioral dissonance (David, 2000).

Mental contamination and cognitive–emotive–behavioral dissonance

Future research in REBT should be focused on the elaboration of some techniques for controlling mental contamination and hopefully thereby increasing the effectiveness of cognitive disputation and the speed with which rBs can be effectively assimilated. There are some fruitful cognitive experimental paradigms that should be explored to elaborate such techniques (for details, see David, 2000). Let me give details of some of them here briefly. *First*, people could be taught explicitly about mental contamination and how to control it. This means that we should teach them to: (1) be aware of the possibility that unwanted mental processing (e.g. previously held maladaptive cognitions) might be triggered in a given situation; (2) be motivated to correct the error; (3) be aware of the direction and of the magnitude of contamination; and (4) attain sufficient control and abilities to correct the contamination. I think that this procedure must be implemented or taught explicitly during cognitive disputation. A preliminary examination of this technique in a single-case experiment, multiple baselines across simple phobia patients, has confirmed its capacity to reduce mental contamination and to facilitate the assimilation of rBs (David, 2000). *Another way* to control mental contamination would be to block the first component that initiates the process of mental contamination, namely the activation of unwanted mental processing. A review of the literature regarding the construct of cognitive inhibition (Dempster and Brainerd, 1995) suggested many possible ways to inhibit the activation of the unwanted mental content. One way would be for a therapist not only to try to change maladaptive cognitions but also simultaneously to provide an incompatible alternative to the maladaptive information. Previous work has found more successful forgetting of maladaptive information when participants have considered an alternative to that maladaptive information (Anderson, 1982). This intervention might work for several reasons. The new incompatible adaptive information has the same function as maladaptive information (to serve a specific task) and it may block the expression of maladaptive information by *lateral inhibition* (for details, see Eysenck and Keane, 2000). Ideally, clients should insist not only on learning to search for alternative adaptive information (the main trend in current clinical work), but also should ensure that such information is logically incompatible with past information (less often emphasized in clinical practice). Indeed, I found such a technique useful in stimulating the assimilation of rBs in the therapy of simple phobia patients (David, 2000). However, our investigations are preliminary and were conducted in single-case experiments. Future studies might offer more solid support for the techniques.

Brief comments about other cognitive processes involved in D and E

According to Anderson (2000), declarative or explicit cognitions are also coded in our implicit memory in procedural forms by practice and automatization. This is why a disputation that only takes place at the level of declarative memory is insufficient to modify such beliefs because they still remain in our procedural knowledge base. This duplication should be taken into account when we elaborate treatment packages to deal with iBs. Taking into account these findings, I think that as well as behavioral homework and techniques, behavioral conceptualization should be clearly visible in REBT theory.

The assimilation of a new effective response (E) may be facilitated by findings from decision-making research. Decision-making models (for details, see Kahneman and Tversky, 2000) in combination with modern knowledge about problem solving (e.g. Hatano and Inagaki, 2000) should be integrated into current REBT practice during the practical problem-solving stage. This knowledge should also be taught as a part of the training program in REBT to equip the REBT therapist with the powerful tools needed to deal with practical problems remaining after emotional problems have been solved.

The potential impact of REBT on the development of cognitive psychology

Cognitive psychology is mainly a basic science while REBT is mainly an applied science. The relationship between basic and applied science is very complex. For example, there are many filters that a basic theory must pass through in order to penetrate an applied science. The first filter is the relevance or usefulness of the principles of the basic theory to clinical work. Much work in cognitive psychology may have little utility in the clinical setting because the knowledge developed from 'normal' populations is not necessarily applicable to clinical populations (Engels et al., 1993). However, supposing that the basic knowledge gained from these studies is relevant to clinical theory, an applied science would try to use such knowledge to elaborate some interventions. There is a second filter through which these interventions must pass in order to impact upon the applied science, namely efficacy. *Efficacy* refers to the capacity to solve clinical problems in a carefully controlled setting. The techniques that survive are then further filtered to check for their effectiveness. *Effectiveness* refers to the capacity of the techniques to solve clinical problems in real clinical settings rather than in laboratory trials. The final filter is the *accommodability*: how the techniques can be directly implemented in a specific clinical context, and what are the costs and benefits associated with this implementation. Most research in cognitive psychology is focused on basic principles and theories. Few types of cognitive research (i.e. applied cognitive psychology research) are oriented to real clinical problems, and even fewer are oriented to the elaboration of clinically relevant techniques. REBT may help bridge the gap between cognitive psychology research and clinical practice. For example, REBT may extend some of cognitive psychology's basic principles to the clinical setting by checking for their usefulness, efficacy, effectiveness, and accommodability. In this way, REBT not only extends the basic research of cognitive psychology but it would gain a strong applied cognitive psychology component, which could be continuously fed and developed by the new basic research in cognitive science.

However, REBT should not only extend the impact of the basic research of cognitive psychology, it should also offer new ideas and research topics for basic research in cognitive psychology. Cognitive psychology has often focused on cognitions as a static phenomenon (Ingram and Siegle, 2001), while REBT is devoted to the modification of affect and behavior by changing cognitions (Ellis, 1994). Therefore, research in REBT may contribute to the basic cognitive psychology by clarifying the role of dynamic cognitive variables in modifying ongoing cognitive processes. Also, REBT's focus on philosophy and cultural differences (Ellis, 1994) may suggest new research topics for cognitive psychology. For example, less is known in cognitive psychology about the influence of cross-cultural differences in the basic cognitive processes involved in psychopathology. REBT could make a significant contribution to cognitive research in this area by publishing clinical data and higher-order clinical theories that could be later analyzed according to the procedures of basic sciences.

Drawbacks of the integration of REBT into the psychological mainstream

Lakatos (1970) stated that mainstream science only exposes the public to its theories and models, and tries to construct a protective belt around its assumptions. This is a useful strategy, which keeps debates focused on theory and driven by empirical evidence. Assumptions are neither verifiable nor falsifiable. They are often assumed simply because an influential founder of the paradigm assumed them. Assumptions are masked and protected because sometimes they differ widely even within an apparently homogeneous theoretical enterprise. For example, cognitive neuroscience seems to be a fairly consolidated scientific enterprise. But a 'bloody war' would start if people were to debate the fundamental assumptions about the relationship between brain and mind. However, this is not the case since this problem remains well-protected and unanswered. In the mainstream, there is no room for debates about assumptions, and in consequence, there is no place for 'spiritual leaders' to guide debates about philosophical assumptions. Mainstream psychology is theory-driven rather than leader-driven.

REBT is a scientifically oriented psychotherapy, but at the same time it is an independent and idiosyncratic system of psychotherapy. Because REBT as a system proudly exposes its philosophical assumptions about life and human beings, it feels uncomfortable to the more defensive mainstream. Furthermore, Albert Ellis seems to be one of the last psychotherapists of the old tradition of 'spiritual leaders', and he is a fervent supporter of REBT's philosophical component. Thus, REBT seems to be both philosophical and leader-driven. Because of these two factors, REBT as a system is incompatible with the way the mainstream works, and thus has not been able to fully penetrate the mainstream. Although many of REBT's ideas have been assimilated into the mainstream (Still, 2001), in some cases the source of these ideas is not cited in order to avoid debates about their philosophical tinge. Ellis (Popa, 2001) has remarked that this has happened many times.

Other CBT schools have had a different fate. For example, both Aaron Beck's and Donald Meichenbaum's approaches have been better assimilated into the mainstream. It was easier for them because they, like more mainstream approaches, protected their philosophical assumptions and focused on their empirical theories. With REBT this is more difficult for the reasons mentioned above. In light of all these facts, one wonders what the future role of REBT will be in the mainstream.

One possibility is that REBT will remain an independent system of psychotherapy, which is scientifically oriented, but whose theory and research continue to have a philosophical flavor. In this form, REBT will retain its identity, but will likely only be brought to the attention of mainstream psychologists through empirically validated REBT packages or specific techniques used in a more integrated therapy. In addition, its theory will continue to frequently inspire researchers though it will often be presented under different names to avoid the philosophical connotations. More than that, and it has happened many times (for details, see David et al., 2002), (a) REBT theory might often be misunderstood in research; (b) incorrect predictions might be derived from it; and (c) some of the existing data might not be properly interpreted. This is the price to pay for preserving the current identity of REBT. It allows the mainstream to incorporate some of REBT's developments, but to continue to neglect REBT as a whole system.

Another possibility is that REBT could change its approach, and begin to stress its theory and models, rather than its philosophical assumptions. In addition, it could begin to assimilate constructs from cognitive psychology, which might attract more mainstream researchers and attention to REBT, and by doing so, might make it more visible and influential to the mainstream. This assimilation of REBT into the mainstream, in turn, could contribute to further developments of REBT theory and practice. We think that REBT does not need *more* research. REBT needs *other kinds* of research and more importantly, it needs *high quality and systematic* research.

No matter what the choice is, REBT has already made valuable contributions to mainstream psychology. However, I believe that the future recognition and development of this contribution will depend on the course that REBT chooses to follow.

References

Anderson, C.A. (1982) Inoculation of counterexplanation: debiasing techniques in the perseverance of social theories, *Social Cognition*, *3*, 129–139.

Anderson, J.R. (2000) *Cognitive Psychology and its Implications* (5th edn). New York: Worth.

Beck, A.T. (1976) *Cognitive Therapy for Emotional Disorders*. New York: International University Press.

Beck, A.T. and Clark, D.A. (1997) An information processing model of anxiety: automatic and strategic processes, *Behaviour Research and Therapy*, *35*, 49–58.

Bond, F.W. and Dryden, W. (1996) Why two, central REBT hypotheses appear untestable, *Journal of Rational-Emotive and Cognitive-Behavior Therapy*, *14*, 29–40.

Bowers, G. (1981) Mood and memory, *American Psychologist*, *36*, 129–148.

Cramer, D. and Fong, J. (1991) Effect of rational and irrational beliefs on intensity and 'inappropriateness' of feelings: a test of rational-emotive theory, *Cognitive Therapy and Research*, *15*, 319–329.

David, D. (2000) *Unconscious Information Processing* (Prelucrari inconstiente de informatie). Cluj-Napoca: Dacia Press.

David, D. and McMahon, J. (2001) Clinical strategies in cognitive behavioral psychotherapy: a case analysis, *Romanian Journal of Cognitive and Behavioral Psychotherapies*, *1*, 71–86.

David, D., Schnur, J. and Belloiu, A. (2002) Another search for the 'hot' cognitions: appraisal, irrational beliefs, attributions, and their relation to emotion, *Journal of Rational-Emotive and Cognitive-Behavior Therapy*, *20*, 93–131.

Dempster, F.N. and Brainerd, C.J. (1995) *Interference and Inhibition in Cognitions*. San Diego: Academic Press.

Denoff, M.S. (1991) Irrational beliefs, situational attributions, and the coping responses of adolescent runaways, *Journal of Rational-Emotive and Cognitive-Behavior Therapy*, *9*, 113–135.

DiGiuseppe, R. (1996) The nature of irrational and rational beliefs: progress in rational emotive behavior theory, *Journal of Rational-Emotive and Cognitive-Behavior Therapy*, *4*, 5–28.

Dixon, N.F. and Henley, S.H. (1991) Unconscious perception: possible implications of data from academic research for clinical practice, *Journal of Nervous and Mental Disease*, *179*, 243–252.

Dowd, T.E. and Courchaine, E.K. (1996) Implicit learning, tacit knowledge, and implications for stasis and change in cognitive psychotherapy, *Journal of Cognitive Psychotherapy*, *10*, 163–180.

Dryden, W., Ferguson, J. and Clark, T. (1989) Beliefs and influences: a test of a rational-emotive hypothesis: I. Performance in an academic seminar, *Journal of Rational-Emotive and Cognitive-Behavior Therapy*, *7*, 119–129.

Ellis, A. (1962) *Reason and Emotion in Psychotherapy*. New York: Stuard.

Ellis, A. (1994) *Reason and Emotion in Psychotherapy* (revised edn). Secaucus, NJ: Birch Lane Press.

Ellis, A. and Dryden, W. (1997) *The Practice of Rational-Emotive Behavior Therapy* (2nd edn). New York: Springer.

Ellis, A. and Grieger, R.M. (1977) *Handbook of Rational-Emotive Therapy*. New York: Springer.

Engels, G.I., Garnefsky, N. and Diekstra, R.F.W. (1993) Efficacy of Rational-Emotive Therapy; a quantitative analysis, *Journal of Consulting and Clinical Psychology*, *61*, 1083–1091.

Eysenck, M.W. and Keane, M.T. (2000) *Cognitive Psychology: A Student's Handbook* (4th edn). Philadelphia: Psychology Press/Taylor and Francis.

Folkman, S. and Lazarus, R. (1988) Coping as a mediator of emotion, *Journal of Personality and Social Psychology*, *54*, 466–475.

Gabbard, G.O. (2000) A neurobiologically informed perspective on psychotherapy, *British Journal of Psychiatry*, *177*, 117–122.

Gilbert, D. (1991) How mental systems believe, *American Psychologist*, *46*, 107–119.

Glenn, S. (2001) A critical look at the assumptions of cognitive therapy, *Psychiatry: Interpersonal and Biological Processes*, *64*, 158–164.

Grieger, R. and Boyd, J. (1977) Psychotherapeutic responses to some critical incidents in RET. In A. Ellis and R. Grieger (eds) *Handbook of Rational-Emotive Therapy*. New York: Springer.

Harran, S.M. and Ziegler, D.J. (1991) Cognitive appraisal hassles in college students displaying high or low irrational beliefs, *Journal of Rational-Emotive and Cognitive-Behavior Therapy*, *9*, 265–271.

Hatano, G. and Inagaki, K. (2000) Knowledge acquisition and use in higher-order cognition. In K. Pawlik and M.R. Rosenzweig (eds) *International Handbook of Psychology*. London: Sage.

Heppner, P.P., Reeder, B.L. and Larson, L.M. (1983) Cognitive variables associated with personal problem-solving appraisal: implications for counseling, *Journal of Counseling Psychology*, *30*, 537–545.

Ingram, R.E. and Siegle, G.J. (2001) Cognition and clinical science: from revolution to evolution. In K.S. Dobson (ed.) *Handbook of Cognitive-Behavioral Therapies*. New York: Guilford Press.

Jacoby, L.L. (1991) A process dissociation framework: separating automatic from intentional uses of memory, *Journal of Memory and Language*, *30*, 513–541.

Kahneman, D. and Tversky, A. (2000) *Choices, Values, and Frames*. New York: Cambridge University Press.

Katkin, E.S., Wiens, S. and Ohman, A. (2001) Nonconscious fear conditioning, visceral perception, and the development of gut feelings, *Psychological Science*, *12*, 366–370.

Kihlstrom, J.F. (1999) The psychological unconscious. In P. Lawrence and J. Oliver (eds) *Handbook of Personality: Theory and Research* (2nd edn). New York: Guilford Press.

Kirsch, I. (1999) *How Expectancies Shape Experience*. Washington DC: American Psychological Association.

Lakatos, I. (1970) Falsification and the methodology of scientific research programmes. In I. Lakatos and A. Musgrave (eds) *Criticism and the Growth of Knowledge*. Cambridge: Cambridge University Press.

Lazarus, R.S. (1991) *Emotion and Adaptation*. New York: Oxford University Press.

LeDoux, J. (2000) Cognitive-emotional interactions: listen to the brain. In R.D. Lane and N. Lynn (eds) *Cognitive Neuroscience of Emotion. Series in Affective Science* (pp. 129–155). New York: Oxford University Press.

Macaskill, N.D. and Macaskill, A. (1996) Rational-emotive therapy plus pharmacotherapy versus pharmacotherapy alone in the treatment of high cognitive dysfunction, *Cognitive Therapy and Research*, *20*, 575–592.

McClamrock, R. (1991) Marr's three levels: a re-evaluation, *Minds and Machines*, *1*, 185–196.

McClelland, J.L. and Rumelhart, D.E. (1986) *Parallel Distributed Processing: Explorations in the Microstructure of Cognition*. Cambridge, MA: MIT Press/ Bradford Books.

Mahoney, M.J. (1993) Introduction to special section: theoretical developments in the cognitive psychotherapies, *Journal of Consulting and Clinical Psychology*, *61*, 187–194.

Marr, D. (1982) *Vision*. San Francisco: W.H. Freeman.

Moeller, A.T., Kotze, H.F. and Sieberhagen, K.J. (1993) Comparison of the effects of auditory subliminal stimulation and rational-emotive therapy, separately and combined, on self-concept, *Psychological Reports*, *72*, 131–145.

Newell, A. (1990) *Unified Theories of Cognition*. Cambridge, MA: Harvard University Press.

Ohman, A. and Soares, J.J.F. (1994) Unconscious anxiety: phobic responses to masked stimuli, *Journal of Abnormal Psychology*, *103*, 231–240.

Popa, S. (2001) Interview with Albert Ellis: The cognitive revolution in psychotherapy, *Romanian Journal of Cognitive and Behavioral Psychotherapies*, *1*, 7–16.

Rescorla, R.A. (1988) Pavlovian conditioning: it's not what you think, *American Psychologist*, *43*, 151–160.

Richardson-Klavehn, A. and Gardiner, J. (1996) Cross-modality priming in stem completion reflects conscious memory, but not voluntary memory, *Psychonomic Bulletin and Review*, *3*, 238–244.

Robins, R.W., Gosling, S.D. and Craik, K.H. (1999) An empirical analysis of trends in psychology, *American Psychologist*, *54*, 117–128.

Schacter, D.L. (1987) Implicit memory: history and its current status, *Journal of Experimental Psychology: Learning, Memory, and Cognition*, *3*, 501–518.

Schacter, D.L. and Tulving, E. (1994) *Memory Systems*. Cambridge, MA: MIT Press.

Segal, Z.V. and Vella, D.D. (1990) Self-schema in major depression: replication and extension of a priming methodology, *Cognitive Therapy and Research*, *14*, 161–176.

Seger, C. (1994) Implicit learning, *Psychological Bulletin*, *2*, 163–196.

Smith, C.A., Haynes, K.N., Lazarus, R.S. and Pope, L.K. (1993) In search of the 'hot' cognitions: attributions, appraisals and their relation to emotion, *Journal of Personality and Social Psychology*, *65*, 916–929.

Solomon, A. and Haaga, D.A.F. (1995) Rational emotive behavior therapy research: what we know and what we need to know, *Journal of Rational-Emotive and Cognitive-Behavior Therapy*, *13*, 179–191.

Solomon, A., Haaga, D.A.F., Brody, C., Friedman, D.G. and Kirk, L. (1998) Priming irrational beliefs in recovered-depressed people, *Journal of Consulting and Clinical Psychology*, *3*, 440–449.

Still, A. (2001) Marginalisation is not unbearable. Is it even undesirable?, *Journal of Rational-Emotive and Cognitive-Behavior Therapy*, *19*, 55–66.

Tobias, B.A., Kihlstrom, J.F. and Schacter D.L. (1992) Emotion and implicit memory. In S.-A. Christianson (ed.) *The Handbook of Emotion and Memory: Research and Theory*. Hillsdale, NJ: Lawrence Erlbaum Associates.

Tsai, A., Loftus, E. and Polage, D. (2000) Current directions in false-memory research. In D.F. Bjorklund (ed.) *False-Memory Creation in Children and Adults: Theory, Research, and Implications*. Mahwah, NJ: Lawrence Erlbaum Associates.

Tulving, E. (1983) *Elements of Episodic Memory*. London: Oxford University Press.

Vernon, A. (1997) Applications of REBT with children and adolescents. In J.

Yankura and W. Dryden (eds) *Special Applications of REBT: A Therapist's Casebook*. New York: Springer.

Walen, S.R., DiGiuseppe, R. and Dryden, W. (1992) *A Practitioner's Guide to Rational-Emotive Therapy* (2nd edn). New York: Oxford University Press.

Wang, C., Jia, F., Fang, R., Zhu, Y. and Huang, Y. (1999) Comparative study of Rational-Emotive Therapy for 95 patients with dysthymic disorder, *Chinese Mental Health Journal, 13*, 172–173.

Wegner, D.M. and Smart, L. (1997) Deep cognitive activation: a new approach to the unconscious, *Journal of Consulting and Clinical Psychology, 6*, 984–995.

Wilson, T.D. and Brekke, N. (1994) Mental contamination and mental correction: unwanted influences on judgments and evaluations, *Psychological Bulletin, 116*, 117–142.

Young, J.E. (1999) *Cognitive Therapy for Personality Disorders: A Schema Focused Approach* (3rd edn). Sarasota, FL: Professional Resource Press/Professional Resource Exchange, Inc.

Ziegler, D.J. (2001) The possible place of cognitive appraisal in the ABC model underlying Rational Emotive Behavior Therapy, *Journal of Rational-Emotive and Cognitive-Behavior Therapy, 19*, 137–152.

Chapter 8

The contribution of social psychology to Rational Emotive Behavior Therapy

Kristene A. Doyle

This chapter is intended to bridge research findings in the field of social psychology to those of Rational Emotive Behavior Therapy (REBT). To date, there is a paucity of literature linking these two areas, which is surprising given that much of what it is that REBT therapists do has substantial roots in social psychological theory and research. Many of the topic areas in the social psychology literature, especially persuasion and influence, have application to both Cognitive Behavioral and Rational Emotive Behavior therapists. The goal of this chapter is to review some of the relevant findings in the social psychological literature in the context of Rational Emotive Behavior Theory and Therapy. It is suggested that practicing REBT therapists take into consideration such findings, particularly in those cases where progress in therapy appears to be halted.

Social psychology has been defined in numerous texts and literature. Relevant to Rational Emotive Behavior Theory is Allport's (1985) definition, in which he states that social psychology is 'a discipline that uses scientific methods to understand and explain how the thought, feeling, and behavior of individuals are influenced by the actual, imagined, or implied presence of others.' This definition is pertinent in that much of the focus of REBT theory is on the interaction between thought, feeling and behavior as a function of one's interpretation of events.

Furthermore, the goal of social psychology is to understand how most people act in a given situation, and is not as concerned with the unique personal characteristics of individuals that may cause them to act differently from each other. The aim of social psychologists is to understand the *general* tendencies in the actions, feelings, and thoughts of individuals (Worchel et al., 2000). This approach is consistent with Rational Emotive Behavior Theory, in so far as Ellis (1957, 1958, 1962) pointed out the innate and acquired irrational, unrealistic, and illogical human tendencies that often encourage disturbance. Ellis has written extensively on the biological basis of human irrationality (Ellis, 1976), and has concluded that practically all people have distinctly innate, as well as socially acquired traits that are irrational. The REBT therapist utilizes this knowledge when working with an individual, but does take into account that individual's unique traits and characteristics. This is not out of line with the field of social psychology, which acknowledges the wide range of human activities and the influence of culture and of the past on human behavior (Worchel et al., 2000).

Historical background of social psychology

Social psychology as a field was largely confined to the western world, particularly North America, until recently (Jones, 1985). Moreover, a review of the development of the field suggests that it is shaped by world events, political currents, and social issues of the time (Harris, 1986). The year 1897 is generally commemorated as the year of the first social psychological experiment. Norman Triplett reviewed official records of bicycle races and observed that a rider's maximum speed was approximately 20 percent faster when he raced in the presence of other riders than compared to when he raced alone. According to Allport (1985), the effect of the presence of others on individual task performance was for the most part the only issue that was studied experimentally for the first three decades of social psychology.

Research in social psychology in the early twentieth century was quite different from what it is today until Kurt Lewin, with a background of applied psychology, came forward. Lewin has been described as the founder of modern social psychology, introducing theory into social psychology. Lewin believed that general propositions that linked human behavior with social situations could and ought to be developed, and tested with the help of experimentation. Lewin helped the field of social psychology begin to view research not just as investigations into separate and unconnected phenomena, but also as a means of testing general theories on human behavior (Worchel et al., 2000).

World War II was the incentive for many studies that were conducted to determine who should say what and in which particular order with the goal of persuading an audience to believe a particular message or adopt a particular position, with significant studies from Asch (1956) and Milgram (1965) (Worchel et al., 2000). Asch (1956) conducted studies on conformity, while Milgram (1965) investigated the area of obedience. During this time, Leon Festinger began questioning how people valuate themselves, and argued that in the absence of objective measures, people compare themselves with others (Worchel et al., 2000).

The mid-1960s through the mid-1970s saw the field of social psychology become increasingly concerned with the way individuals perceive and interpret social events. During the 1980s and 1990s cognitive approaches were emphasized, as was the role of culture in social behavior (Worchel et al., 2000).

With this brief and by no means exhaustive review of the historical development of the field of social psychology, it becomes obvious that many of the areas of interest that have developed, such as persuasion, attitude change, and communication, are very much applicable to the field of Rational Emotive Behavior Theory and Therapy. The remainder of this chapter will focus on the application of social psychological research findings to REBT.

The role of persuasion in Rational Emotive Behavior Therapy

Ellis (2001), in a presentation given at the American Psychological Association Annual Convention, stated that recent findings in social psychology and personality have supported two of the main theories of REBT. According to Ellis (2001), REBT posits that humans are born and reared with strong constructivist and problem-solving tendencies that assist them to survive and live reasonably happily. REBT also hypothesizes that humans are also biologically, and as a result of their social rearing, prone to interfere with their own well-being and make themselves anxious, depressed, self-pitying, angry, and so on. According to Ellis (2001), modern social psychology agrees in numerous ways with REBT's constructivist position by specifying that even with their frequent irrational, self-defeating, and socially sabotaging tendencies, humans also have the ability to make themselves aware of their destructiveness and to purposefully work to change and reconstruct their thinking, feeling, and behaving. Furthermore, Ellis (2001) points out how Aronson et al. (1999) demonstrate how social psychologists can assist people to be more constructive and rational when they indulge in the innate and acquired tendencies to defeat themselves and others. For example, these authors describe how if people stop and think about engaging in a harmful act, they may often stop themselves from committing it. This can be likened to the hedonic calculus, an exercise often done in REBT, in which the advantages and disadvantages of a particular thought, feeling, or self-defeating behavior are listed and weighed.

Rational Emotive Behavior therapists dedicate a large percentage of the therapeutic session to the identification and disputation of irrational beliefs (rigid, dogmatic, absolutistic self-defeating beliefs). REBT practice involves the therapist working hard, sometimes harder than the client, at persuading them to replace irrational beliefs with more rational (flexible, self-preserving) beliefs. Essentially, REBT practice includes attempts at *persuasion* – persuading clients to see that their current way of thinking, feeling, and behaving is somehow self-defeating.

The job of a Rational Emotive Behavior therapist is akin to an advertiser trying to persuade us to buy a particular product. They could also be compared to newscasters, who supposedly are objective, and can have a tremendous impact on our opinions as they determine which events are given exposure and how much exposure is given (Aronson, 1995). Typically, therapists hope to be objective as well, and to respect the agenda of the client. But it would be remiss to ignore the fact that therapists can impact client opinions by deciding what and how much of something they are exposed to. Therefore, it would be beneficial to examine, scrutinize and determine how certain social psychological research findings can be used to assist clients to overcome their innate and natural tendencies to at times be self-defeating.

One of the main difficulties that emerges in therapy is when a client holds on strongly to a belief or self-defeating behavior, sometimes even acknowledging that the current way of thinking or behaving is destructive. At such times, the findings on persuasion might prove helpful in aiding clients to relinquish such beliefs and/or behaviors. It is important to review and understand Richard Petty and John Cacioppo's (1986) theory of the elaboration likelihood model. This model states that we are inclined to think deeply about a persuasive argument if the issue is one that is relevant and important to us. The theory posits that there are two major routes to persuasion: the central route and the peripheral route. The central route relies on solid arguments based on relevant facts and figures and involves the prudent, thoughtful deliberation of message content. The central route gets people to think about issues. High elaboration indicates the central route, and requires that the receiver have both motivation and the ability to process the message carefully. Therefore, a client with a career as a computer programmer may do better when the REBT therapist takes the central route to processing. On the other hand, the peripheral route involves simple cues (e.g. an attractive source), and takes short cuts in cognitive processing: therefore, rather than attempting to engage a person's thinking, cues are provided that stimulate acceptance of the argument without much thinking (Fraser and Burchell, 2001). Low elaboration indicates the peripheral route and is likely in the absence of motivation and ability. Therefore, for certain clients, such as adolescents, taking the peripheral route to persuasion may be the recommended course. By providing examples of controversial public figures such as Madonna, who appears to hold the belief that 'I don't need others' approval', acceptance of this belief may emerge faster because the peripheral route was engaged. Taking the elaboration likelihood model's theory into account, emphasizing one route over the other depending on the type of client may result in better outcome, which may include the client's willingness to engage in an alternative, rational way of thinking or behaving. The manner in which any issue is presented can either stimulate thinking or trigger almost immediate agreement, depending on the route that the communicator is taking.

Communicator variables as they relate to belief change

Another area in the social psychological literature that may be relevant involves communicator variables. It has been found that a communicator can be effective if it is clear that the person has nothing to gain (and perhaps has something to lose) by persuading us. Taking this into consideration, it is recommended that after presenting an empirical dispute (i.e. where is the evidence for this belief?), or logical dispute (i.e. how does it logically follow that because you *want* something it therefore *must* be that way?), the REBT therapist, very casually and almost apathetically, state something like the following to the client: 'Look, go ahead and continue thinking the way you are. I'm not losing *anything* by you maintaining your belief on this issue or continuing to engage in this behavior. In fact, it's hard work for me to challenge your beliefs – so let's move on to another area, okay? What else would you like to work on?' Could this approach be criticized as sneaky? Probably. But has this approach been effective? Often. Clients sometimes dedicate more time to disagreeing with their therapist and trying to prove that they are correct, rather than listening to the words and arguments of their therapist. It is often when the therapist puts a stop to the back-and-forth banter and appears to 'give in', that their clients get concerned and actually begin to listen to disputes and entertain the idea of incorporating them into their behavioral repertoires.

The field of persuasion frequently discusses the concept of trustworthiness. Findings have suggested that the trustworthiness of a person can be increased if the audience is absolutely certain the person is not *trying* to influence them. Believing the person is acting spontaneously increases the likelihood of being persuaded (Aronson, 1995). One implication of this finding for therapists may be to play a bit like the 'scattered therapist' with some of your more well-functioning, cognitively astute clients. Research has indicated that the more educated a person, the more skeptical, and studies show that people who are skeptical believe their skepticism makes them immune to persuasion. This is not true, however. While working on one issue with such a client, the calculating REBT therapist may be able to persuade them on a different belief that the client has in the past refused to give up by spontaneously interjecting something about that issue at a random time.

Fear arousal and belief change

One of the main tenets of Rational Emotive Behavior Theory is disputation of irrational beliefs from cognitive, behavioral and emotive levels. This has definite relevance to social psychology research on logical versus emotional appeals. When determining which type of appeal to make, consideration should be made of the effects of various levels of a specific emotion on opinion. Suppose you wish to arouse fear in your clients as a way of inducing opinion change. It is recommended that consideration be made of whether it would be more effective to arouse a small amount of fear, or rather a large amount capable of scaring the client.

When thinking about this issue, it makes sense that a good scare can have the effects of motivating action; on the other hand, there is the argument that too much fear can be incapacitating and might impede the person's ability to attend, understand and act on the message. Research shows that if a communication arouses a great deal of fear, we tend *not* to pay close attention to it (Aronson, 1995). Therefore, it might be advantageous to assess how fearful or afraid clients are when discussing particular beliefs, situations, emotions, or simply the idea of change. If therapists fail to do so, some of their clients may appear to be processing and thinking about what is being discussed, but may not actually be doing so. It is not a good idea to assume that though clients do not overtly appear afraid or fearful, that they are not actually so.

On the other hand, there is also a finding that the more frightened a person is by a communication, the more likely he or she is to take positive preventative action. However, people who have a reasonably good opinion of themselves are most likely to be moved by high degrees of fear arousal. People with low opinions of themselves are least likely to take immediate action when confronted with a communication arousing a great deal of fear. However, after a time delay, such individuals tend to behave very much like those individuals with high self-esteem. Interestingly, if immediate action were not necessary but instead action could be taken later, people with low self-esteem are more likely to take that action if they were exposed to a communication arousing a great deal of fear (Aronson, 1995). Therefore, it would be important to consider whether or not immediate action or behavior is necessary and then induce fear based on that.

While the social psychology literature uses the term self-esteem when discussing the research on fear arousal and persuasion, REBT as a theory discards such a concept, and instead, encourages Unconditional Self-Acceptance (USA). This is defined as 'an unqualified and nonjudgmental attitude towards oneself' (Dryden and Neenan, 1996, p. 146). The surrendering of self-rating is encouraged by REBT therapists in response to how complex humans are, and in so doing, one can never be a failure or a success, even when one fails or succeeds. Having said that, from previous findings, one recommendation being made is that prior to really getting into disputing, REBT therapists preferably should assess for USA on the part of the client. If a high degree of USA is present, then quicker and greater success may be achieved by disputations arousing a high degree of fear. If, on the other hand, there is an indication of a low degree of USA, then it may be a better decision to arouse a lesser degree of fear arousal.

Aronson (1995) has indicated that people with a low opinion of themselves (in REBT terms this would be likened to very conditional self-acceptance and a tendency to self-down) may have great trouble coping with threats to themselves. Therefore, a high-fear communication may overwhelm and paralyze them. If REBT therapists come on too forceful in their disputes in the hope of stimulating change, they may actually be doing their clients a disservice. Low or moderate fear arousal may be more palatable in the moment. As mentioned previously, if clients are given time, and it is not crucial that they act immediately, they will be more likely to act if the message 'scares the crap out of them'.

An important adjunct to the aforementioned is research by Howard Leventhal and his associates that shows that fear-arousing messages containing specific instructions about how, when, and where to take action are much more effective than recommendations not including such details (Aronson, 1995). A significant finding from this research for REBT therapists to consider is that a high-fear communication may produce a much greater *intention* to stop or start a particular behavior; however, unless it is accompanied by recommendations for *specific behavior*, it produces little behavior change. A practical application of this finding is in the case of a client who is engaging in excessive drinking behavior. Simply reviewing the history of alcoholism in the family, the detrimental effects alcohol has on the body's organs, and the negative consequences alcohol consumption is having on the individual's life (e.g. occupational, academic, and/or social functioning) may be enough to induce a great deal of fear in the client as well as an intention to stop the behavior; however, without recommending or having the client generate specific alternative, self-preserving behaviors to overcome the self-defeating behavior, you may simply have a fearful client who intends to stop drinking, but never really does so. Interestingly, specific instructions *without* a fear-arousing communication are relatively ineffective (Aronson, 1995). Thus, it appears that the combination of a fear-arousing communication *with* specific recommended behaviors is what will effect change in certain types of clients.

In line with the previous discussion on the impact of self-esteem on persuasibility (in REBT terms 'self-acceptance'), is an important research finding that indicates that as a person's confidence weakens, they become less prone to listen to arguments against their beliefs. Therefore, the very clients you most want to convince and whose opinions might be the most susceptible to being changed are the ones least likely to continue to expose themselves to a communication designed for that purpose (Aronson, 1995). In such cases, therapists may want to prioritize goals of therapy, first working on the client's Unconditional Self-Acceptance and confidence in themself, and then working on disputing irrational beliefs and persuading clients to relinquish such self-defeating thoughts.

Another factor to consider when trying to persuade your clients regarding belief change is that most people are deeply effected by one clear, vivid, personal example than by an abundance of statistical data (Aronson, 1995). It appears that from this finding that as a therapist, more success in persuading clients may ensue, if, rather than bombarding them with a load of data and arguments for or against a particular belief, you self-disclose one clear, real example supporting your argument. Many times, perseverating on empirical, logical, and functional disputes proves ineffective after a certain period of time. The use of such disputes tends to have an effect in the beginning of therapy; however, incorporating self-disclosures that are timely and calculated can have an equally strong, sometimes stronger, impact. You may find that after you provide a client with a vivid personal example, in later sessions they will not recall all of the disputations you may have considered to be brilliant, but rather the personal example. The reason for this is not known at present. However, it may simply be a function of the client's viewing their therapist as another human being who too has experienced negative activating events and unhealthy negative emotions. The therapist can serve as a model for clients, demonstrating that hard work at disputing irrational beliefs and conquering self-defeating behaviors does pay off. This can all be done through the use of self-disclosure.

One- versus two-sided arguments

Another area of social psychological research pertinent to the practice of REBT is that of one-sided versus two-sided arguments. Research shows that the more well-informed the audience, the less likely they are to be persuaded by a one-sided argument and the more likely they are to be persuaded by an argument that brings out the important opposing arguments and then proceeds to refute them. On the other hand, an uninformed person, or the less cognitively intact or the less REBT-savvy client is less apt to know of the existence of opposing arguments, or be compelled by them even if they are pointed out. If the counter-argument is ignored, the less-informed members of your audience are persuaded; if the counter-argument is presented, confusion may arise (Aronson, 1995). The difference between one-sided and two-sided arguments is best shown via an example. Let's say that a mother comes in for therapy with the complaint that her three-year-old son is consistently banging his head on the wall. She tends to make herself angry, start yelling, and sometimes becomes physical with him. She knows she does not want to mother that way. A one-sided argument in this case would be just focusing on why it would be better for her to give up her demand that her son be different than he is. A two-sided argument in this example would look at the benefits of giving up her demands as well as the reasons for keeping her behavior such as getting results in the short run (by stopping the head-banging behavior).

REBT therapists oftentimes automatically go through a complete hedonic calculus or cost–benefit analysis, presenting both sides to clients when disputing. However, this approach may not be appropriate for some of our clients when we take into consideration the concepts of one- versus two-sided arguments. By doing a hedonic calculus and listing both sides to a behavior (i.e. the positive and negative) with some of our clients, therapists may actually be less elegant and be confusing the issue.

In addition to the cognitive level of clients, another factor to consider is the initial position of the client. If a client is predisposed to believe your argument, a one-sided presentation has a greater impact on his or her opinion than a two-sided presentation. Therefore, during the initial session with your client when you are explaining the B→C connection, which is defined as 'the hypothesis that individual's evaluative beliefs not only precede but also largely determine their emotional states or consequences' (Dryden and Neenan, 1996, p. 11), a goal would be to get a sense of whether or not your clients are buying into this idea. This may be one way to gain a sense of whether or not your client is predisposed to believe your arguments.

If, in this assessment, it emerges that your client is leaning in the opposite direction, that is, endorsing A→C thinking (defined as 'thinking engaged by individuals who believe that others or life events directly cause their emotional problems' (Dryden and Neenan, 1996, p. 2), then a two-sided refutational argument is more persuasive.

Position of client belief and how it relates to disputation

Let's suppose that you have a client who strongly disagrees with your point of view (presumably the more rational point of view). The question becomes whether or not you will be more persuasive if you present your position in its most extreme form or if you modulate your position by presenting it in such a way that it does not seem very different from your client's position. It is important to remember that most humans have a strong desire to be correct. When someone comes along and disagrees with us, we may often feel discomfort because it suggests that our opinions or actions may be 'wrong' or based on misinformation. The greater the disagreement, the greater the discomfort. To reduce this discomfort, we may change our opinions or actions. The greater the disagreement, the greater our opinion change will be (Aronson, 1995).

However, if a particular communication differs considerably from a person's own position, it may be outside that individual's 'latitude of acceptance' and the individual will not be very influenced by it (Hovland et al., 1957). Research suggests that the greatest opinion changes appear to occur when there is a moderate discrepancy between your message and the opinions of your clients.

It is important to bear this finding in mind when working on persuading clients. For example, if a client comes to therapy with the demand that her boss not speak to her in a degrading way, her core irrational belief (at the bottom of the levels of abstraction) is that 'the world *must* be the way I want it to be'. The REBT therapist may not be able to dispute at this level because it is simply outside that particular client's latitude of acceptance. In such situations, it may be more therapeutic to stay at a lighter level of abstraction. The chance of losing your clients is probably reduced.

Therapist- and client-related factors

According to Aronson (1995), there are at least four ways in which clients can reduce their discomfort that results from a discrepancy between their beliefs and therapist opinions: (1) they can change their opinion; (2) they can induce the therapist to change his or her opinion; (3) they can seek support for their original opinion by finding others who share their point of view, despite what the therapist says; (4) they can denigrate their therapist and convince themselves the therapist is stupid and thereby invalidate the therapist's opinion. However, it would be difficult to denigrate a therapist who is perceived to be a highly trustworthy expert on the issue under discussion. Thus, it follows that if a therapist's credibility is high, the greater is the discrepancy in opinion between therapist and client, the greater is the influence exerted on the opinions of the client. If, on the other hand a therapist's credibility is doubtful, therapists will produce maximum opinion change in their clients if there are moderate discrepancies in opinion. Therefore, if as a therapist you work with populations such as those who are court-mandated, or adolescents, or spouses who are coerced into therapy, you may have more success when disputing if your position is only slightly discrepant to your client.

A client-related factor to consider regarding degree of persuasibility is the frame of mind your client is in prior to the dispute. The client can be made receptive to a dispute if they have been well fed and are relaxed and happy (Aronson, 1995). The following suggestion may appear to be facetious; however, it is anything but that. It is suggested that REBT therapists seriously consider having clients eat a meal prior to therapy. It has been my experience that for many clients, particularly those with anger control difficulties, when they come into session in the evening and repeatedly dismiss all of my long, hard work, and I assess when the last time it was that they ate, it is often some time in the morning. Furthermore, when we take a look at their day, we find that they typically had many more outbursts as well as difficulty disputing any irrational beliefs that popped up, compared to days when they were eating more regularly. In addition, my experience after three years of co-leading the Women's Group at the Albert Ellis Institute in New York indicated how much difficulty controlling irrational beliefs and processing in-session disputes the women had when they were neglecting their self-care. The idea of proper nutrition and scheduled meals should be taken seriously as a factor in the persuasibility of clients.

Conversely, clients can be made less receptive and less persuadable. One way to decrease their persuasibility is by forewarning the individual that an attempt is going to be made to persuade them (Aronson, 1995). This is especially true if the content of the message differs from their own beliefs. From this, it is deduced that it is *not* a wise idea to indicate to your clients that you are going to dispute their irrational beliefs. Rather, it is probably wise to just go ahead and do it. It's similar to watching a baseball game and the sportscaster states that they will return after 'a word from our sponsor'. Most people take the opportunity to use the bathroom, get a refreshment, etc. It's almost as if it is a license to shut down for a moment, until the game comes back on.

Brehm's theory of reactance

Another relevant area of social psychology literature for REBT theory and practice is Brehm's theory of reactance, which suggests that when our sense of freedom is threatened, we attempt to restore it (Brehm, 1966). Aronson (1995) has indicated that persuasive disputes, if blatant or coercive, can be perceived as intruding upon one's freedom of choice, activating a person's defense to resist the messages. One of the defining characteristics of REBT is the active–directive, forceful nature of its therapists. Much of this is due to its founder, Albert Ellis's style. While it would be misleading to suggest that all REBT therapists mimic Dr Ellis's style, REBT therapists generally tend to be more forceful than other cognitive-behavioral therapists. One precaution to consider taking is not appearing *too* confrontational, especially in the beginning of therapy. If therapists are too forceful in the early stages of therapy, there may be less chance of success at disputing the irrational beliefs, and furthermore, therapists may unintentionally inoculate their clients against future disputes. The inoculation effect (McGuire, 1961) suggests that if people receive prior exposure to a brief communication that they are then able to refute, they tend to be 'immunized' against a subsequent full-blown presentation of the same argument. The empirical literature in this area suggests that prior exposure to weakened forms of counter-arguments (which often involves a brief reference and then refutation of these arguments) is more effective in bestowing resistance to strong subsequent attacks than is prior presentation of supportive arguments (Lindzey and Aronson, 1969). This finding has clear implications for REBT practice.

Another important finding is that, all other things being equal, when faced with information that opposes important beliefs, people have a tendency, whenever feasible, to invent counter-arguments *on the spot*. By doing so, they are able to prevent their opinions from being unduly influenced and protect their sense of autonomy (Aronson, 1995). The good news is that it is possible to overcome some of this resistance, by somewhat distracting your clients while the dispute is being presented. Through distracting, minds become occupied, thereby preventing clients from thinking up counter-arguments to your disputes. One recommendation to consider is teaching your clients progressive muscle relaxation prior to your challenging their irrational beliefs. After they have mastered the techniques, as you get into disputing irrational beliefs, have clients do the relaxation training so as to occupy their mind and inhibit the construction of counter-arguments.

Festinger's theory of cognitive dissonance

According to the theory of cognitive dissonance, an unpleasant state of tension or dissonance occurs when an individual simultaneously holds two cognitive elements that have psychologically opposite implications (Lindzey and Aronson, 1969). In response to the unpleasant state of tension, people are motivated to reduce it, by doing one of the following: (1) changing one or both cognitions in such a way as to render them more compatible with each other; or (2) adding more cognitions that help bridge the gap between the original cognitions (Aronson, 1995).

The theory of cognitive dissonance predicts that it feels good to have intelligent people on our side and less intelligent individuals on the other side (in terms of endorsement of a particular belief). Therefore, a stupid argument in favor of one's own position arouses some dissonance, because it takes into question the intelligence of the people who agree with it or the general intelligence of the belief. Similarly, a reasonable argument on the other side of the issue also arouses some dissonance because it raises the possibility that the other side (or argument) is right. In response to the dissonance that is aroused, an attempt to *not* think about the arguments, or not to learn them very well, or even to forget them, may result. People may tend to remember plausible arguments agreeing with their own position and the implausible arguments agreeing with the opposing position (Aronson, 1995). In line with this last statement is the phenomenon known as the 'confirmation bias', which refers to our propensity, whenever we hold a particular idea or theory about the world, for ourselves, or others, to search for evidence which supports our view(s) and avoid or disregard the evidence which challenges that theory (Fraser and Burchell, 2001). Clients will frequently present with mounds of evidence supporting their disturbed, dogmatic, illogical beliefs, irrespective of all the evidence that challenges such beliefs.

Following a decision, especially a difficult one that involves a great deal of time or effort, people almost always experience dissonance. This is because the chosen alternative is seldom entirely positive, and the rejected alternatives are rarely completely negative (Aronson, 1995). One way for clients to reduce such dissonance is to seek out exclusively positive information about the decision that they have made. The implication for REBT therapists is to, in session, continually present or bombard clients with information supporting the healthier rational belief. Another consideration to make is having clients do a homework assignment of *referenting*, but a modified version of such. Referenting involves listing the advantages and disadvantages of specific courses of action (Dryden and Neenan, 1996). A modified referenting exercise would involve only listing the advantages of the new rational belief, rather than also listing the disadvantages of the irrational belief. In other words, as a therapist you want to selectively expose clients to the rational belief. Another reason for doing this is because after a decision, people try to gain reassurance that their decisions were wise by seeking information that is certain to be reassuring (Aronson, 1995).

Aronson (1995) reviews cognitive dissonance and discusses an interesting historical reference to make a point. After analyzing the Pentagon papers from the Vietnam War, Ralph White suggested that dissonance prevented the US leaders from seeing information that was discordant with the decisions they had already made. White reported, 'There was a tendency, when actions were out of line with ideas, for decision makers to align their ideas with their actions' (Aronson, 1995, p. 192). It would be useful to learn from this historical reference and apply it to the practice of REBT. Consider having clients, in the *beginning* of therapy, do behavioral assignments against their irrational beliefs. Have your clients *act* how they want to *think*. Another reason for encouraging clients to do this is because often clients are tentative about their own prior beliefs and attitudes and thereby use their observation of the behavior as an indication of what those beliefs are. This is Bem's concept of self-referencing (Aronson, 1995).

Foot-in-the-door technique

When an individual makes a small commitment, it tends to set the stage for larger commitments. The behavior needs to be justified, and in response to this attitudes are changed. This change in attitude affects future decisions and behavior (Aronson, 1995). Expanding this concept to practice with clients, getting the difficult client involved in a much smaller aspect of the alternative belief (i.e. that there is the possibility that a rational alternative even exists) may produce positive results. It should be noted that the smaller aspect has to be so easy that the client will not argue against it. This action serves to commit the client to the belief. Once they are committed, the likelihood of their complying with a larger request in the future increases.

Limitations and recommendations

Much of the social psychology literature, and the psychotherapy literature in general, focuses on the concept of self-esteem. The theory and practice of

Rational Emotive Behavior Therapy disagrees with this concept, and instead argues for Unconditional Self-Acceptance, Unconditional Other-Acceptance (UOA), and Unconditional Life-Acceptance (ULA) (or High Frustration Tolerance). REBT suggests that conditional self-acceptance, or self-esteem, results in people evaluating themselves as a good or worthy person when they perform adequately or do well, and as a bad or unworthy person when they perform inadequately. Feelings of depression often emerge when people fail at significant tasks and/or get rejected by others. Feelings of anxiety may also result for those who perform well, because there is always the possibility that they may not succeed in the future or be accepted by others in the future (Ellis, 2001). If individuals gave themselves USA, received UOA from therapists and family, and had ULA (high frustration tolerance), perhaps some of the aforementioned research findings would be quite different.

The desire for self-justification is an important reason why people who are strongly committed to an attitude on an issue tend to resist any direct attempts to change that attitude. Such people are impenetrable to the disputes you will pose. However, if a person has USA and is given UOA, then the desire for self-justification would not be necessary. As such, individuals may be more willing to relinquish certain self-defeating attitudes and beliefs, and practice alternative, self-preserving ones.

One recommendation for future developments is that REBT practitioners and researchers look more seriously into the empirical findings of the field of social psychology. It was not until Dr Ellis was asked to do a talk on the relationship of Rational Emotive Behavior Therapy to social psychology at the American Psychological Association in 2001 that he was brought up to date with the research findings of social psychology. In his paper, Dr Ellis rightfully points out that so much of his attention has been focused on treating individual clients that he has been distracted from the area of social psychology (Ellis, 2001). Furthermore, REBT theory and practice would benefit from research being conducted utilizing concepts such as Unconditional Self-Acceptance, Unconditional Other-Acceptance, and Unconditional Life-Acceptance. This is because much of the research to date that has been conducted in the field of social psychology has been done with the concept of self-esteem. The field of social psychology might benefit from incorporating USA into its theory and research.

Furthermore, in general, REBT as a theory has not done a very good job of testing its hypotheses and assumptions in empirically valid studies. Although there are a large number of studies that have been conducted examining REBT's efficacy, to date there is a paucity of literature compiling this outcome data. Because REBT has been lacking in this area, and has been more focused on promoting the theory, the relevant findings in not only the field of social psychology, but in others as well, have been, if not ignored, at least not attended to. As a general recommendation, to enhance its theory and practice, REBT might consider reviewing and integrating both theory and findings from other areas of psychology, sociology, and philosophy.

Another limitation of social psychology theory to REBT theory concerns the goal of social psychology. As stated earlier in this chapter, the goal of social psychology is to understand how *most* people act in a given situation, and is not necessarily concerned with the unique personal characteristics of individuals that may cause them to act differently from each other. Although REBT theory rests upon the assumption that practically all people have distinctly innate and socially acquired traits that are irrational, the theory is concerned with the unique belief system, emotional experiences and behavioral patterns of the *individual*. In fact, a common practice among REBT practitioners is the development of individual client schema sheets, both the current irrational schema of the client, as well as the alternative, rational schema sheet. The rationale behind such sheets is to have clients practicing, rehearsing, and incorporating the rational schema into their belief system. If these schema sheets were developed based on the findings of social psychological findings without respecting, acknowledging, and utilizing the client's unique characteristics, they would not only be inapplicable to clients, but also probably ineffective. Rational Emotive Behavior therapists preferably should continue developing such individualized treatment interventions, but may also benefit from examining and applying some of the relevant social psychology findings.

The field of social psychology and REBT have a number of strengths to offer one another. Perhaps a greater understanding of the general tendencies as well as the individual, unique qualities of individuals will result if social psychology and REBT researchers and practitioners look to each other and integrate theory and empirical results.

References

Allport, G.W. (1985) The historical background of social psychology. In G. Lindzey and E. Aronson (eds) *Handbook of Social Psychology*, Vol. 1 (3rd edn, pp. 1–46). New York: Random House.

Aronson, E. (1995) *The Social Animal*. New York: W.H. Freeman.

Aronson, E., Wilson, T.D. and Akert, R.M. (1999) *Social Psychology* (3rd edn). New York: Longman.

Asch, S. (1956) Studies of independence and conformity: I. A minority of one against a unanimous majority, *Psychological Monographs, 70(9)*.

Brehm, J. (1966) *Explorations in Cognitive Reactance*. New York: Academic Press.

Dryden, W. and Neenan, M. (1996) *Dictionary of Rational Emotive Behaviour Therapy*. London: Whurr.

Ellis, A. (1957) *How to Live with a Neurotic: At Home and at Work*. New York: Crown.

Ellis, A. (1958) Rational psychotherapy, *Journal of General Psychology*, *59*, 35–49. Reprinted: New York: Albert Ellis Institute.

Ellis, A. (1962) *Reason and Emotion in Psychotherapy*. Secaucus, NJ: Citadel.

Ellis, A. (1976) The biological basis of human irrationality, *Journal of Individual Psychology*, *32*, 145–168. Reprinted: New York: Albert Ellis Institute.

Ellis, A. (2001) *The Relationship of Rational Emotive Behavior Therapy (REBT) to Social Psychology*. Paper presented at the American Psychological Association Annual Convention, San Francisco, 26 August.

Fraser, C. and Burchell, B. (2001) *Introducing Social Psychology*. Cambridge: Polity Press.

Harris, B. (1986) Reviewing 50 years of the psychology of social issues, *Journal of Social Issues*, *42*, 1–20.

Hovland, C., Harvey, O.J. and Sherif, M. (1957) Assimilation and contrast effects in reaction to communication and attitude change, *Journal of Abnormal and Social Psychology*, *55*, 244–252.

Jones, E.E. (1985) The historical background of social psychology. In G. Lindzey and E. Aronson (eds) *Handbook of Social Psychology*, Vol. 1 (pp. 1–46). New York: Random House.

Lindzey, G. and Aronson, E. (1969) *The Handbook of Social Psychology*, Vol. 3 (2nd edn). Reading, MA: Addison-Wesley.

McGuire, W.J. (1961) Resistance to persuasion confirmed by active and passive prior refutation of the same and alternative counterarguments, *Journal of Abnormal and Social Psychology*, *63*, 326–332.

Milgram, S. (1965) Some conditions of obedience and disobedience to authority, *Human Relations*, *18*, 57–76.

Petty, R.E. and Cacioppo, J.T. (1986) The elaboration likelihood model of persuasion. In L. Berkowitz (ed.) *Advances in Experimental Social Psychology* (pp. 123–205). Hillsdale, NJ: Erlbaum.

Worchel, S., Cooper, J., Goethals, G.R. and Olson, J.M. (2000) *Social Psychology*. Stamford, CT: Wadsworth/Thomson Learning.

Chapter 9

Contributions of General Semantics to REBT theory

Susan Presby Kodish and Bruce I. Kodish

Introduction

Albert Ellis has noted the contributions of General Semantics to his work. "As I think can be seen by many of the parallels between rational-emotive therapy (RET) [REBT] and Korzybski's General Semantics (GS), the two disciplines overlap in many important respects. This is hardly coincidental, as I was distinctly influenced, when formulating and developing RET, by several of Korzybski's ideas" (1993, p. 25). Of what concern is General Semantics to REBT practitioners now, beyond noting its place in the historical antecedents of REBT?

REBT focuses on how internal processes mediate between stimulus and response. More specifically, the activating event, beliefs, consequences (ABCs) sequence serves as the central formulation of both theory and practice. As a focus of interventions, primacy is given to "beliefs" (although interactions among various aspects of human functioning are recognized). Over the years, Ellis and others have expanded on and modified REBT theoretical underpinnings and practice interventions. For example, a long list of irrational beliefs gradually has been reformulated as three branches of one underlying source of irrationality: a *demand* that I, others and the world *must* be the way I want them to be. This ongoing revision shows a recognition that all has not been said and done, and has strengthened the work and helped to keep it alive.

We believe that an understanding of the intricacies of General Semantics has much to contribute in further developing and strengthening REBT theory, and hence practice. In this chapter, we present some basics of General Semantics, including recent theoretical findings regarding these basics. We then spell out some General Semantics techniques derived from these formulations which REBT practitioners can add to their disputing repertoires in order to guide their clients towards better effects in their lives.

We start with a brief overview of this discipline. Those who wish to delve further can consult a range of General Semantics references.[1]

Some basics

General Semantics was formulated as a practical, interdisciplinary philosophy–science of human evaluation by Polish-American scholar and teacher Alfred Korzybski (1879–1950). "Semantics" as used here refers to "evaluation", that is, how and to what effect humans derive and make sense of their experiences. In other words, evaluation as used in General Semantics is similar to, yet broader than, the sum total of the REBT model; it summarizes the whole of human–environment interactions.

While a concern with language appears central to the discipline, General Semantics involves much more than linguistic 'meanings'. Rather it focuses on the neurologically-based organism-as-a-whole-in-an-environment responses *not only* to words and other symbols but to *any* events in terms of the 'meanings', significance, etc., to the individual ([1933] 1994, p. 24).[2] These organism-as-a-whole-in-an-environment responses are not merely verbal, but operate on non-verbal levels; "'happening-meanings' not to be found in dictionaries or books" (Bois, 1996, p. xlii). As noted in REBT theory, they involve your combined 'thinking'–'feeling' (we can talk about 'cognition' and 'emotion' as if they exist separately, but do they in actuality?).

General Semanticists emphasize the inevitable *neurological* aspects of evaluation. Korzybski noted that symbols, words, theories, assumptions, etc., result from nervous system processes. These and other events make a difference to humans by means of their physico-chemical, neurological effects. Indeed, Korzybski coined the terms "neuro-semantic" and "neuro-linguistic" to highlight the major role of these neuro-evaluational, neuro-linguistic factors in ourselves and in the environments (culture, etc.) that we inherit and use.

Time-binding

A concern for human values appears central to General Semantics. In exploring the relations of values to human knowledge, Korzybski proposed the notion of "time-binding" as the basis for his theory (Korzybski, [1921] 1950).

Time-binding involves:

> the characteristic human ability, using language and other symbols, to transmit information across time; the potential for individuals to learn from their own and other people's experiences; the potential for each generation to start where the last generation left off; the potential to become aware of this ability.
>
> (Kodish and Kodish, 2001, p. 213)

The notion of time-binding implies "humans as a *naturally* cooperative class of life" (Pula, 1994, p. xv). From this comes a vision of individual and social ethics noted by Harry Weinberg in his General Semantics classic, *Levels of Knowing and Existence* ([1959] 1973, p. 159):

> Thou shalt not knowingly warp the functioning of any nervous system . . . So act as to make thyself a better time-binder; so act as to enable others to use their time-binding capacities more effectively.

General Semantics thus involves an ethic – positive time-binding – based on our human potential to learn from the past, progress in the present, and contribute to the future. The cooperation inherent in positive time-binding allows us humans to even further develop our time-binding capacities – to become more fully human.[3] We shall see how a fundamental ethic of REBT, unconditional self and other acceptance, is allied with positive time-binding and related aspects of General Semantics.

General Semantics and psychotherapy

The history of the development of General Semantics in the 1920s and 1930s may provide further insight into the relation of the discipline to psychotherapy and, specifically, REBT.

As a veteran of World War I, Korzybski deeply felt the disparities between successful time-binding in regard to narrow, technical developments (e.g. in World War I tools of war) contrasted with the failure of time-binding in broader social/cultural developments (e.g. the use of war to solve human problems). He began to see these extremes of human time-binding behavior as forming a continuum of sanity and insanity.

At one end of this continuum exists "sanity", which he considered human evaluating at its best – exemplified by what scientists and mathematicians do when they are working at their best (if not in the rest of their lives). "Insanity" represents human evaluating at its worst – exemplified by how those confined to mental hospitals approach life. (In the 1920s, Korzybski studied psychiatric cases at St Elizabeths Hospital in Washington DC under the guidance of William Alanson White, MD). Korzybski labeled the so-called 'normal' person hovering between the two extremes "unsane", a term suggested to him by psychiatrist Philip Graven (Korzybski, 1990, p. 162).

Thus, Korzybski treated science and mathematics as forms of human behavior with some possible relevance to healthy human living. Using the methods and results of scientific practice, he derived General Semantics, a teachable, practical system for improving how we function individually and in groups. Some people have found this strange. However, others, like Albert Ellis, have taken seriously Wendell Johnson's contention that

"Korzybski's greatest contribution to our thinking was this proposition, that . . . scientific method[s] be taken out of the laboratory and be put to use in everyday life" (Johnson, 1972, pp. 33–34).

Korzybski called for an "extensional orientation" towards living. This consists of orienting ourselves primarily to non-verbal happenings and 'facts', with the ability to use higher-order verbal approaches as needed. Johnson asserted that such an extensional, scientific approach "reduces essentially to three questions . . . 'What do you mean?' . . . 'How do you know?' and 'What then?'" (1972, p. 37). "I have discovered", he said, "that these three are about the most liberating questions you can imagine" (p. 37).

As noted below, these central, liberating, epistemological questions of GS convey its practical, scientific orientation and may suggest some of its potential for enhancing and advancing positive time-binding efforts; they can be used to enhance psychotherapeutic theory and practice.

Language and behavior

A particular 'holistic' view of language, culture, consciousness and behavior seems central to the applied, evaluational approach of General Semantics. This view, called "linguistic relativity", has a history in western culture going back at least several hundred years to the work of Leibniz, Vico, Hamann, Herder, Kant, von Humboldt and linguistic anthropologists Edward Sapir and Benjamin Lee Whorf, among others (Alford, 1980). In sum, language and culture are understood as unified and inseparable (non-elementalistic) phenomena.

Without denying trans-cultural similarities among humans, the principle of linguistic relativity implies that, as linguistics scholar Penny Lee (1996, p. 87) wrote:

> although all observers may be confronted by the same physical evidence in the form of experiential data and although they may be capable of "externally similar acts of observation" . . . a person's 'picture of the universe' or 'view of the world' differs as a function of the particular language or languages that person knows.

As Korzybski formulated it, the culturally inherited structure of our language, including terminology, grammar, etc., relates to assumptions, premises, implications about the structure of ourselves and the world. "We read unconsciously into the world", Korzybski wrote, "the structure of the language we use" (1994, p. 60).

Despite a decades-long domination of linguistic studies by formal analysts like Noam Chomsky and Steven Pinker, with little or no sympathy for linguistic relativity, there exists renewed and growing interest in this principle and a growing accumulation of scientific evidence that supports it.[4]

The General Semantics view of linguistic relativity appears unique among other versions for two reasons. First, because of its explicit *neurological* emphasis, which views cultures as neuro-evaluational, neuro-linguistic environments. Second, because the work of Korzybski and other General Semanticists focuses quite specifically on applied aspects of this relativity. By becoming more aware of our language and its implicatory structure, we can nudge our orientation in a saner, more 'fact'-based, extensional direction.

In the next section, we illustrate the basic mechanism through which this influence occurs, and its relation to REBT theory. The practical suggestions which follow this provide many neuro-semantic, neuro-linguistic techniques which – if used – can influence perception and behavior in positive directions that enhance REBT practice.

General Semantics theory and its contribution to REBT theory

Three things about Korzybski's General Semantics tend to get stressed by Ellis: overgeneralizing (e.g. use of "all", "everyone"); dichotomizing (either/ or); and E-Prime (English minus all forms of the verb "to be"). Important as these are, they represent only a small part of the General Semantics system. In this section, we present and elaborate on this system, making connections to REBT theory, as a basis for considering how the theory of General Semantics can more broadly inform REBT practice, presented in the next section.

The abstracting process

We start with a model of the neurological abstracting process that incorporates the main components of General Semantics.[5] As you read, contemplate how the following components relate to your own and your clients' lives.

1.   A general plenum of ever-changing, energetic space–time happenings which comprises "all" by definition; the broken outer line indicates that the plenum goes on indefinitely.
2.   Within this plenum, a localized space–time event which comprises the happening of interest at a particular moment.
3.   The immediate nervous impact of the event, as experienced through each individual's senses. At this level, we enter the realm of what Korzybski called "abstracting", the process by which an individual's nervous system transforms sub-microscopic, energetic events into internal non-verbal and verbal experiences. Abstracting occurs on different levels. Each subsequent 'higher' level involves further abstracting from previous

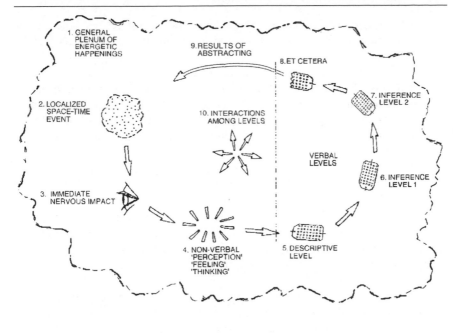

1. GENERAL PLENUM OF ENERGETIC HAPPENINGS

9. RESULTS OF ABSTRACTING

8. ET CETERA

7. INFERENCE LEVEL 2

2. LOCALIZED SPACE-TIME EVENT

10. INTERACTIONS AMONG LEVELS

VERBAL LEVELS

6. INFERENCE LEVEL 1

3. IMMEDIATE NERVOUS IMPACT

4. NON-VERBAL 'PERCEPTION' 'FEELING' 'THINKING'

5. DESCRIPTIVE LEVEL

Abstracting Process

Figure 9.1   Abstracting process.

'lower' levels. At each level, some particulars get left out, while similarities tend to get emphasized. In other words, categories are created and details can be overlooked. Although our discussion of abstracting begins, by convention, with an 'initial' nervous impact, we want to make clear that we *do not* accept a linear causal, stimulus–response view of behavior with an 'initial' stimulus from the environment 'setting off' behavior. In our Korzybskian view, abstracting involves an ongoing, circularly causal, organism–environment transaction guided by the internal processes (including higher-level abstractions such as beliefs, etc.) of an individual adapting the environment to her- or himself.[6]

4. Our individual non-verbal reactions, including 'perception', 'feeling', 'thinking' without words (assumptions, premises, expectations, etc.), etc. At this non-verbal level, we create our experiences of what we call 'objects' from the space–time plenum of events.

5. Our individual first-order use of language in relation to the above. This can include naming and description of observations of any or 'all' of the above. This can be considered the level of statements of 'facts'.

6. Our individual second-order language use in relation to the above. This can be thought of as the first level of stating inferences about what we've abstracted so far.

7. Our individual inferences about our prior inferences and other abstracting; in part this can include generalizations as well as further reacting to reactions.
8. An "et cetera" level, which indicates that we can continue to abstract from our abstractions, theoretically unendingly. The higher levels of abstracting include scientific theories at a date; i.e. our 'knowledge' about the workings of the universe – tested through laboratory experiments and field observations – which comprise what we know about the plenum of sub-microscopic happenings.
9. An arrow returning to the plenum, indicating that the results of our abstracting at a particular time become part of the plenum from which we further abstract.
10. Arrows in several directions moving out from the center of the model, indicating that the various levels of abstracting occur simultaneously and interactively. When we speak about them as if they are separate (elementalism), we introduce an artifact of language.

Language, despite the limitations of the abstracting process, enables us to use our human ability to communicate among ourselves and across generations and to build testable theories that may improve life. We do well, however, to remain conscious of these limitations. One way of expressing a central goal of General Semantics is "consciousness of abstracting". We consider the practical implications and applications of this in the next section.

By viewing abstracting as a mapping process we derive the basic principles of General Semantics: *A map is not the territory. A map is not all of the territory. A map is self-reflexive.* These non-Aristotelian premises (going beyond but incorporating Aristotelian logic and viewpoints) represent a non-absolutistic, process orientation which recognizes individuality of particular conditions and purposes, etc. in daily life (Berman, 1989, p. 189). With it we adopt an attitude of generalized uncertainty while still allowing for a limited definiteness open to revision.

Now, let's consider further the map–territory premises. Immersed in, and comprised of a sub-atomic, energetic process of ongoing flux and change, we use our senses to abstract what becomes our individual experience of 'reality'. So even at a non-verbal, "unspeakable", sensory level, we have created perceptual maps that are not the sub-atomic territory. Thus General Semantics falls within the realm of constructivist theories.[7]

These perceptual maps inevitably are not identical to that presumed territory and necessarily leave out aspects of it, due to human biological limitations and our personal physical limitations and histories. Our perceptions form our non-verbal worlds.

On the verbal levels, we then can talk about our non-verbal experiences. However, our words cannot capture all of those perceptual experiences, and cannot fully express the non-separable, "un-speakable" aspects of non-verbal sensing, feeling, thinking and behaving. We can learn how to make our language more closely fit our non-verbal reality, but our word maps are not the non-verbal 'reality' they represent, nor can we ever completely map it with words.

Further, our nervous systems allow us to self-reflexively create verbal maps of our verbal maps, potentially unendingly. We can spin ever-more-general categories, hypotheses, etc., for better and worse. These higher-level verbalizations influence our perceptions and non-verbal experiences in an ongoing way. In addition, our maps can be seen as mappings of our own nervous system processes along with whatever else we're mapping.

People can orient themselves primarily by means of definitions and higher-order verbalizations. We refer to this as an "intensional orientation". Nigh all of us have probably had experience with clients who prefer to talk abstractly, grandly, endlessly in lieu of practicing new and different behaviors.

In contrast to this, with an "extensional orientation" (discussed previously) we can use higher-order categories, generalizations and hypotheses to our benefit, while orientating ourselves primarily to "facts" and behavior, i.e. to our non-verbal experiences. This enables us both to develop sound theories and live our daily lives on a sound factual basis.

Much of General Semantics involves learning how to live extensionally, how to map more accurately, use language more productively than destructively, and adjust to ongoing flux and change. For example, Korzybski invented terminology and techniques to help achieve more accurate mappings. Terms such as "organism-as-a-whole-in-an-environment" can help you to maintain something of a sense of process when you translate your perceptual experiences into necessarily static language. Using General Semantics, you can also pay attention to your non-verbal sensing, non-verbal assumptions, etc. We develop these aspects further below.

What General Semantics theory suggests for REBT theory

A few words about our perspective on General Semantics and REBT: we both have been studying, practicing, writing about and teaching General Semantics for many years. We also both have had extensive experience with REBT, Susan as an REBT psychotherapy practitioner (now coach) and Bruce in relation to his work as a physical therapist (B. Kodish, 2001, pp. 140–142). We have used both disciplines to improve our own functioning. We consider REBT one of the most sound and effective forms of therapy available, particularly since useful techniques from other approaches can be adapted and used within its overarching model. We have also found that General Semantics has provided us with important additional perspectives and techniques.

So now let's consider what General Semantics theory suggests for REBT theory. We approach this from the perspective of the abstracting process model presented above, in conjunction with REBT's ABC model.

Activating events provide the customary starting point for REBT theory. What do we mean by "activating event"? A person 'encounters' a certain event which sets off a series of reactions, etc. But is the activating event a single entity? From a General Semantics perspective, no. Rather, the A is comprised of, at the least, a sequence involving the immediate nervous impact of the sub-microscopic event plus initial non-verbal, and even verbal, transactions. This suggests that intervening at these initial levels of abstracting may help people to open up possibilities for experiencing a so-called 'single' activating event in a variety of ways.

Consequences are what people generally think of as their problem. These can be emotional, relational, and/or behavioral, as formulated by the person. As a form of psychotherapy, REBT theory tends to stress the emotional, while allowing for other consequences. The theory allows for reacting to reactions, one of its major strengths. This is consistent with a General Semantics perspective. But General Semantics theory takes the process further, since in GS we more explicitly formulate and use levels of abstracting as a theoretically unending, self-reflexive "chain reaction". Delineating this process allows for becoming more conscious of it at many levels, opening up possibilities for avoiding and ameliorating problems which emerge from not clearly separating each level from prior and subsequent ones.

In REBT, beliefs are viewed as the intermediary between A and C, that is, as the cause of C. This core Ellis formulation, seemingly simple, yet deeply profound, gives people with varying intellectual, educational and emotional strengths and detriments, an opportunity to gain control over their reactions. These beliefs are viewed as more and less rational, more and less fact-based, leading to more and less functional consequences. They are considered to include both basic assumptions and self-talk.

In General Semantics we view what comprises the REBT B as an even more complex entity, occurring at multiple levels. Returning to the abstracting process model, we note that beliefs involve both non-verbal and verbal levels. They influence our perceptions, our non-verbal initial assuming–sensing–feeling–thinking at a given moment, and our verbal behavior at descriptive and inferential levels. Further, our beliefs are related to our individual and cultural generalizations and other higher-order theories. Each of these aspects provides an explicit intervention point.

Let's consider levels of abstracting from the perspective of language use. As amply noted in REBT theory, how we talk to ourselves has profound effects on our functioning. In General Semantics we pay particular attention to our ability to use and misuse language.

A concern for General Semanticists is the relations among the verbal levels and how these levels relate to our non-verbal experiences. Distinguishing among these levels seems especially important for answering the REBT question, "Where is the evidence?" In General Semantics, sharply distinguishing between statements of fact and statements of inference goes a long way towards being able to answer this and other questions. Statements of fact are seen as residing, verbally, at the descriptive level of the abstracting process model; all verbalizations beyond this involve inferences. Learning how to apply this distinction has a special place in General Semantics training.[8]

How about the self-reflexive aspect of the General Semantics view of abstracting? This is represented in REBT theory in the explicit way in which Ellis and others have noted the importance of reacting to reactions in creating dysfunction and resolving it. This is broadened in General Semantics by considering every aspect of our functioning as representing an individual "take" on the world. What I see isn't what's "out there", nor is it what you see. What I take as givens aren't what you take as givens; my conclusions are not the necessary and sufficient ones for everyone, etc.

To summarize, General Semantics theory enhances REBT theory by dealing more explicitly with the abstracting process which underlies the ABCs. This can lead to a more nuanced practice, with options that are consistent with the overarching REBT theory.

How General Semantics can inform REBT practice

General Semanticists have derived from General Semantics theory, and incorporated from other approaches, many ways to move from unsanity to sanity. These involve perceptual, other non-verbal, and verbal techniques congruent with the theory and practice of REBT. REBT practitioners can use these General Semantics techniques to enhance their repertoires to help their clients dispute and therefore attain positive new effects in their lives. We suggest that you exemplify these techniques by using them when you interact with clients, and explicitly teach them to clients for their own use.

Perception

Some aspects of the nature of perception – how we construct what becomes our 'reality' – seem of particular concern for our work with clients. We each perceive differently, as noted above, influenced by our individual and species characteristics. Relevant individual differences can be such factors as height and acuity of senses, as well as basic assumptions and premises. When understood and accepted, this notion promotes a "to-me-ness" attitude that can improve relationships – reduce arguments, encourage openness to the view of others, etc. It can also contribute to a celebration of uniqueness and unconditional self and other acceptance.

How can we convey information about perception to our clients? We often use experiments which demonstrate how we each see differently: for example, individual differences in the construction of multiple colors from a seemingly black and white figure (Gregory, 1987). Especially powerful with a group, these can also be done with one person.

More simply, note the way we create a "disc" when viewing a fan in motion, which when still, appears as individual blades. Thusly, we create 'objects' from the sub-microscopic plenum of events (Korzybski, 1994, pp. 382–383).

Another approach is to introduce them to so-called "optical illusions" (Block and Yuker, 1992). These demonstrate how our 'perception', as a form of non-verbal abstracting, consists of our active attempts to construct a world out of cues we receive (Hoffman, 1998). These attempts are based on past abstracting, which includes assumptions, inferences and expectations, both verbal and non-verbal.

In a sense, we make 'bets' about what is going on. These perceptual 'bets', hypotheses or inferences, are made unconsciously in fractions of seconds and give us some predictability in dealing with the incomplete information that our senses provide. An awareness of this process can help your clients avoid absolutistic reliance on what they perceive; hence can help them to reduce error and argument.

Non-verbal awareness

We live and experience our lives on the silent, non-verbal level of existence, although it seems that we are endlessly talking to ourselves. (For the moment we are putting aside the 'fact' that our words also exist in some sense on the silent level.) This self-talk, if intensional, can prevent us from functioning well. If we talk to ourselves extensionally, we can help ourselves to get in better touch with what is happening within and around us.

Eventually, however, a large part of living extensionally involves learning to turn down and turn off the volume of the words inside our heads. So an important part of General Semantics training involves practice looking, listening, tasting, 'feeling', etc., at the silent, unspeakable level. We want to convey an attitude towards living that involves awareness of ourselves as organisms-as-wholes-in-environments.

As human evaluators we mainly transact with words, symbols and other events in terms of their significance or 'meanings' to us. The 'meanings' that we make, our evaluations, are not just verbal. What do you do when you walk by a bakery? Observe what other people do. What non-verbal differences can you note between walking by a bakery and walking by a drug store, for example?

Facial expression, tone of voice, 'body' posture, all involve 'meanings' beyond the words that we hear. Such so-called 'body' language expresses the non-verbal thinking–feeling of each of us. These non-verbal behaviors not only convey 'meanings' to others, but to ourselves as well. You not only smile with happiness, but can create a good mood by smiling.

By learning how to contemplate non-verbally, your clients can prepare themselves to behave extensionally. Freeing themselves as much as possible from their beliefs about what they 'should' see, they can become better observers as they test their higher-order abstractions.

Perhaps few of us are concerned, as was Korzybski, with building general systems of evaluation. However, most of us are concerned with building better ways of evaluating, with improving the quality of our lives. We often recognize that this quality involves some sense of a vast 'something' that we cannot put into words but that somehow connects us with our environments.

In General Semantics, we seek to encourage such contemplation and so greater creativity, aesthetic appreciation, sense of well-being, communication, etc. We also seek to connect such contemplation with our higher-order verbal evaluating, in recognition of the inevitable connections between silent-level and verbal-level functioning. We seek, as expressed by Charlotte Schuchardt Read, "To *feel* ourselves as time-binders, considering 'time-binding' not just intellectually but as participating in the human experience of millenniums" (1965/1966, p. 50).

Many disciplines and philosophies touch on this. For example, Zen practices and other forms of meditation, hypnosis, 'healing' practices, etc., point people towards experiencing such connections. In General Semantics, we particularly use sensory awareness.[9] REBT therapists would do well to experiment with, and evaluate the results of, incorporating non-verbal techniques in their work.

Personal scientists

General Semantics, as an *applied* theory of knowledge (epistemology), focuses on helping people to become personal scientists, also a concern of REBT (Ellis, 1988, p. 23). We don't need to have laboratories or degrees in scientific studies to improve how we observe, form hypotheses, and, most especially, check them out; in other words, how we challenge our beliefs, our assumptions, with evidence.

When we have a problem, bump our noses against some questionable assumption(s), we can make a decision to follow steps used by scientists in formulating, checking and revising hypotheses about such usually subconscious notions.[10] These steps can be summarized by the following already noted questions, which we do well to ask when we want to use science as an approach for everyday life: What do I (and you) mean? How do I (and you) know? What then?[11]

What then? Elaborate on this approach with your clients, assign homework based on it, and find out how this works for both you and your clients.

Personal time-binding

REBT practitioners are aware of how frequently we talk to ourselves. We can use this internal chatter for worse and better. When we label ourselves "stupid" or similar negative higher-order abstractions, we create a negative time-binding environment for ourselves. When we make perfectionistic demands on ourselves, unconditionally and absolutistically telling ourselves what we "must" do, as Ellis emphasizes throughout his writings, we diminish our chances of fully realizing our potentialities. Instead, we can extensionalize our internal chatter, just as we extensionalize our talk with others. For example, we may use conditional "shoulds", such as "If I want good relationships, I should accept other people and take responsibility for how I act."

We can not only take responsibility for our behavior, but take responsibility for treating ourselves well. Thus, your clients can learn how to use their time-binding capacities most effectively by cooperating with themselves – unconditional self-acceptance.

Part of time-binding involves each of us learning from ourselves, learning how to make the most of our individual experiences. We refer to this as personal time-binding. With personal time-binding, we recognize that we communicate with ourselves as well as with others. We also recognize that each one of us can focus on the personal legacy we want to leave for future generations.

This does not have to involve money, as is frequently believed. Similarly, it does not have to involve writing books or developing scientific theories. Rather, having decided what results you want to perceive, you can decide to act in such a way in your daily life that you bring them about. Your clients can decide to contribute to their own well-being, as well as that of others; the effects can reverberate in untold ways into the future.

English minus absolutisms (EMA)

Ellis has written some of his books in E-Prime, English minus the use of the verb "to be". While many general semanticists find this useful as a practice exercise, we also consider it unnecessarily limiting to use all of the time.

We advocate, as did Korzybski, avoiding the "'is' of identity" (he is a therapist) and the "'is' of predication" (she is narcissistic). This helps us to avoid identifying individuals with linguistic categories and qualities we ascribe. In addition, as a broader alternative, we espouse an approach to language use that General Semanticist and linguistics scholar Allen Walker Read has formulated and labeled EMA, short for English Minus Absolutisms.

Even while remaining aware that the 'meanings' of words are in us, we do well to eschew certain words which seem to carry an absolutistic baggage inappropriate for life in a process world. According to Read, "When we find ourselves using the very common absolutisms such as *always, never, forever, eternity, pure, final, ultimate,* and so on, we could say to ourselves, was that term necessary? Could we frame our sentence in some other way?" (1985, pp. 11–12).

Using the whole system of General Semantics will tend to change the structure of your language towards EMA. By explicitly altering the structure of your language to avoid absolutisms, you can gradually nudge yourself, including your non-verbal behavior, to function less dogmatically and more tentatively, as befits a fallible human being. This can have very positive effects on your relationships. Susan finds that one of the most powerful things she can do in her coaching work is to introduce EMA to clients and encourage them to use it. Dramatic positive improvements in relationships are often reported at the next session.

Indexing

The use of indexing comes from mathematics, where variables are given subscripts to specify them, for example x_1, x_2, x_3, etc. In our everyday language, the variables we're concerned with consist of the words we use. We consider any statement at least somewhat indeterminate or 'meaningless' in an extensional sense until we specify or index our terms. Our word categories lead us to focus on similarities rather than differences. Necessary and useful as this seems, however, no two individual people or things in any particular category are ever exactly the 'same' in all aspects. No matter how similar they seem, differences remain. REBT practitioner$_1$ is not REBT practitioner$_2$. Seemingly depressed client$_1$ is not seemingly depressed client$_2$.

By using indexes, you remind yourself of the important differences among individual people, 'objects', events, etc. Almost automatically you can avoid identifying your categorial map with the individuals you're categorizing. This helps you to avoid identifying your words with your non-verbal experiences and the non-verbal territory. While maintaining links to other individuals in a category, indexing gives each individual a unique separate sub-category.

How will we respond to individual humans if we continually index to remind ourselves that, for example, 'psychoanalyst'$_1$ is not 'psychoanalyst'$_2$, 'insurance salesperson'$_1$ is not 'insurance salesperson'$_2$? Perhaps we need not only less discrimination against individuals because of the categories we put them in, but also more discrimination among individuals by noticing how they differ. For example, clients who say, with despair, that "I'm just like my mother", can be helped by being led to consider the differences between them.

You can also use indexes to help you to evaluate in terms of continuums or degrees. Without indexes it seems easy to say, "You either feel depression, anxiety, etc., or you don't". Placing "depression" and "anxiety" on continuums, as often suggested in psychology rating scales, you can index them, say with 0 indicating no pain or anxiety and 10 indicating the maximum imaginable. In this way, you can more realistically note the degree nature of these variables. You can begin to notice and encourage degrees of improvement in yourself and others rather than expect instantaneous, all-or-nothing results.

In addition, you can use indexes to enhance how you deal with second-order problems. You can talk about anxiety$_2$ about anxiety$_1$, fear$_2$ of fear$_1$, enjoyment$_2$ of enjoyment$_1$, hate$_2$ of hate$_1$, etc.

Dating

With indexing we have a way of indicating differences among individuals, matters of degree, levels of abstraction, and environmental conditions. We can easily recognize a need for some way of indicating (indexing) differences over 'time' when we look in the mirror. When our clothes are altered, we want new measurements to be taken each time. Even more importantly, we want to take into account differences over time in our relationships, work situations, etc., so that we can make the most useful adjustments to changing circumstances.

To make our words and statements – our evaluations – more extensional in regard to the time factor, in a process world of 'change', General Semanticists advocate dating, applying a date to the terms we use and statements we make. A client can get "unstuck" from old patterns by recognizing that she/he$_{2001}$ is not the same as she/he$_{1970}$, for example.

Dating can help you to realize that no particular individual 'is' exactly the 'same' from moment to moment. You today are not you 10 years ago. In what ways have you changed? Some individuals, like a good tailor, seem 'naturally' more extensional and seem more likely to take the time factor into account. Most of us, including your clients, need the reminding that dating our terms and statements gives us.

Non-allness

Here we discuss several aspects of changing language use to support a multi-valued, rather than an either–or, orientation. How can you help clients take into account that their maps do not represent all of the territory, their maps do not necessarily match the maps of others? How can you help them to open themselves to a variety of alternatives when solving problems?

An extension of EMA involves moving away from such phrases as "'the' 'best' way" and towards "a better way" or "some better ways" to do something. Talking about "'the' solution" rather than "a solution" or "some solutions" contains a hidden assumption of absolutism or allness, that this is the only way, period! Using *a, an,* or *some*, rather than *the*, can help you to look for causes and multiple factors rather than 'the cause' and single factors.

Qualifying phrases that specify the situation under which you are making a statement, and that acknowledge your role as evaluator, allow you to make quite definite statements extensionally. Such phrases as *as far as I know, under these circumstances* and *to me* can help you to qualify and limit what might otherwise sound like over-generalizations. Using phrases such as *up to a point* and *to a degree* can help nudge you away from either–or evaluating.

Lotfi A. Zadeh, a professor of Electrical Engineering, developed (1995) what he calls "fuzzy logic", a multi-valued approach to engineering which has enabled the production of ever more complex, condition-sensitive equipment of various sorts. General Semantics can be seen as a methodology for the daily application of "fuzzy logic"; what has been found so effective in the engineering world can be applied usefully to everyday life. How can we best deal with a whole range of possibilities in between all-or-nothing, either–or choices? First, by recognizing that they exist; then, by delineating what can be found in the shades of gray between black and white. In this way, we give up false expectations for precision and certainty and gain greater relevance, accuracy and reliability. We recognize that we can have degrees of knowledge, of information, of success.

What kinds of situations might those concerned with REBT encounter? An example from Susan's practice involves a man and woman who are married. Let's consider the question: To what extent are they a "couple"? They were approaching a visit to her parents' home, usually a tense situation. Susan asked them to describe what had happened in the past. As they talked, she noticed that the woman seemed so pulled toward her family that the man seemed peripheral. In this situation they were not functioning as a couple, even though by virtue of being married they had assumed this status. Susan helped them to develop strategies which involved them working together during the visit. On returning, they reported great improvement. They now seemed a couple in her parents' home.

In relationships, you may find it useful to recognize when you've put yourself or others into a certain category, like couple or friend, assumed some definite non-variable definition and meaning for this category and then bumped into some problems. These problems may be partly created by your assumptions about the meaning and definition. By recognizing degrees of 'coupleness', of 'friendness', etc., you can avoid some difficulties.

Problems often can be ameliorated by viewing such areas of life as ethnicity, conception, dying, sexual orientation, disability, etc., as matters of degree. You're not either totally in control or not responsible, totally well or disabled, etc. The techniques of General Semantics presented in this chapter and elsewhere can be taught to clients in order to help them deal with the complex, fuzzy middle-ground (Pula, 1998; Kodish and Kodish, 1995).

"Et cetera" (etc.) has a prominent place in General Semantics. The term comes from the Latin for "and other things". Looking for and enumerating examples when we speak and write helps us get extensional about our higher-order abstractions. Explicitly using "etc." helps us to remember that, even after we've done this, we haven't said it all. When we thus have an et cetera or non-allness attitude, we ask ourselves: What might I have left out? What else? What other effects does this have, etc.? It seems useful to us to remember "etc." whenever we see a period, encouraging ourselves to move from a "period and stop" attitude and towards a "comma and more" attitude.

IFD disease

Our clients frequently seem caught in what Wendell Johnson called 'IFD disease': idealization, which leads to frustration, which leads to demoralization (depression) (1989, pp. 14–15). Idealization can be viewed as synonymous with perfectionism, an important focus in REBT. In General Semantics we focus specifically on the IFD sequence as part of helping ourselves and others move from action-stopping idealization to change-promoting extensionalized goals, etc.

For example, many clients often set goals phrased as higher-order abstractions, such as "I want to be a success", or "I want to be happy". Phrased in this way as absolutes, these goals seem unattainable; how would you know where to begin and how would you know when you got 'there'? As phrased, they function as terms which suggest opposites, in an either–or way. Either I'm a 'success' or a 'failure'; either I'm 'happy' or 'unhappy'.

Such clients can help themselves by applying various extensional techniques to these terms (and goals). Thus, you can find less absolutistic terms to describe your wishes, eliminate the "'ises' of identity and predication", index and date 'success', acknowledge that individuals create their own definitions of goals and can re-evaluate them, etc.

Instead of "I want to be a 'success'" you might say, "I want to achieve such-and-such a result; I will follow these steps, starting on these dates, re-evaluating on this date", etc. With 'concrete', non-absolutistic goals, you can evaluate each step as you take it. At any point, then, you're less likely to evaluate yourself as a 'failure'; rather, you might say, "I'm not doing as well at step four as I'd like. What can I do differently?"

Extensionalizing leads to an emphasis on *doing* rather than on being; on *using* and *evaluating* what you know, not just collecting information. We find that this change in emphasis leads to much improvement in people's lives.

Implications for theory, therapy and the future

Ellis has written, "[REBT] parallels much of the thinking of the General Semanticists. But it also provides a detailed technique of psychotherapy which is so far absent among followers of Korzybski" (Ellis, 1962, p. 328).[12] As we have noted here, we agree about these parallels and therefore we don't consider General Semantics to conflict with REBT.

However, some practitioners may find that some of our suggestions take them quite far outside of their accustomed ways of working. REBT, in its most pristine form, has seemed largely word-based. We have presented some techniques which involve non-verbal experiments (although therapists would embed them in verbal preliminaries and follow-ups). For example, perceptual demonstrations involve more than just a dialogue between client and therapist. Similarly, sensory awareness and other non-verbal work shifts the focus away from words. That's the point of doing it!

We see General Semantics and REBT as largely educational. This perspective is shared by Ellis and other REBT practitioners, as exemplified by The Living School, the Albert Ellis Institute's former school for children. However, therapists vary in their degree of willingness to "teach" clients as part of doing therapy and counseling; adding General Semantics techniques involves additional "teaching".

Thus, we envision some stretching and attendant discomfort for some practitioners. However, we believe that both clients and therapists will be rewarded with positive effects.

Integrating General Semantics into REBT theory, hence practice, may require some explicit focus on General Semantics in REBT training programs and/or attendance at General Semantics seminars.[13] Although we recognize that this may add to an already-full training sequence, we also consider this training worthwhile.

Such integration will involve more explicit recognition in REBT theory of organism-as-a-whole-in-an-environment components and interactions; in other words, the theory will explicitly be broadened. (We say "explicitly" because Ellis makes clear in his writings that he recognizes these components and interactions.) How this will affect ongoing theory and practice remains a question to be explored.

Let's return to the notion of education. REBT may be and stay "marginalized" within the fields of psychotherapy and counseling and, more specifically, within the general cognitive behavior field (*Journal of Rational-Emotive & Cognitive-Behavior Therapy*, Spring 2001). However, because of their deeply philosophical and teachable nature, both General Semantics and REBT suggest ways of developing and promoting sanity outside of the therapy room. We've already mentioned The Living School. General Semantics and REBT teaching materials for classroom, parental and children's use have been developed. How might these be incorporated into school programs? What other applications are possible, in other areas of life?

An indication of such applications can be found in the Table of Contents of *Developing Sanity in Human Affairs*, the papers from the 1995 Eleventh International Interdisciplinary Conference on General Semantics (Kodish and Holston, 1998). Topics on General Semantics applications and research include: critical thinking, cultural diversity, violence, the language of medical practice, assisted suicide, media literacy, news media ethics, the work of drug prevention counselors, and the effects of TV commercials on children in schools.

Our own work also illustrates applications that go "outside the box". Bruce combines General Semantics, an REB-orientation and physical therapy techniques in working with clients to ameliorate and prevent back and other pain problems (B. Kodish, 2001). In her personal coaching practice, Susan uses what she calls REB-Coaching, which includes General Semantics.[14]

Therapists and others often speak of prevention – a worthwhile goal. Can we take the notion of prevention even further than "the absence of pathology" and into considerations of "full humanness"? What kinds of possibilities might emerge as REBT and General Semantics "teachers" combine their contributions towards positive time-binding as they work with their clients, speak, write, and otherwise live their lives?

In his article "Can we develop a worldwide *extensional* ethic?" Kenneth L. Baldwin (1998, p. 425) suggested what such full humanness might look like in terms of what he called an "extensional ethic":

> If we humans choose to do so, we can develop an extensional ethic here on earth, an ethic built on the facts of human experience rather than words passed down from heaven . . . It insists that we, the language-using species, communicate truthfully and factually with each other about our experienced reality so that we don't destroy ourselves with mutual suspicion and adversarial struggles.

Can we move significantly towards this vision? As Baldwin (p. 422) put it:

> I think the answer to the question posed by the title of my paper is a conditional "yes" – yes, we can develop a worldwide *extensional* ethic – *if* general semanticists, humanists, and scientists work persistently to promote a fact-based extensional orientation directly amongst *peers*, without wasting our or their efforts on high-level abstractions like "family values" or "this society". Whether we *will* develop an extensional ethic is another question. If we ourselves get caught up in abstractions without facts, in either–or judgements or naming and

blaming games, we will be unable to teach and model the kind of fact-related thinking needed to make success more likely.

Notes

1 See, among others: Alfred Korzybski's works, *Manhood of Humanity* ([1921] 1950), *Science and Sanity* ([1933] 1994), *Collected Writings* (1990); Susan Presby Kodish and Bruce I. Kodish, *Drive Yourself Sane: Using the Uncommon Sense of General Semantics* (2001); Wendell Johnson, *People in Quandaries* ([1946] 1989); *General Semantics Bulletin*; *ETC.*; numerous articles at the Institute of General Semantics website, www.general-semantics.org, and the International Society for General Semantics website, www.generalsemantics.org.

2 Herein, we follow the usage that applies double quotes to indicate both direct quotes and terms or phrases used by someone but not necessarily indicating a direct quote, and single quotes to indicate a quotation within a quotation. We also use single quotes to mark off terms and phrases which seem in varying degrees misleading. These "safety devices" alert readers to take care when using terms such as 'semantics', 'meaning', etc. They also mark off terms used metaphorically or playfully. The use of hyphens, as in the term "organism-as-a-whole-in-an-environment" provides another linguistic safety device. Connecting the terms with a hyphen creates a new "non-elementalistic term" which can help to emphasize how the separate words refer to inseparable non-verbal events.

3 See Abraham Maslow's *Toward a Psychology of Being* (1968). He came to prefer the term "full humanness" over "self-actualization" because many people misunderstood and misused the latter, and it became associated with self-indulgence. For Maslow, and from a General Semantics perspective, full humanness involves not only developing our idiosyncratic potentials (self), but our cultural potentials – our ability to contribute to world betterment.

4 Suzette Haden Elgin's book, *The Language Imperative* (2000), provides a readable entry into issues surrounding linguistic relativity, especially in relation to multilingualism. See Dan Alford's website, http://sunflower.com/~dewatson/alfordIndex.htm and Penny Lee's book *The Whorf Theory Complex: A Critical Reconstruction* (1996) for more extensive, scholarly treatments of linguistic relativity and Whorf's work. *Evidence for Linguistic Relativity* (Niemeier and Dirven, eds) and *Explorations in Linguistic Relativity* (Pütz and Verspoor, eds) indicate some of the accumulated evidence for the linguistic relativity principle. Related developments by Sydney M. Lamb and others in "neurocognitive linguistics" uphold Korzybski's vision and Whorf's presentiments of the importance of neuro-linguistic research in this area.

5 This model combines two previous ones developed by Korzybski: the Structural Differential and Process of Abstracting models (see *Drive Yourself Sane* – Kodish and Kodish (2001) – for further discussion of these) with modifications by us to emphasize interactivity and feedback loops.

6 In the 1940s, Korzybski quickly saw that the new science of cybernetics provided a framework for talking about the cyclic process of abstracting that he had previously described. In recent years, feedback control mechanisms have been most comprehensively applied to human behavior in the Perceptual Control Theory (PCT) of William T. Powers and associates. This important work supports the approaches developed by Korzybski and Ellis by providing an explicit and exact basic theory which views "behavior [as] the process by which we act on the world to control perceptions that matter to us" (Powers, 1998, p. 17).

See Cziko (2000), Marken (1992), the PCT website: www.ed.uiuc.edu/csg. See also *Back Pain Solutions* by Bruce I. Kodish (2001), which presents a specific application of PCT to a clinical problem.

7 "Modern constructivism examines those processes of perception, behavior, and communication which we human beings use to *create* our individual, social, scientific, and ideological realities, instead of *finding* them ready-made in the outside world, as we all naively assume" (Watzlawick, 1990, p. 132).

8 See Sanford Berman's *Why Do We Jump to Conclusions?* (1969); Irving Lee's *Language Habits in Human Affairs* (1994), Chapter 9: Descriptions and inferences; and William V. Haney's *Communication and Interpersonal Relations* (1986), Chapter 8: The inference–observation confusion. Also see Haney's *Uncritical Inference Test*, a valuable learning aid for exploring this distinction, available from the International Society for General Semantics, Box 728 Concord, CA 94522; phone: 925-798-0311; fax: 925-798-0312; e-mail: isgs@generalsemantics.org; website: www.generalsemantics.org.

9 See Charles Brooks, *Sensory Awareness* (1974); also the Sensory Awareness Foundation website: www.sensoryawareness.org.

10 Elaborated in *Drive Yourself Sane* (Kodish and Kodish, 2001).

11 Modified from Johnson (1972, p. 38).

12 Actually, General Semanticists have made contributions to psychotherapy theory and practice from Korzybski's time to the present. See Baldwin (1997), Benoit (1993), Caro et al. (1993), and Presby (1982) for relatively recent examples of psychotherapy approaches developed by General Semanticists.

13 The Institute of General Semantics sponsors one-day, weekend and week-long basic seminars, as well as advanced training seminars on particular topics. Contact information: Martha Santer, Institute of General Semantics, 86 85th Street, Brooklyn, NY 11209-4208; phone: 718-921-7093; fax: 718-921-4276; e-mail: Institute@General-Semantics.org; website: www.general-semantics.org.

14 Discussed in her article 'Rational emotive behavior coaching' (2001).

Bibliography

Alford, Dan (1980) A hidden cycle in the history of linguistics, *Phoenix*, 4, numbers 1 and 2. Available at http://sunflower.com/~dewatson/dma-2.htm.

Baldwin, Kenneth L. (1997) *Stop Hurtful Words and Harmful Habits: A Life Therapy Guide to Personal Growth*. Highland City, FL: Rainbow Books.

Baldwin, Kenneth L. (1998) Can we develop a worldwide extensional ethic? In Susan Presby Kodish and Robert P. Holston (eds) *Developing Sanity in Human Affairs* (Contributions to the Study of Mass Media and Communications, 54), pp. 420–426. Westport, CT: Greenwood Press.

Benoit, Dominique (1993) General semantics and psychotherapy, *General Semantics Bulletin*, 57, 52–64.

Berman, Sanford I. (1969) *Why Do We Jump to Conclusions?* Concord, CA: International Society for General Semantics.

Berman, Sanford I. (1989) *Logic and General Semantics: Writings of Oliver L. Reiser and Others*. San Francisco, CA: International Society for General Semantics.

Block, J. Richard and Yuker, Harold E. (1992) *Can You Believe Your Eyes? Over 250 Illusions and Other Visual Oddities*. New York: Brunner/Mazel.

Bois, J. Samuel with Foreword by Gary David (ed.) (1996) *The Art of Awareness: A*

Handbook on Epistemics and General Semantics (4th edn). Santa Monica, CA: Continuum Press.

Brooks, Charles V.W. (1974) *Sensory Awareness: The Rediscovery of Experiencing.* New York: Viking Press.

Caro, Isabel, Ballestar, Carolina and Alarcon, Cristina (1993) A therapeutic use of general semantics: the development of the cognitive therapy of evaluation, *General Semantics Bulletin, 57*, 31–51.

Cziko, Gary (2000) *The Things We Do: Using the Lessons of Bernard and Darwin to Understand the What, How, and Why of Our Behavior.* Cambridge, MA: MIT Press.

Elgin, Suzette Haden (2000) *The Language Imperative.* Cambridge, MA: Perseus.

Ellis, Albert (1962, 1977) *Reason and Emotion in Psychotherapy.* Secaucus, NJ: Citadel Press.

Ellis, Albert (1988) *How to Stubbornly Refuse to Make Yourself Miserable about Anything – Yes Anything!* Secaucus, NJ: Lyle Stuart.

Ellis, Albert (1993) General semantics and rational-emotive therapy. Alfred Korzybski Memorial Lecture 1991. *General Semantics Bulletin, 58*, 12–28.

Ellis, Albert (1996) *Better, Deeper, and More Enduring Brief Therapy: The Rational Emotive Behavior Therapy Approach.* New York: Brunner/Mazel.

Gregory, Richard L. (1987) Benham's Top. In R.L. Gregory (ed.) *The Oxford Companion to the Mind* with the assistance of O.L. Zangwill, pp. 78–79. New York: Oxford University Press.

Haney, William V. (1986) *Communication and Interpersonal Relations: Text and Cases* (5th edn). The Irwin Series in Management and the Behavioral Sciences. Homewood, IL: Irwin.

Hoffman, Donald D. (1998) *Visual Intelligence: How We Create What We See.* New York: Norton.

Johnson, Wendell ([1946] 1989) *People in Quandaries.* San Francisco, CA: International Society for General Semantics.

Johnson, Wendell with Dorothy Moeller (1972) *Living with Change: The Semantics of Coping.* New York: Harper and Row.

Journal of Rational-Emotive & Cognitive-Behavior Therapy (2001), *19*, Spring, 1.

Kodish, Bruce (2001) *Back Pain Solutions: How to Help Yourself with Posture-Movement Therapy and Education.* Pasadena, CA: Extensional Publishing.

Kodish, Susan Presby (2001) Rational emotive behavior coaching, *Journal of Rational-Emotion & Cognitive Behavior Therapy.*

Kodish, Susan Presby and Holston, Robert P. (eds) (1998) *Developing Sanity in Human Affairs* (Contributions to the Study of Mass Media and Communications, 54). Westport, CT: Greenwood Press.

Kodish, Susan Presby and Kodish, Bruce I. (1995) Fuzzy logic and general semantics in everyday life, *General Semantics Bulletin, 62*, 16–22.

Kodish, Susan Presby and Kodish, Bruce I. ([1993] 2001) *Drive Yourself Sane: Using the Uncommon Sense of General Semantics* (rev. 2nd edn). Pasadena, CA: Extensional Publishing.

Korzybski, Alfred ([1921] 1950) *Manhood of Humanity: The Science and Art of Human Engineering* (2nd edn). Lakeville, CT: The International Non-Aristotelian Library.

Korzybski, Alfred (1990) *Collected Writings: 1920–1950* (Collected and arranged by

M. Kendig. Final editing and preparation for printing by Charlotte Schuchardt Read, with the assistance of Robert P. Pula.) Englewood, NJ: Institute of General Semantics.

Korzybski, Alfred ([1933] 1994) *Science and Sanity: An Introduction to Non-Aristotelian Systems and General Semantics* (5th edn). Englewood, NJ: The International Non-Aristotelian Library.

Lamb, Sydney M. (1999) *Pathways of the Brain: The Neurocognitive Basis of Language* (Current Issues in Linguistic Theory, 170). Philadelphia: John Benjamins.

Lamb, Sydney M. (2000) Neuro-cognitive structure in the interplay of language and thought. In Martin Pütz and Marjolijn Verspoor (eds) *Explorations in Linguistic Relativity* (Current Issues in Linguistic Theory, 199). Philadelphia: John Benjamins. Also available at www.ruf.rice.edu/~lamb/lt.htm.

Lee, Irving J. ([1941] 1994) *Language Habits in Human Affairs* (2nd edn, edited by Sanford I. Berman). Concord, CA: International Society for General Semantics.

Lee, Penny (1996) *The Whorf Theory Complex: A Critical Reconstruction*. Philadelphia: John Benjamins.

Marken, Richard S. (1992) *Mind Readings: Experimental Studies of Purpose*. Chapel Hill, NC: Control Systems Group/New View Publications.

Maslow, Abraham H. (1968) *Toward a Psychology of Being* (2nd edn). New York: Van Nostrand Reinhold.

Niemeier, Susanne and Dirven, René (eds) (2000) *Evidence for Linguistic Relativity* (Current Issues in Linguistic Theory, 198). Philadelphia: John Benjamins.

Pinker, Steven (1994) *The Language Instinct: How the Mind Creates Language*. New York: Morrow.

Powers, William T. (1998) *Making Sense of Behavior: The Meaning of Control*. New Canaan, CT: Benchmark Publications.

Presby, Susan (1982) General semantics and the process of psychotherapeutic exchange, *General Semantics Bulletin*, *49*, 115–123.

Pula, Robert P. (1994) Preface. In Alfred Korzybski, *Science and Sanity: An Introduction to Non-Aristotelian Systems and General Semantics* (5th edn, pp. xiii–xxii). Englewood, NJ: The International Non-Aristotelian Library.

Pula, Robert P. (1998) General-semantics and fuzzy logic/sets: similarities and differences. In Susan Presby Kodish and Robert P. Holston (eds) *Developing Sanity in Human Affairs* (Contributions to the Study of Mass Media and Communications, 54), pp. 82–95. Westport, CT: Greenwood Press.

Pütz, Martin and Verspoor, Marjolijn (eds) (2000) *Explorations in Linguistic Relativity* (Current Issues in Linguistic Theory, 199). Philadelphia: John Benjamins.

Read, Allen Walker (1984) Changing attitudes toward Korzybski's general semantics, *General Semantics Bulletin*, *51*, 11–25.

Read, Allen Walker (1985) Language revision by deletion of absolutisms, *ETC.: A Review of General Semantics*, *42*, 1, 7–12.

Read, Charlotte Schuchardt (1965/1966) Exploring relations between organismic patterns and Korzybskian formulations, *General Semantics Bulletin*, *42*, 7–12.

Watzlawick, Paul (1990) *Münchhausen's Pigtail: Or Psychotherapy & 'Reality' Essays and Lectures*. New York: W.W. Norton.

Weinberg, Harry L. ([1959] 1973) *Levels of Knowing and Existence* (2nd edn). Lakeville, CT: Institute of General Semantics.

Whorf, Benjamin Lee (ed. John B. Carrol) (1956) *Language, Thought & Reality: Selected Writings of Benjamin Lee Whorf.* Cambridge, MA: MIT Press.

Zadeh, Lotfi A. (1995) Fuzzy logic: issues, contentions and perspectives. Alfred Korzybski Memorial Lecture 1994. *General Semantics Bulletin, 62,* 12–15.

Chapter 10

Evolutionary psychology and Rational Emotive Behavior Therapy

Nando M. Pelusi

Until recently, most psychologists viewed the human mind as a *tabula rasa*. Increasingly, proponents of evolutionary psychology (EP) agree with biologist William Hamilton when he asserted 'the human *tabula* was never *rasa*' (Ridley, 1997). Although distinctly differing from animals, humans display concordance with other animals, and demonstrate similar instincts – including emotional and behavioral expressions.

The practice of psychotherapy has historically had grounding in social theory. Theory examines the organism and its interaction with the environment. However, it assumes that instruction gets received from the environment (whether stimulus–response, or stimulus–organism–response), and the organism 'learns'. Psychology, then, has a culture-based, scientific, but somewhat arbitrary foundation, unencumbered by the Darwinian underpinnings that have infused the study of animals in biology. That is the 'standard social science model' so described by Cosmides and Tooby (2000).

Philosophies that explore human nature often ignore biological tendencies and constraints. Today, that bias seems to be waning. Some current psychologists are attempting to rest their endeavors on the platform of evolution (McGuire and Troisi, 1998). The concept of evolution in human nature has received a mixed reaction among professionals and the public (owing to the effects of historical misapplication plus misrepresentation). One area that has had scant attention is the application of evolution to psychotherapy.

This paper is an extension of William J. Ruth's prescient call to 'open the floodgates' of evolutionary psychology and REBT (Ruth, 1993). The gates have not opened, and may just now start to trickle with the exploration of applying evolutionary insights to psychotherapy and to REBT in particular.

Humans have evolved from ancestors who lived mostly in the African savannah for 100,000 years or so. This is accepted as fact by most educated investigators. Evolution of species is not 'just a theory' as some American presidents have said. It is a fact on the same order of certainty as that the

Earth orbits the Sun. The uncertainties lie in some of the specifics about exactly how and why traits, species and groups have evolved (Ridley, 1996).

Our existence was once one of the greatest mysteries. As Dawkins (1989) has remarked – the mystery has been solved, and Charles Darwin solved it. He found the mechanism that explains by entirely naturalistic means how we came about. He called this deceptively simple mechanism 'Natural Selection'. He distinguished it from the artificial selection that dog breeders, pigeon breeders, and flower growers used. A conscious *selector* is not necessary for natural selection to take place. That is, selection still takes place because individual organisms show differential survival rates and reproduction rates. The surviving individuals that reproduce pass on the genes that provide the progeny with characteristics of the survivors. However, the next generation of gene-carriers will encounter new competitors, environments, and obstacles. And so on. Notice that the 'good of the species' is not of concern, but merely individuals acting in certain ways which help them survive and reproduce – or not. Evidence points to 'selfish' genes. An interesting paradox is that selfish genes create altruistic individuals (Dawkins, 1989). Therein lies the genesis of evolutionary psychology explored in this paper, along with its contributions to REBT, the kernel around which many cognitive therapies have grown.

Despite the important accomplishments of psychology in the last hundred years, the science has relied on competing theories of what constitutes human nature. All branches of science with the exception of the 'social sciences' have embraced the powerful unifying principle of evolution. For many reasons, with varying validity, evolution has not commanded respect in the study of humans for much of the last century. Animal behavior and purposes, on the other hand, have gotten profoundly understood in evolutionary terms. Although Darwin was the first evolutionary psychologist, the discipline lay dormant for a century after his death. He wrote, 'In the distant future I see open fields for far more important researches. Psychology will be based on a new foundation, that of the necessary acquirement of each mental power and capacity by gradation. Light will be thrown on the origin of man and his history' (Darwin, 1859, p. 488).

The proximate and ultimate views of human behavior

Recent articles and books have explored the usefulness of looking into the past – the evolutionary past, that is. In essence, the position holds that there are two levels from which to view (in our case) human nature. One is the *proximate* level. That includes our experiences, our families, our beliefs, our socio-economic status, our activating events (the A in REBT's famous ABCs), etc. The other level is the *ultimate*, or evolutionary, level. This includes our profound and sometimes-implicit ideas, our preferences, and even our tendency towards demandingness (an important mindset in

REBT). A consideration of some of the evolved mechanisms that have enabled our ancestors to survive and reproduce is examined via the ultimate perspective. EP has spawned literature in this regard which looks at emotions, moods, behaviors, and the tendency towards thinking in systematic and predictable ways as having adaptive significance. These emotional and cognitive tendencies have not been designed by forethought, but instead by natural processes of natural selection. This involves blind variation of forms and the cumulative selective retention of forms (Cziko, 1995).

Evolution and psychology

The evolutionary view of behavior is not a subset of psychology, as is the study of vision or language. It is more of a viewpoint. It informs the whole of psychology, offering unifying insights into what seem like disparate psychological findings. This chapter is not a 'combining' paper (like REBT and addictions, or REBT and feminism, REBT and whatever). Also, it is not a collection of techniques appended onto REBT philosophy (like Lazarus's multi-modal therapy, Beck's 'cognitive therapy', and the myriad other collections of techniques therapists have invented). This paper seeks the infusion of the considerable insights offered by the biological sciences onto the considerable philosophic and therapeutic insights of Ellis and REBT. Some of this paper includes speculation. Some Popperian hypothesizing follows, in order to see EP as a falsifiable viewpoint, since many of the details are just recently emerging to bolster what proves a powerful heuristic.

Cosmides and Tooby (2000) have conducted research on and have explored the evolved aspects of emotion. They define evolutionary psychology as

> [A]n approach to the psychological sciences in which principles and results drawn from evolutionary biology, cognitive science, anthropology, and neuroscience are integrated with the rest of psychology in order to map human nature. By human nature, evolutionary psychologists mean the evolved, reliably developing, species-typical computational and neural architecture of the human mind and brain. According to this view, the functional components that comprise the architecture were designed by natural selection to solve adaptive problems faced by our hunter–gatherer ancestors, and to regulate behavior so that these adaptive problems were successfully addressed. Evolutionary psychology is not a specific subfield of psychology, such as the study of vision, reasoning, or social behavior. It is a *way of thinking* about psychology that can be applied to any topic within it – including the emotions.

EP extends the premise that as physiology and morphology evolved, so did our psychology. The emotional characteristics found recurrently in humans also evolved to solve certain problems encountered in the ancestral environments. We ascribe mind to others. This is the source of attributions. Humans attribute purpose and meaning to actions, facial expressions, and sounds made by others. We are designed by natural selection to easily assume that others possess a mind, and to attribute telltale intentions to others (and sometimes to inanimate objects).

Dylan Evans (2001) contends that emotions evolved to solve specific problems in the past. If our minds are made up of modules, each affecting different adaptive purposes, our emotions evolved to unify those competing modules into a coherent focus. Emotions are thus a superordinate evolved structure, which organizes us into effective action. Our desire to sleep is incompatible with our desire to escape a rushing tiger. Thus, our emotion (fear) makes us super-alert, and appropriately reactive.

Ellis (1976) has compiled evidence for the biological basis of irrational behavior. In this prescient monograph he argues that humans systematically seem to subvert their goals and continually think and act in self-defeating ways. He concludes that such persistent recurrence of disturbance even among the brightest humans clearly points to a biological tendency towards both rationality and irrationality. In two early excellent articles, Ruth proposed that REBT seemed distinctly poised to incorporate what he called the 'genetic postulate' in explaining why demandingness persisted. His challenges went mostly ignored. Ruth sought to understand the evolutionary significance of musts. Ruth's two main postulates are (1992):

1. A cognitive tendency for demandingness and grandiosity in humans has evolved and is partly genetically coded because it facilitated adaptive behavioral and emotional responses as a means of securing critical evolutionary advantages in basic survival and increased reproductive success.
2. A cognitive readiness to learn and/or create demanding and grandiose thoughts during early childhood may be viewed as an adaptive strategy that has been naturally selected to increase the likelihood that critical maturational goals are achieved for specific developmental drives.

The postulates relate to (1) the evolved nature of demandingness, and (2) the evolved *readiness*, or preparedness, to easily learn demandingness when young.

EP provides no values for psychotherapy. Instead, it provides a framework for insights on human nature and emotions. Most proponents of EP deny that any practical insights for psychotherapy exist within this framework. Certainly, any treatment for therapy had better be tested empirically.

However, as EP can inform psychology, some adherents of EP suspect that a rich opportunity for informing psychotherapy using evolutionary insights awaits investigation. Glantz and Pearce (1989) have outlined an explanation for common discoveries in psychotherapy using evolution. For example, they found that status seeking in males is related to self-rating. Self-rating is found in many depressed and anxious clients.

Terms and concepts in EP

NATURAL SELECTION

Natural selection consists of two parts. The first part is random mutation (chance). The second part is *non-random* cumulative selection. Thus, it is a theory of successive generations getting better adapted, until there is a dramatic change in the environment. Four basic assumptions underlie natural selection (Ridley, 1996). Natural selection occurs when entities (1) reproduce, (2) inherit traits, (3) vary in characteristics and traits, and (4) vary in fitness (to survive and reproduce). Once these basics are fulfilled, evolution occurs, and explains adaptation of organisms to their environments.

Natural selection occurs at both the level of the individual and the level of the gene. Thus, we carry genetic code that comes from our parents, and pass on code to our children. The currency of evolution is this code. However, it only gets passed on when carried successfully by individuals who have inherited those characteristics that are adapted to a particular environment (Dawkins, 1989). Since environments change rapidly, some characteristics prove useful in one situation but not in another. Peter Grant studied the beaks of finches and studied natural selection as it occurred on the Galapagos Islands (Weiner, 1994). Variations in beak shape showed differential rates of survival for finches, depending on climate changes. When rains made berries unavailable, the larger, pliers-like beaks got passed on because nuts got cracked. When dry climates prevailed, the longer, pincer-like beaks survived to extract nutrients from berries. Of course, the owner of the particular beaks lived or died by their characteristics.

THE EEA

The Environment of Evolutionary Adaptation, or EEA, is a statistical composite of the kind of environments our ancestors have faced in the last 100,000 years or so. We know, for example, that our ancestors had to survive, find food and shelter, compete for mates, form alliances, and raise viable offspring.

MISMATCH THEORY

EP posits that many of our discomforts emerge from a mismatch between the natural ancestral environments from which we descended and the modern one we currently live in, which differs dramatically in key ways. Emotions and behaviors that evolved in one environment may prove maladaptive in another. Fear and anxiety, for example, may have proven adaptive in an environment in which predators could lurk in any shadow. Thus, EP examines cognitions and emotions by examining how they may have aided our ancestors in survival and procreation.

TRADE-OFFS V. PERFECTION

Evolution knows no perfection, no 'ideal'. Perfection is a meaningless concept from an evolutionary point of view. Natural selection scavenges and retrofits design forms. The designs that survive are those that get passed on. However, what is adaptive in one environment may be a liability in another. Melanin in the skin is one example. High degree of pigmentation is a great advantage in very sunny climates, where skin is thereby protected from UV light. However, lower levels of pigmentation would get selected in colder, darker climates, to allow for absorption of scarce light for vitamin D.

Diagnosis: proximate and ultimate causation of dysfunction

Two very different kinds of explanations exist in biology and even psychology. Darwin's contribution included an enlargement of scientific explanation. Proximate explanation refers to characteristics we can see. The proximate is subject to direct experimental manipulation. Proximate and ultimate (or evolutionary) are not competing explanations. It is not necessary to choose between them. They both provide insight into why certain behaviors and emotions tend to occur. Jealousy, for example, has both a proximate and an ultimate cause. Suppose your spouse is flirting with a rival (proximate). You have evolved a defense against rivals' seeking to control access to your partner's procreative and parental investment (ultimate). The latter is the evolutionary psychology contribution to understanding emotions and behaviors. Notice that jealousy is not endorsed merely because it helped our ancestors stave off rivals in the environment of evolutionary adaptation (EEA). Although certain reactions, like jealousy, may be somewhat culturally influenced this does not negate that a strong genetic component is at play.

Emotions as a superordinate structure

Most sexual organisms give birth to progeny that are not exact copies. Also, they can give birth to many more than can survive. This sets up conditions in which organisms compete for scarce resources. Those surviving the elements, disease, competitors, and which possess mechanisms that motivate the search and successful attainment of mates get to do the only thing that has currency in evolution: pass on genes. Note that there is no conscious selector, nor any form that is better under all conditions. Natural selection is Darwin's description of what happens in nature, i.e. random variation, with selective retention of forms. The only genetic instruction required is 'duplicate me'.

The individual and the gene's-eye view

In *The Selfish Gene*, Dawkins ([1976] 1989) clarified the dual perspective biologists take when assessing behavior. We as individuals live some brief period of time, but our genes are potentially immortal. We (the phenotypes) are manifestations of the genes (the genotypes). We have evolved as a result of, but also as carriers of, our genes. Several questions emerge from taking this gene's-eye view. How do our genes influence us? Are we the mere products of our genes? Do our genes determine our behavior? What of the role of environment? Although we are products of our genes, we are not slaves to genes. Built in to us is the capacity to select our perceptions by altering our behaviors. Thus, we have goals (conscious and unconscious) which we pursue, but have freedom to select among them, depending on a host of factors, including our cultural experiences.

The return of the unconscious

EP restores the unconscious to a proper role in psychology. Behaviorists eliminated cognition and the unconscious altogether. EP, instead, entirely scraps the Freudian mythological unconscious, and replaces it with a testable theory – one in which the unconscious processes can be evaluated for their genetic advantages. An evolutionary unconscious is one in which propensities have no hydraulic metaphor, but can be tested (for example, ovulating women prefer men who demonstrate features associated with higher levels of testosterone, such as larger brow and chin, more masculine appearance; while non-ovulating women prefer men with relatively lower levels of testosterone, such as more feminine-looking men, whose lower testosterone may presumably make for better 'dads').

Answering how questions and why questions

In REBT we seek to answer the 'how' questions – questions such as 'How do I get myself so upset, and how can I get myself less upset-able?' A focus of EP is to seek to answer the 'why' questions. (And not just 'why me?') EP seeks to answer questions such as 'Why do I get myself so upset; why do I maintain my upsetness so rigidly; and why do I slide back after I've worked so hard?'

Theoretical assumptions of EP

ASSUMPTION 1: HUMAN UNIVERSALS

Brown (1991) demonstrates that some tendencies served an adaptive purpose for all humans irrespective of culture, race, and experience. These traits, behaviors, and passions are found universally today in all areas of the world that have been examined. Buss (1999) investigated 37 cultures around the world, and collected data from a sample of over 10,000. These data suggest that social emotions such as jealousy, desires for specific traits in a mate, are similar throughout human populations. Emotions became part of human nature because they served the individuals possessing them. In evolutionary psychology an adaptive emotional trait is defined as thoughts/feelings/behaviors that aid and abet an individual (not necessarily the social group) to both survive and pass on genes.

ASSUMPTION 2: HUMAN PSYCHOLOGY IN THE EEA

Human psychology adapted via natural selection to environments very different from the modern one. We descended from individuals who felt emotions, and who develped cognitive, emotive, and behavioral tendencies that helped them to survive in the Pleistocene era. This is a period of roughly 100,000 years. The period consisted of what is called the environment of evolutionary adaptation (EEA). This place is a statistical composite rather than an actual place.

ASSUMPTION 3: THE CURRENT MISMATCH

Today our social environment differs in key respects from our original. Social alliances that constituted most of our environment of evolutionary adaptations no longer exist today. For example, far fewer humans existed – illness, the elements, and predators would probably have killed or seriously debilitated us by age 30 (Williams, 1997).

Common misunderstandings about evolutionary psychology

The Naturalistic and Moralistic Fallacies

Two common fallacies occupy the same continuum. The first is the Naturalistic Fallacy. This is the idea that 'If it is natural, then it is good'. The Naturalistic Fallacy implies that if something exists, then we ought to endorse it. Or that we ought to do it even if we don't like it, since it is good and right. This idea is false for many reasons, and evolutionary theorists often reject it. No values are implied when reporting the facts as best we can discern. For example, a diagnosis of cancer is a fact, and perhaps true. However, no implication that cancer is good is ever gleaned from such a fact. When EP highlights propensities in humans that we find distasteful, such as xenophobia, homicide, infanticide, racial suspicions, deception, this in no way implies tacit endorsement.

The second fallacy, the Moralistic Fallacy, states that what ought to exist is what actually exists. Or *can* exist. For example, if we find, say, 'equality' a good social value, we may be prone to force this onto our observations. As with the Naturalistic Fallacy, that a value is good does not mean it always can be achieved in nature. If 'equality' is a good thing to possess (*ceteris paribus*), a Procrustean mission to enforce it may prove more disastrous than virtuous. The goal is good, but nature is valueless. It only knows pitiless indifference (Dawkins, 1989). That does not imply that we ought to follow it, but only that we had better acknowledge a tenet of evolution: selective fitness. The Moralistic Fallacy (if it is good, it is so) ignores, minimizes, or disparages any information that is inconsistent with our beliefs (e.g. differences in height, IQ, charm, productivity, talents).

A good goal would be to avoid falling into either fallacy. Buss, McGuire, and other well-known investigators of evolutionary psychological theories, highlight other misunderstandings about evolutionary theory as applied to behavior (Buss, 1999; McGuire, and Troisi, 1998).

Some irrational beliefs about evolutionary psychology (partly derived from Buss, 1999)

This EP view overlaps with the REBT precept that distinguishes 'is' from 'ought'. Ellis logically disputes beliefs that conflate *is* to *ought* and 'would be better' to 'must be'.

1.   The belief that human behavior is genetically determined

This belief denies the truly integrationist framework presented in EP. Evolved adaptations and environmental cues hold conversations in which each stage results from each prior stage. Buss uses the example of calluses.

Our skin is not genetically determined to create calluses but builds them during specific interactions with the environment. Another example is the suntan. A suntan is both genetic and environmental.

2.   The belief that 'evolutionary' implies 'unchangeable'

Knowledge of our functioning allows for more effective changing of behaviors. Although change remains difficult, the power gained from knowledge about our basic functioning and why it occurs can illuminate the process of change. For example, knowing that we talk to ourselves, and have demands are useful pieces of knowledge. Knowing does not endorse or condone. Another example is anger. Excessive anger and jealousy may have conferred advantages in the ancestral environment, and thus may make change difficult. However, properly attributing the emotional difficulty prevents self-downing and quitting on working it through.

3.   The belief that evolutionary theory cannot account for our emotional, cognitive, and social flexibilities and abilities

Human culture emerges from what humans do, and has been called an 'extended phenotype' (in Dawkins's expression). Genes have evolved behaving organisms which carry them, and those organisms, in turn, create culture. This implies that we will tend to create cultures and technology that 'make sense' to our evolved common sensibilities. Thus, we have innate heuristics, or 'rules of thumb'. For example: 'When someone helps me I want to help them in return.' Our computational abilities evolved to maximize survival and reproduction in the ancestral environment.

4.   The belief that we are optimally designed

All adaptations carry costs. They are compromises between survival and reproductive goals and not every one of our adaptations will work smoothly with every other adaptation that we have. A desire for fat, adaptive in the past, can prove maladaptive today and can create health problems because we do not have efficient mechanisms to limit our intake. Scarcity limited intake. Furthermore, 'optimal' implies a specified environment. Environments, and situations, constantly change. Our most useful adaptations may well prove to be those cognitive-behavioral elements that allow us to form new adaptations. Rather than our possessing any particular adaptation, a super-adaptation (say, a mind) may help us navigate via reasoning ability. Niches change; creatures that do not anticipate or keep pace with changes are no longer with us. Most REBT therapists are familiar with Ellis's 'Fallible Human Being' and his Anti-Perfectionism in psychotherapy. EP incorporates an inherent anti-perfectionist way of thinking.

5.   The belief that evolution implies always maximizing gene reproduction

The goals we have may be products of the evolutionary process, but they do not embody the process itself. Our ancestors pursued goals and motives that put us here. We possess, by inheritance, a similar psychology. Those psychological traits need not consciously pursue genetic furtherance. They merely tend to make desirable those proximate behaviors that affect genetic replication. This includes the desire for love, family, sex, friendship, affiliations and health. The result: ideas, art, music, or science. Whether these pursuits turn out to maximize genetic reproduction is unaffected by the fact that we have the propensities as evolved by natural selection.

Humans have big brains in comparison with our body size, and although natural selection endowed us with, say, a sex drive, it endowed us with a capacity to foresee the consequences of our behaviors. We can intervene, and (with conscious effort) subvert our emotive/behavioral propensity. Thus, today we might use contraceptives. We need not think in terms of the dichotomy 'socially constructed' versus 'natural'. As Pinker (1997) notes '[T]he dichotomy between "in nature" and "socially constructed" shows a poverty of the imagination, because it omits a third alternative: that some categories are products of a complex mind designed to mesh with what is in nature.' So we have influences from genes (but only as a rule of thumb, or heuristic, never a fixed determinant, with respect to behavior).

6.   Evolution is inconsistent with human hopes

Human values appear to be transcultural and genetically sculpted; behaviors connoting empathy, succor, nurturance, and caring have been observed in other primates as well as in the larger group of our human siblings (de Waal, 1996). More inclusive views of evolution, e.g. complexity theory, suggest that cooperation is essential for any system, molecular or organic, to attain continuity through time and against entropy's march (Kauffman, 1995). Humans and many close-species relatives compensate for personal flaws through the formation of alliances and conservation of the personal resources found in our kin and in other members of a social group. Human hopes are an expression of those same processes.

Here are a few more objections described by McGuire and Troisi (1998):

7.   Evolutionary theory doesn't apply to humans

Evolution is not merely reconstructing phylogeny and relatedness among species. It is a theory unifying all species, and how individual species, including humans, have evolved into the creatures they are, with the propensities they have. Abuse from step-parents, sibling rivalry, and parent–offspring conflict make sense with evolutionary thinking.

8. EP ignores individual learning

The capacity to learn, as well as other traits, has gotten selected in humans. The question from EP is not 'Learned or innate?' but 'How easy is it to learn, given our evolution?' For example, learning to speak is acquired easily, but learning to read or write or play the piano takes much more direct instruction.

9. Culture provides an alternative to evolutionary thinking

Culture and biology are not distinct entities, since the ability to absorb and construct culture is an evolved trait. As McGuire and Troisi, p. 29 assert, 'Behavioral predispositions shape culture and are shaped through it.'

10. Evolutionary hypotheses cannot be tested

Hypotheses that make sense evolutionarily can be tested, such as those by Buss (1994) that in most societies male sexual jealousy should be more intense than female. Buss reports that males and females differ in what they find most evocative of jealousy. Males find physical sexual infidelity more upsetting than protestations of love and commitment, while women tend to report the reverse.

Mental disorders from an evolutionary perspective

One EP theory of depression take the view that depression, like fever, is an adaptive response to loss of status, which means loss of resources, which means loss of mating opportunities. Males who lose status and females who lose beauty are at risk for depression. The social competition theory of depression is based on the idea that depression is an evolved response to loss of status, or to an unsuccessful attempt to gain status (Stevens and Price, 1996; Nesse and Williams, 1994). A drastic change in strategy might prove beneficial, and feeling depression causes a powerful motivation to withdraw and retrench. The social competition theory claims that depression allows you to withdraw unproductive activity in one niche to seek a more productive niche. A change in strategies might be helpful to our ancestors who may have needed to switch strategies to adapt. Depression has the dubious advantage of making you accept a change in course. It benefits genes, if not your happiness in the short run. Focusing on one's failures may feel bad, but it may protect you from competitors who would get bolder in attacking you, thus further eroding your status.

Goulin and McBurney (2001) elaborate on some hypotheses by Nesse and Williams (1994) which suggest a variety of explanations for the persistence and prevalence of psychological disorders. These disorders are called so because they produce behaviors that effect self-defeating results.

1. Some psychological problems may not be 'disorders', but actually defenses, analogous to fever or cough. An example is nonclinical depression or low mood.
2. Some psychological problems are side effects of genes which confer fitness benefits in specific situations, analogous to sickle-cell anemia. An example may be schizophrenia.
3. Frequency-dependent selection. An example is the behavior of a sociopath. Genes operate in tandem and in competition with other sets of genes, and they adapt to the prevailing opportunities.
4. Some disorders may reflect the absence or malfunctioning of a particular module, analogous to defective color vision. An example is infantile autism.
5. A mismatch may occur between the current environment and the one that prevailed over much of human evolution. Social anxieties, 'awfulizing', overgeneralizing, self-downing are examples.
6. Some disorders represent the extremes of the distribution of multi-gene traits. The population will always include scatter around the optimum value for any trait that is affected at several loci. Depression is an example.

How EP theory contributes explanatory power to REBT

Why humans musturbate

Musts as restraints from risking costly behavior

Musturbation causes us to function less well than when operating from preferences. This is a central tenet of REBT philosophy (Ellis, 1977). Musts tax us emotionally. With the costs incurred via musturbating, and its universal prevalence among humans, it follows logically that musturbation provided some adaptive benefit *in the EEA* or it would have gotten more and more rare. Musts may not make us happier, or help us perform better, but my speculation is that musts *prevented* behavior that would have had survival or procreative costs. 'I must be approved' *prevented* individuals from risking – or deviating from social norms. 'I must do well' coiled us to freeze or to spring and give it our all – all or nothing. Why? Because despite costs to contentment (which in terms of genetic currency has a value of zero) our musts prevented us from risking unless we were 'certain' of success. Today, we don't need that certainty, and we care about our contentment even if our genes do not get passed on. Some of us choose not to pass on our genes. Genes have made organisms that can choose (by conscious use of technology not available in the EEA, such as condoms) whether to pass on genes. Making sex and love desirable was one way to pass on genes. However, genes cannot foresee, and today we have sex with birth-control technology. (Some speculate that the technology is creating a new generation inheriting incompetence at birth control.)

Musts as propellants for risky 'high-yield' behavior

This function of musts is suggested by the fact that musts elicit all-or-nothing thinking. Musts, by definition, raise the stakes to absolute levels: kill or be killed, topple or be toppled. Alpha males operating on musts may not have had more contentment – but via irrational jealousy, prevented competitors from passing on genes. A 'rational' male in the EEA may have found himself dead or cuckolded, and probably not passing along genes to the next generation. In the EEA some behaviors were high-risk, but had very high genetic payoff – for example, toppling an alpha male meant inheriting his harem. Without the 'craziness' to propel, the plotting and scheming, and then the will to take action, we might 'rationally' stay safe and passive. Those that did were not our ancestors. The all-or-nothing effect of musts dichotomizes the emotions.

Musts as deterrents to others from encroaching

Demanders display their emotions. An angry person has trouble hiding that fact. Others easily spot an angry face. You are less likely to engage in a fight with a person you believe is a 'nut' who will come back at you with everything they have. If a rival senses we are 'rational', they know we probably will not take extreme or homicidal action, and probably will not spend an inordinate time hounding them. Thus, musts not only propel us to take life-and-death risks with high genetic payoffs, but, in addition, it deters others who know that our own irrationality will also propel us to defend (to the death – if need be) our genetic claim. Such crazy determination cannot be faked. Musts make the 'mutually assured destruction' (MAD) strategy believable, and thus effective. Demandingness gets selected – not for happiness – but for genetic effects.

Musts as laser-like targeting of goals

Musts create emotions that galvanize our attention on things that would have genetic consequences. They relate very closely to the three main musts targeted in REBT: doing well (attaining status and resources), getting loved and approved (finding mates, alliances), feeling anger (manipulating others), and damning the conditions (redirecting precious resources of energy and time). Mere preferences could cause us to relax our focus, allowing competitors to best us.

Musts as alarm

Musts make us upset. Upsetness about something makes it priority and tends to overshadow competing concerns. This is bad for our enjoyment, but good for the genes we carry. Consider the case where an upstart rival is making a play for your partner(s). Demanding that this challenge must not occur 'churns up your gut', as Ellis would say. However, that same churning will not be ignored and does not go away unless some drastic actions are undertaken. Drastic emotions leading to drastic actions (like murder) have probably evolved to solve status issues, which ultimately affect genetic success (Daly and Wilson, 1988). Various data suggest that most homicides are committed by men on other men, usually in relation to a rivalry over females, but also over status (which redounds to access to females). Disrespectful slights, verbal offenses, and gestures, are often met with rage, especially when females are involved. This is a universal emotion – not found exclusively in 'western cultures' (Brown, 1991).

Musts as social manipulation

Musts contribute to social manipulation. Whether the emotion is anxiety, depression, or anger, others are affected (the etymology of the word refers to emotion). We facilitate our non-obvious, genetic goals (unconsciously) by feeling emotions that take prepotency. Disturbed behavior instructs others on how to respond to us. Machiavelli noted that a feared leader amasses more power. Remember that these emotion tendencies evolved in conditions found in the EEA.

Musts as obstinate resistance to conformity

Stubbornness and obstinacy can also be very effective. Strong feelings of anger when getting 'pushed' beyond one's limit gave rise to reactions that could overcome social pressure. Ellis often refers to force and vigor in the disputation process. By emphasizing this, he implicitly acknowledges the effect of obstinacy and resistance to conformity.

Musts solve the commitment problem

Why do couples commit to each other? A purely 'rational' person might decide to dispassionately leave a troubled relationship. Most couples agonize over a split, often for many months after a relationship has ended. Couples often consult psychotherapists and read about relationships. Indeed, they often feel and want their partner to feel passion, not take part in rational decision-making about them. Musts get us to pursue the daunting and arduous task of finding a mate. 'I need a mate.' Once we find that person, it recalibrates to the famous passions of 'I need this particular person, no other will do' and 'It must work out'.

Musts may not make us happy, but they give us extreme emotions both to get us in relationships and to stay there as long as it takes to have procreated and raised a child in the EEA. Couples experiencing trouble at 4 or 7 years into a relationship run up against this, the selected waning of their musts. After the genes have gotten on, the incentive is to replace these musts with new ones designed to uproot someone despite social and other costs: 'I must find myself' and 'I need to feel free'. These new musts create loads of misery for some couples who find them difficult to ignore. When passions are gone, musts are gone, and they are replaced with new musts. A specific relationship has reached genetic senescence after a period of genetic procreation.

Sexual selection and musts

Another powerful process in operation was also discovered by Darwin – namely, the one called 'sexual selection'. This process examines how females respond to male traits, and thus select certain attributes. For example, selection occurred which resulted in individuals who had more or less demandingness. Females select mates using many criteria. Often, females are attracted to males possessing power, status, and ambition, or traits that denote the possibility of attaining those (confidence, persistence, social intelligence, perceptiveness). Female chimpanzees have been known to engage in extra-pair copulations (EPCs) with lower-status males. This presents us with the possibility that females with youthful mates (with good genes) may have had EPCs with older males (with high status), and vice versa.

Evolution and disputing

In REBT a central tenet involves vigorous disputing of irrational beliefs. Often those beliefs are held rigidly, and recur after seemingly being eliminated. Edelstein and Steele (1997) make the analogy of disputing as brushing your teeth – you had better do it daily, or the tartar (and musts) come back. Clients may get discouraged without an explanation as to why such tenacity is exhibited by irrational beliefs – and why such persistent disputing is required.

Evolution and attribution

Individuals occasionally get into and stay in relationships that prove harmful, often believing that that bad relationship is with a soul mate. They believe that they cannot find another partner. This fear can be attributed to evolved tendencies instead of self-delusions such as 'this must be my only true soul mate'.

Anxiety and the false-alarm theory

Anxiety is costly. The cost of dying once, however, is far more than the cost of misery from chronic alarm (from the gene's-eye view). Anxiety damages tissue, prevents enjoyment, and hinders creativity. However, the prevalence of anxiety suggests that it had utility for our ancestors. A smoke detector that under-reports smoke would allow us to sleep through dangerous levels of smoke. We carry danger-detectors, which, overall, tend to err on the side of caution. In addition, mismatch theory would predict that we would make a mountain out of a social molehill, escalate the desire for social approval into a need, and get upset when risking social failure. Why is it so hard to give up the idea that we 'need' to do well? The answer speaks deeply of our evolved psychological tendency. The more we know of this tendency the more tenacious we can be at correcting it.

Depression, status, and resource-holding potential in males

Ellis contends that a central must is 'I must do well and be loved'. This is viewed in evolutionary theory like the depressed person's assessment of resource-holding potential (similar to Beck's cognitive triad of self, future, and world). Assessments about the self, future and world would have proven quite important to a person's ability survival and their access to resources. Men and women would be concerned about resources (men, to get and keep a mate, and a woman, to adequately care for her children).

Testable and empirical hypotheses

One of the goals of science is to make hypotheses that are testable or *in principle* testable. EP contains both versions. Buss (1999) demonstrates several studies relating to love and sex strategies, jealousy, and predictable emotions and desires observed in many cultures. Daly and Wilson (1988) have explored homicide in the context of genetic relatedness.

Consistencies between REBT and evolutionary theory

REBT has espoused a philosophy about human nature that overlaps considerably with an evolutionary approach.

RATIONAL AND IRRATIONAL THINKING

Several types of evidence support REBT's hypothesis that humans have a tendency to think both rationally and irrationally (Ellis and Dryden, 1987). Virtually all humans, including bright and competent people, show major irrationalities. Irrational, disturbed behaviors are found across cultures and times. We continue to act in self-defeating ways despite experiences, teachings of parents and peers. Insight into one's own self-defeating behaviors seems to help only partially to change them. We often return to irrational habits after having worked hard to overcome them, and delude ourselves that we can avoid the consequences of poor behavior. Why is this? This persistent and systematic tendency requires explanation. Ellis attributes it to being an FHB – 'a fallible human being'. However, what makes us such fallible human beings, with such predictable propensities to musturbate in nauseatingly recurrent ways? An examination of our evolutionary past makes interesting and useful predictions.

EGO AND DISCOMFORT DISTURBANCES

REBT posits that two fundamental forms of emotional/behavioral problems are ego disturbance and discomfort disturbance (Ellis, 1977). According to REBT, humans make demands on people (including themselves), and also make demands on the world and the conditions they are in. In ego disturbance, we find a damning of self or others. This involves a status assessment of self and others, which usually involves a rating of the person's inherent worthiness. In discomfort disturbance, or low frustration tolerance, we find that humans compulsively seek pleasure and immediate gratification, and have a tendency to avoid responsibilities even when it leads to great disadvantages.

DISTURBANCE ACQUISITION

Ellis (1984) posits that events do not disturb us. Rather, we bring our innate (and individual) ability to disturb ourselves to the experiences we have. This is an implicit 'selection' model of disturbance acquisition. Unlike behaviorists, but like behavior geneticists, he does not believe that the environment 'imprints' or 'instructs' us, so much as that it provides experiences, which we then evaluate in order to fashion our beliefs.

UNDESIRABLE EMOTIONAL AND BEHAVIORAL CONSEQUENCES

REBT focuses mainly on disturbances and how they are maintained, more than how they are acquired. Targets include undesirable Cs. Three insights from REBT theory include: (1) that disturbances result mainly from biased, absolutistic thinking, (2) that people remain disturbed by reindoctrinating themselves in the present with irrational beliefs, and (3) that by diligently working in the present and future to think, feel, and act against irrational beliefs they are likely to change them and make themselves less disturbed (Ellis and Dryden, 1987).

INTERPLAY OF COGNITIVE, EMOTIONAL, AND MOTOR COMPONENTS

REBT involves (cognition) disputing irrational beliefs logically, empirically, and functionally. In addition, power and forcefulness are often used (emotion). *In vivo* weekly assignments and goals are agreed upon, which make a client act against their tendency (motor). This interplay gets examined naturally in psychology and in EP when we consider the close fit between receptor, emotional, and motor characteristics in regard to an adaptive, self-interested, purpose.

RECOGNITION OF HIERARCHY (SOCIAL STANDING)

Attachment and affiliation seem to be important elements in human contentment. Ego, self-downing, aggrandizement, etc., are reactions, evolved tools, that meet selfish needs, and even the most humble sufferer malingers just a bit. Changes in hierarchic position also have implications for the amount and persistence of demands on the client. Changes in rank may simplify or complicate life. Simplification usually implies that life becomes manageable or boring; making life complicated makes it exciting or overwhelming.

Attribution effects of EP on REBT

Clients tend to rate themselves. Ellis focuses on what he calls 'self-downing' as a major problem (Ellis, 1977). However, self-esteem, and self-disesteem, could act in the service of our genes (even if not in the service of our long-term happiness). Attributing one's tendency to do poorly to biology helps a client avoid the self-downing attributions that form the emotional problem.

While co-leading a group with Albert Ellis in the early 1990s, I remember him upbraiding a young man whining about the type of life he thought he deserved. Ellis said, in typical pithy prose, 'The universe doesn't care about you, it's not for you or against you, it just doesn't give a shit.' The implication was clear: there is no providence. This is exactly the view that most serious evolutionists take.

Resistance and rigidity

Why do we tend to rigidly hold on to dysfunctional beliefs? Why do we tend to systematically believe that desires are necessities? Humans demonstrate a propensity for what Ellis (1977) has called the three main musts:

I.   I must do well, and be loved or approved, or I'm no good.
II. You must treat me well, or you're no good.
III. Conditions in the world must be fair or favorable to me, or I can't stand it.

The escalation of a preference to do well into a 'need' is understandable given the resources that accrue to the successful among us. Most significantly, males get access to females, and females compete for the attentions and commitments from the best males (those showing resources or potential for resource-holding). This is the currency of the gene. With respect to the rigidity with which individuals hold their beliefs, it follows that quick summation of beliefs would prove a powerful heuristic. Beliefs are streamlined thoughts. We do not have to rethink positions on things, so that our beliefs increase the immediacy of appropriate responses to the environment. It requires little conscious thought to do most of the things we do. Beliefs about people tend to resist change. Mindsets get formed about people often before we know anything about them (Etcoff, 1999), such as someone who looks different, sounds different, or even has a weird name, like 'Nando Pelusi'. Albert Ellis did his own research on boys with peculiar names and how they fared worse in social status. However, we also form beliefs about ourselves. We form a sense of 'self-esteem', or 'self-rating', relative to some standard. When we fall short of some real or imagined standard, we form images of ourselves that tend to linger into adulthood. Harris (1998) has amassed interesting data about this, where she asserts that our self-images and esteem are much more influenced by relations with peers than with parents.

Evolutionary psychology and cognitive distortions

ATTRIBUTION EFFECTS

We often unconsciously attribute and explain events in the world. We also often hypothesize cause and effect without consciousness. Cognitive-behavioral therapists help make those processes more conscious for clients, and make them aware of their role in perceptions, attributions and the effects of deeply held beliefs.

> **Case illustration**
>
> A 28-year-old woman compulsively continues to see a man who mistreats her. She believes that he is the only man for her, and that it must work out with him.
>
> Example of dispute: 'You continue to think he's the *only* man for you, and go back to needing him, even though you feel bad after spending time with him, and know that this is not a long-term relationship. You may be responding not so much to him, as much as to your evolved tendency to *rigidly believe* you must keep him – regardless of cost. In Stone Age times, your ancestors might have responded to that genetic impulse – as you do – even at great cost to themselves. Let's dispute the belief that may have helped your genes in ancient times, but is a complete mismatch with today's world, and doesn't help *you* and your goals. Do you have to follow your genetic legacy?'

A brief case illustration follows for some of the common cognitive distortions:

OVERGENERALIZING

In the EEA, the cognitive distortion we call 'overgeneralizing' would probably serve us well. Consider that a failure during that period would be part of the entire social landscape. We would all be on the cover of the *Stone Age Enquirer*. Any success or failure would tend to brand you, making social risks very costly. Getting a negative reputation would be hard to overcome.

MIND READING

In the EEA, social alliances would select for individuals with talent for understanding intentions of others. The ability to perceive emerging social alliances and potential enemies would prove useful. However, others don't often make their intentions explicit. In order to 'read' what a person may do, we attribute a mind, and intention. We assume others have similar emotional and cognitive states to our own.

A 45-year-old man with a graduate degree gets divorced and plunges into a painful depression. He rigidly believes that no other woman will want him. We discuss the nature of, and possible origins of, overgeneralizing: 'Your tendency to assume and believe that no woman would want you may make you unhappy, but keep your genes viable into the next generation. However, you carry that genetic legacy today, which you can choose to override once you know it. In addition, it may not even help your genes today since we live in a world with millions of potential females unlike in the Stone Age.'

Evolutionary psychology and diagnosis in REBT

The C in REBT

Undesirable emotional consequences

DEPRESSION

This is a readjustment in social status. Depression statistically results after decrease in your esteem in the eyes of your social group or significant others. A typical A is not doing well, and not getting love or approval. Humans are prone to making these important desires into musts, and thus precipitate depression. One conscious individual goal is enjoyment of life, but survival and procreation may not have a 100% relationship today with happiness. Another way to say this: our genes do not care about our happiness even if we do.

ANXIETY, SHAME AND GUILT

These are threats to social status.

Undesirable behavioral consequences

IMMOBILITY, PASSIVITY AND SHYNESS

Threats to social status, which redound to decreased access to sexual partners, may cause us, in the conditions of the Pleistocene to avoid socially risky behaviors.

Males and females may differ in what constitutes social risk. For a male, loss of prestige might mean loss of access to sexual or love partners. To females, loss of reputation as trustworthy may mean loss of access to a committed man, although she may find no shortage of short-term sexual partners. A male's potential investment of time and energy in sex is minuscule compared to the nine months of pregnancy a female may face.

For males, social shyness costs far more than for females. But the risk of losing social standing (he believes) is far worse (from the point of view of his genetic furtherance). Females find social shyness a problem when it prevents them from accepting attention from males. Gay men and lesbians face the same problems with respect to their desires and frustrations. The only difference is the sex of the object of their desires. Males (straight or gay) generally desire attractive young partners, and females (straight or lesbian) desire reliable, strong, high-status partners. This constitutes some evidence for our innate proclivities.

GUILT

A powerful emotion of anxiety (about potentially getting found out for some misdeed) and self-downing (about actually getting found out) would be necessary to keep ourselves, as the carriers of genes, from transgressing the expected social norms. Those norms come not from consensus, but from emotions that have gotten selected for their effects on genes (Dawkins, 1989).

EP and disputation

Depression emanating from the two main irrational beliefs (iBs), I must do well and be loved, and the world must treat me favorably: 'I must do exceptionally well and excel in several respects.' In the world of our ancestors, we had a chance of doing exceptionally well and excelling at something. We had a good chance of being the best at something in our village, since the village consisted of 100 or so members who lived a briefer time. Today, the media portray genetic 'freaks' with unlikely combinations of advantages. Claudia Schiffer and Brad Pitt were not the neighbors we needed to compete against to gain access to partners. Today, we compare ourselves to exemplars of genetic fitness with unlikely combinations of genes. The emerging 'science of beauty' is described by Etcoff (1999) to include traits that exude survivability. In the modern world, with instant media access, where world-class performers are our competition, that must has little chance of aiding our pursuit. Instead, we would retreat until we found another niche for competence. Today, all niches are likely to be close to the 'wall' for human capabilities, and competition is keener in several respects: niches change faster, and more individuals compete for them. This salubrious effect on us all does not serve to increase happiness, but makes us less happy (Frank, 1985).

More people currently populate the world than have existed in history. Thus, we're not contenders for supremacy in any field (except for a short while). However, biologically, we have the same drives and impulses as our ancestors throughout the span of one hundred centuries (100,000 years).

Why do we backslide after making progress in therapy? The evolutionary perspective only augments the overall answer, but does not replace the proximate answer: you slide back because you tell yourself 'It is too hard' or 'I must not fail, I must be loved'.

Attribution: 'Why do I keep backsliding this important area of my life?' Evolutionary answer: Because we are born, raised and *evolved* to escalate our desire for approval into a necessity, since it helped our ancient ancestors.

The Handicap Principle

Highlighting irrational adherence to the Handicap Principle

In selection several forces operate. One is natural selection, which determines differential survival. However, sexual selection simultaneously affects reproductive success (Darwin, 1878). Sexual selection depends somewhat on survival selection (natural), but not entirely. For example, a male praying mantis reproduces at the expense of survival, since his head is bitten off during sex. We all may have experienced some hot dates – but this is ridiculous. Therefore, sexual selection occasionally favors risks to survival. This *riskiness* denotes good genes to females, and thus prompts male display behavior with high risk, but high mate-payoff.

The Handicap Principle and disputation

Holding resources is one of the main ways males attract the attention of females. Males compete for females by demonstrating fitness in a variety of ways. One way is genetic fitness. Genetic fitness is displayed not just by looking healthy, but also by displaying the ability to overcome obstacles. Bowerbirds show architectural finesse, as well as the ability to procure materials and defend their bowers from competitors. Similarly, men drive cars that display wealth, do daring deeds that risk cost or injury, and 'waste' money on 'useless' items such as jewelry, flowers, expensive dinners. In fact, romantically speaking, the more useless and wasteful the expense, the better it is. A necklace that costs $700 is much more romantic than a washing machine that costs $700. A Mont Blanc pen costing $200 is more romantic than a lifetime supply of Bics for $200. The handicap is wasteful and risky, and displays fitness. It is not overtly 'rational'. However, the rationality is deep and genetic.

Disturbance and depression

The biologists Zahavi and Zahavi (1997) call this the Handicap Principle. They documented cases among various species. Males display to females (via a peacock's tail, for example) that they can maintain a handicap and still survive, and fight off predators and competitors. These displays work better when they are hard to fake. Displaying a Rolex, a Ferrari, or a Manhattan apartment is hard to fake. A fake Rolex looks like a fake Rolex in the escalating game of cheater and cheater-detection. You either have access to the real thing, or not. Men who waste, take on a handicap, actually displaying their genetic superiority by overcoming the self-imposed obstacles. One would expect expensive clothing to be more durable. But most expensive clothing is not more durable, but less! This demonstrates to prospective females that men can afford to purchase and wear such trifling items.

Disturbance itself may constitute a handicap principle. This self-imposition is not necessarily a conscious one. No psychodynamics at all is implied here. This cognitive process was designed by natural selection to help in the competition for genetic furtherance. This says 'My rigidity, my self-defeating behavior, makes me principled, and thus, a good catch.'

Smoking, alcoholism, overeating, gambling, fighting, and other known risky behaviors carry an added hidden allure: the Handicap Principle is in effect. The more publicity smoking gets for engendering disease, the more young people give it cachet by trying to look 'cool'. They are accepting the handicap that confers desirability on them.

Discrepancy in depression rates for males and females

Women show higher rates of depression than men, but men have much higher rates of suicide when depressed. This suggests that depression may serve different functions for males and females. Males may show relative resistance to depression since it would prove an unattractive quality to females. Men who got depressed (or showed depressive qualities) would command fewer resources.

Biological and theoretical underpinnings for REBT

Need for approval, need to do well, rage at injustice, and passivity in the face of frustration are common REBT targets. However, understanding the basis for such recalcitrant emotions helps the therapist know what she is up against, and helps the client accept himself with his deeply rooted tendency to do those things.

Displaying the costs by 'referenting', and rethinking the powerful impulse to waste, risk, and incur heavy costs, is all in the service of the genes (which may differ from what makes the individual more content in the long run).

Drawbacks of combining REBT with EP

Combining REBT with any approach runs the risk of diluting what essentially is a parsimonious and powerful theory of psychotherapy with a potentially non-essential view (e.g. REBT and witchcraft, REBT and crystals, REBT and my-own-politics). However, as noted, evolutionary theory is not a mere addendum to REBT, but a way of perceiving human nature that is gaining respect from ever-widening circles. Nonetheless, while evolutionary theory itself may be unquestionably true, the specifics about how it actually applies are eminently questionable. Especially questionable are applications for psychotherapy. For example, empirical investigation into EP may show that it adds little or nothing to disputation for the average client. Or, indeed, that it slows or confuses the disputation process for the average client. This has yet to be tested.

No systematic or formalized psychotherapy currently exists combining the insights of evolution. Mainly, several colleagues and I have infused the diagnosis and disputation aspects of REBT with evolutionary biology and psychology. Therefore, this chapter addresses the theory, but only suggests possible application techniques.

Other potential drawbacks include falsely deriving morals from the pitiless process of natural selection, or from science itself. The Moralistic and Naturalistic Fallacies are two errors discussed here. Evolutionary views of human behavior are often incomplete. Currently, they address human universals, but research into individual differences remains to be conducted. The questions about EP continue from those concerned about misuse, and these concerns had better get treated with respect. Another drawback involves the reaction from persons who are religious, or schooled in the 'standard social science model'. Care can be taken to prevent offense when possible. The debate is far from over, and both sides have valid arguments about risks in viewing humans from an overly *reductionistic* point of view.

Summary

This chapter attempts to show how evolutionary psychology (EP) and evolutionary thinking can deeply inform our understanding of human nature and the acquisition and maintenance of human disturbances. EP can provide perspectives on REBT diagnosis and on why clients easily disturb themselves from both the proximate (thinking) and the ultimate (evolved tendency). EP provides an understanding of the 'mismatch' between our past and present; that is, between our evolved basic biology and psychology and our current social, economic, and practical environment. EP informs REBT by examining the gene's-eye view, and how it may differ from the individual's-eye view. Disputation in REBT can be informed by understanding *why* humans get demanding, and understanding the evolved human universals that include passion, pleasure, desire and love, as well as jealousy, anger, guilt, depression and anxiety. EP informs the *why* individuals resist changes to their demands. EP provides clues to answering the general *why* questions previously ignored and providing great explanatory power. The EP explanations can give us insights into whether we want to go along with the schemes of our genes. In fact, EP helps psychotherapy join the rest of the scientific community by dispensing with the arbitrary 'standard social science model', and basing psychotherapy on general laws known to affect all species at every level. The potential drawbacks of committing the Moralistic and Naturalistic Fallacies exist, but are outweighed by the sheer breadth of insight offered by EP.

References

Brown, D.E. (1991) *Human Universals*. New York: McGraw-Hill.

Buss, D. (1999) *Evolutionary Psychology: An Introduction*. New York: Allyn and Bacon.

Cosmides, L. and Tooby, J. (2000) Evolutionary psychology and the emotions [electronic version]. In M. Lewis and J.M. Haviland Jones (eds) *Handbook of Emotions* (2nd edn). New York: Guilford.

Cziko, G. (1995) *Without Miracles*. Cambridge, MA: MIT.

Daly, M. and Wilson, M. (1988) *Homicide*. Hawthorne, NY: Aldine.

Darwin, C. (1859) *The Origin of Species*. London: Murray.

Darwin, C. (1878) *The Expression of Emotions in Man and Animals*. London: Murray.

Dawkins, R. (1989) *The Selfish Gene* (new edn). New York: Oxford University Press.

de Waal, F. (1996) *Good Natured*. Cambridge, MA: Harvard University Press.

Edelstein, M. and Steele, D.R. (1997) *Three Minute Therapy: Change Your Thinking, Change Your Life*. New York: Open Court.

Ellis, A. (1976) The biological basis of human irrationality, *Journal of Individual Psychology*, *32*, 145–168. Reprinted by the Albert Ellis Institute, New York.

Ellis, A. (1977) *Anger: How to Live Without it*. Secaucus, NJ: Citadel Press.

Ellis, A. (1984) The essence of RET-1984, *Journal of Rational-Emotive Therapy*, *2*, 1, 19–25.

Ellis, A. and Dryden, W. (1987) *The Practice of Rational-Emotive Therapy*. New York: Springer.

Etcoff, N. (1999) *Survival of the Prettiest*. New York: Doubleday.

Evans, D. (2001) *Emotions*. London: Oxford University Press.

Frank, R.H. (1985) *Choosing the Right Pond: Human Behavior and the Quest for Status*. New York: Oxford University Press.

Glantz, K. and Pearce, J. (1989) *Exiles from Eden*. New York: Norton.

Goulin, J.C.H. and McBurney, D. (2001) *Psychology: An Evolutionary Perspective*. New York: Prentice Hall.

Harris, J.R. (1998) *The Nurture Assumption*. New York: Free Press.

Kauffman, S. (1995) *At Home in the Universe*. New York: Oxford University Press.

McGuire, M. and Troisi, A. (1998) *Darwinian Psychiatry*. New York: Oxford University Press.

Nesse, R.M. and Williams, G.C. (1994) *Why We Get Sick*. New York: Times Books Random House.

Pinker, S. (1997) *How the Mind Works*. New York: Norton.

Ridley, M. (1996) *Evolution* (2nd edn). Cambridge, MA: Blackwell Science.

Ridley, M. (1997) *The Origins of Virtue*. New York: Viking.

Ruth, W. (1992) Irrational thinking in humans: an evolutionary proposal for Ellis' genetic postulate, *Journal of Rational-Emotive & Cognitive-Behavior Therapy*, *10*, no. 1, Spring.

Ruth, W.J. (1993) Evolutionary psychology and rational-emotive therapy: time to open the floodgates, *Journal of Rational-Emotive and Cognitive-Behavior Therapy*, *11*, no. 4, Winter.

Stevens, A. and Price, J. (1996) *Evolutionary Psychology*. New York: Routledge.

Weiner, J. (1994) *The Beak of the Finch*. New York: Vintage.

Williams, G. (1997) *The Pony Fish's Glow*. New York: Basic Books.

Zahavi, A. and Zahavi, A. (1997) *The Handicap Principle: The Missing Piece of Darwin's Puzzle*. New York: Oxford University Press.

Chapter 11

Theoretical developments in REBT as applied to schizophrenia

Peter Trower

REBT and other cognitive behavior therapies have traditionally been applied to mental health problems that are clearly at least partly psychological, and have a form and structure in which emotional and behavioural disturbance can be seen to be a function of dysfunctional or irrational beliefs, given certain adverse life circumstances, and a genetic and environmentally derived vulnerability. In other words, they are problems that can be assessed in terms of the ABC model. Such is the case, for example, in anxiety disorders, major depression and many other axis 1 disorders in DSMIV (American Psychiatric Association, 1994).

In contrast, REBT has not normally been viewed as appropriate for mental disorders believed to be largely biological. Perhaps the most prominent of the disorders viewed as largely biological and for which REBT has not therefore been considered appropriate are schizophrenia and other psychotic disorders. However, I am proposing in this chapter that REBT can be appropriately used, particularly when the underlying theory is developed in a number of ways and integrated with other models. Such developments can, it is argued, radically change the possibilities for cognitive interventions in schizophrenia (Chadwick et al., 1996). These theoretical developments in REBT to be outlined in this chapter can be divided into four areas. The first area is concerned with the overall conceptualization of schizophrenia, and I critically compare the standard biomedical view with an alternative REBT/CT view to show that the issue of 'appropriateness' is largely a question of theoretical assumptions. The second area concerns developments at the level of the syndrome of schizophrenia, the third at the level of the symptoms, and the fourth – most ambitiously – is a step towards the development of an alternative model to the biological model as an explanation for the syndrome and symptoms of schizophrenia.

Throughout this discussion I will be utilizing the widely accepted REBT definitions of A, B and C, where A (activating event) encompasses perceived facts (either internal such as sensations or external such as events seen or heard) and inferences about the facts, B (belief) encompasses evaluations about the As, in particular the primary must and the derivatives of self–other downing, awfulizing and low frustration tolerance. Finally, C (consequence) encompasses the emotional and behavioural consequences that follow from the specific Bs, given the specific As.

Theoretical assumptions in schizophrenia – a critique

The biomedical model is the prevailing model of schizophrenia, sometimes explicitly, sometimes implicitly. It is well accepted in the cognitive tradition that models and theories are forms of belief, and beliefs enable us to generate our understandings (assessments) and actions (interventions) for a problem, but they also have a down side, in that they can blind us to alternative understandings and action (intervention) possibilities. This down side is particularly intractable if our theory is implicit rather than explicit, and is thereby unconsciously assumed rather than consciously questioned. This should be familiar, because it is the *sine qua non* of the cognitive approach. I wish to argue that the commonly held version of the biomedical model contains a core dysfunctional assumption, and one that is held implicitly, not explicitly. This assumption guides us to think of schizophrenia as a biological illness or disease, and hallucinations (for example) as symptoms of this illness, just like dementia is an illness and hallucinations are symptoms of dementia. What 'treatment' do we think of for hallucinations? The implicit medical model guides us towards physical/ physiological/biochemical interventions. This is because the model directs our thinking, and blinds us to alternatives that depart too sharply from the underlying assumptions.

So, to return to my opening question, should we avoid cognitive approaches to schizophrenia? The answer it seems is (often) yes – they are not appropriate to the treatment of schizophrenia conceptualized as an illness. A second, less extreme, position is to do meta-level interventions only – to develop rational beliefs about *having* schizophrenia – but don't try to tackle schizophrenia itself.

A truly cognitive approach like REBT does seem to be at the opposite pole from the medical model – probably why it has not been thought to be appropriate for schizophrenia. The main difference is that in a cognitive theory the patient isn't just the helpless victim of an underlying illness that causes their symptoms but perceives, interprets, evaluates, decides and actively responds to experiences and events and processes, and their emotions and behaviour are largely a consequence of those appraisals. Some, like Ellis, make the strong claim that the Beliefs (defined as stated earlier as evaluative beliefs) directly cause the Consequent emotions and behaviour, given the situation the person is in. In other words, a person feels and behaves as a consequence of the way they evaluate events, not the events in themselves, or, to quote Epictetus as Ellis often does, it is not things in themselves that disturb us but our interpretations of them. This model has long been established, of course, in depression and anxiety disorders and many other emotion-based problems. Thus Jean selectively perceives and misinterprets feedback she gets from her boss as meaning she is not good enough. She then irrationally assumes that this means she is not as good as she should be, and then derives the conclusion that she is worthless, and becomes depressed.

But this model seemed hardly appropriate for schizophrenia, the true mental illness, marked as it supposedly is by a biological deficit, lack of insight and discontinuity from 'normal' human experience. But in fact this is exactly what I and my colleagues do argue. By applying this model to schizophrenia, we open up a whole new dimension for assessment and intervention, at both the syndrome level and the symptom level, as proposed in the next two sections.

Developments in REBT for the 'syndrome' of schizophrenia

The syndrome level refers to the traditional biological model of schizophrenia as a mental illness with a largely genetic origin, manifested through characteristic symptoms, and treated principally by medication. As suggested above, this remains the prevailing model in most mental health services in the United Kingdom, Europe and the United States. Described in this way, the role of REBT has to be confined to treating schizophrenia at a meta-level. This involves assessing schizophrenia as an Activating event for the client, containing distorted inferences which trigger irrational evaluations at B about the awfulness of having schizophrenia (or worse, being schizophrenic), leading to consequent emotional and behavioural disturbance at C (though even this approach is hardly encouraged in a biomedical model that emphasizes lack of this, or any other, insight). In this approach the therapist elicits the chain of inferential interpretations the individual makes about having the illness, until she has established the critical A, and uses this to identify the iBs. Thus far, this is familiar territory, recognizable as a fairly standard, though not common, application of REBT. However, this approach can be enhanced by reconstruing the schizophrenia syndrome not as a simple monolithic A with which the individual has been afflicted, but viewing the syndrome more as a dynamic process with a changing pattern over time, and this process can be deconstructed into component ABC parts.

We start the analysis with the C, and will often find this will focus on depression. Depression in schizophrenia is a rather neglected field of study, although depression-like pathology has been acknowledged in the literature since the earliest observations (Bleuler, 1950), and is a common (Siris, 2000) and serious problem in that it precedes suicide in this population, particularly if associated with hopelessness (Drake and Cotton, 1986).

The most widespread assumption in routine psychiatric practice is the 'intrinsic' theory, namely that depression, if present, is an intrinsic part of the illness, and as such should be present at one or more stages during the course of an acute psychotic episode (Hirsch and Jolley, 1989). In this view, it is assumed that depressive symptoms are ameliorated as psychotic psychopathology recedes and are not expected to re-emerge after recovery – unless as an intrinsic part of a relapse along with other first-rank symptoms.

However, results from Birchwood et al. (1993) and Rooke and Birchwood (1998) show that depression often follows sometime after an acute psychosis, and that this may be a psychological response (demoralization) to an apparently uncontrollable life event (the psychosis) and its attendant disabilities. In other words, a distinction can be made between two types of depression – that which is deemed to be a symptom of schizophrenia itself, and 'post-psychotic depression' (PPD) which emerges in the so-called recovery period after remission of the acute phase and which is a reaction to the experience of having had a psychotic episode, hospitalization, loss of status and other sequelae.

This was shown definitively in our recent longitudinal study (Birchwood et al., 2000a). In this study 36 per cent of patients developed depressive symptoms of at least moderate severity during the 12 months following the resolution of an acute episode. There was clear evidence that this post-psychotic depression was different in type from the depression that a sample of this population had during their acute episode.

If post-psychotic depression is not a symptom of schizophrenia but a psychological reaction to it, then the next task is to examine the depressive beliefs that individuals have during PPD about their illness. In a further analysis, Iqbal et al. (2000) showed that those who went on to develop PPD (but prior to the onset of actual PPD) reported significant loss, humiliation and entrapment arising from their psychosis, and were more likely to attribute the cause of their psychosis to the self. They also had lower self-esteem and were more self-critical than their non-depressed counterparts. During PPD, patients reported greater insight into their illness, further lowering of self-esteem and a further increase in their appraisals of loss, humiliation, entrapment, shame and self-blame. It seemed clear that insight meant increased awareness of the perceived consequences of their psychosis.

This research shows there are a number of inferences at A which are potential triggers of iBs. In particular, the onset of psychosis was reported as leading to the loss of valued roles and goals ('I am capable of little value as a result of my illness'), and that the social stereotype of mental illness is a stigma which marginalizes the individual in society, and from which the individual feels he cannot escape, and is therefore trapped ('I am powerless to influence or control my illness') and humiliated ('I cannot talk to people about my illness'). Although not specifically investigated in terms that would conform to the irrational beliefs according to REBT theory, it is not difficult to speculate that such inferences would trigger core evaluations associated with depression, particularly of self-downing and awfulizing. Further research could usefully investigate demanding thinking behind these derivatives in these clients, in particular that they should not have a mental illness, and consequently to have one inevitably means they are worthless and that their situation is awful.

The structure of A

So far we have shown that people who have had one or more psychotic episodes may become depressed at C because they draw inferences at A about their psychosis which trigger irrational beliefs at B, though the latter have yet to be fully investigated. However, we can take this analysis further by looking at the structure of the chain of inferences at A. Generally speaking, REBT theory has little to say about the structure of the inference chain. Usually the inference chain is derived pragmatically, by for example asking the client to further describe what it is about the A (or their last inference about the A) that is most depressing, thus obtaining a series of inferences that are connected in the client's mind. However, in our research into PPD we have drawn upon a theory from evolutionary psychology which proposes a structure to inferences, a theory from which we can make predictions about what form the chain of inferences will take. The theory we use is social rank theory (Gilbert, 1992; Price and Sloman, 1986).

According to this theory, social rank is a key dimension of social organization in group-living animals, particularly humans. In order to maintain group cohesion and avoid injury, individuals need to have internal psychobiological mechanisms that enable them to accept their rank position rather than engage in continuous conflict. Those in lower rank positions employ de-escalation strategies that involve biological changes that automatically force the animal to back down or submit to the dominant individuals, and to signal their acceptance of their lowly status. In animals and humans subordinate individuals may be tense, vigilant to down-rank attacks, and lack confidence. There is now considerable evidence that in many depressed states people see themselves as inferior and of low rank compared to those around them, are shame-prone with low self-esteem which Gilbert (1992) referred to as 'involuntary subordinate self-perception'. However, depression also involves two other crucial conditions. First, there is a recognition of defeat (in which the individual no longer struggles to change its low rank position, i.e. is in a state of 'hopelessness'). The second related condition is entrapment, in which the individual desperately wishes to be free but believes they cannot escape from their low rank position. My view is that a 'must' is implicit in this entrapment, and according to REBT theory, would be causal in the depression.

It is clear from the findings of our research on PPD that the depressed participants expressed inferences and evaluations that – like depressed clients in general – were consistent with social rank theory. We concluded that PPD is dependent upon the individual's own experience of psychosis and how he or she appraises its implications for the self, specifically in terms of loss of social roles and goals, self-blame, shame, and humiliation and feelings of defeat and entrapment. The effect of powerful and oppressive experiences (or shattering life events, such as psychotic illness) according to this theory initiates an internal defensive mechanism that compels the individual to see the world in dominant–subordinate rank terms and themselves as subordinate low-rankers. What this means, however, in terms of the theory, is that the individual's belief system will conform to a predictable structure, the 'involuntary subordinate self-perception' that Gilbert (1992) refers to. Thus, the A will be something like 'X is powerful and superior (e.g. psychiatrist/social worker/the 'system'/the family, etc.) and the B 'I am powerless and inferior'. In the case of X being an individual, e.g. a psychiatrist, an inference might be 'X has given me a diagnosis of schizophrenia. He thinks I am insane', and B might be 'and therefore I surely am'. Allied to this chain of thoughts may be an inference 'nobody will like me/want to employ me any more' followed by 'I won't have any friends, a job, won't be able to have a girl-/boyfriend, have a car, a house, a family, etc.' This may be followed by a B which may take the form of a low-rank term such as 'I'd be nobody, lowest of the low, an outcast, nothing, a weirdo.' Here, of course, we will often come close to cognitions that sit close to the boundary between an inference about the self and an iB about the self, which we would normally seek to clarify. The next type of inference or evaluation may be concerned with defeat and entrapment, such as 'I'm finished. It's hopeless. I'm helpless. I'll never be any good again.'

In summary, social rank theory gives us a theory which can guide the cognitive assessment stage of REBT and help to identify and lay bare the inferences and evaluations for later questioning and challenging, all of which will be aimed at enabling the client to develop an alternative conceptualization to the 'involuntary subordination self-perception'.

Developments in REBT at the symptom level

So far, we have discussed developments at the syndrome level – the appraisal by the individual of the experience of having had a psychotic episode. However, can we make further progress with the psychotic episode itself, or even with the symptoms that largely identify the episode? The next stage of the argument is that indeed we can (with suitable theoretical development) – that the psychotic episode itself has an internal structure, and can be further deconstructed, again utilizing the ABC framework. In this section we shall examine the key positive symptoms from this perspective, namely voices, delusions and paranoia.

Voices

In a biomedical model, hallucinations may be understood as simply the symptoms that result from the mental illness. This is one type of A–C theory which appears to bypass any mediating cognitive processing: the illness A causes the symptoms – in this case voices – C. Treatment is directed at the voices at C, along with other symptoms, including depression, which would be grouped together at C, or is directed at A, the underlying causal 'illness', if the physiological and biochemical substrates can be identified. In practice, the goal is usually to eradicate the symptoms. An alternative A–C formulation is to regard the voices as an A which directly cause emotional turmoil (e.g. depression, anxiety, anger) and dysfunctional behaviour (e.g. shouting at the voice). In this case the A is the target of intervention. Both types of formulation are common in mainstream psychiatric settings.

The question arises, do voices have to be conceptualized in A–C terms, or can they be understood in a cognitive or ABC model, in which individual appraisal is the crucial variable? This is a fundamental issue, since there is no scope for an REBT or any cognitive approach in an A–C model, and since this is the prevailing model, this is presumably why no attempt was made until comparatively recently to develop a cognitive approach to psychosis at the symptom level.

To try to get an answer to this question (can voices be conceptualized in an ABC model?), we need to hypothesize whether voices should be treated as Cs, Bs or As. Early attempts at applying a cognitive formulation tried to understand the voices as Bs or inferential As – generally speaking as somehow cognitions about events which had taken on a very concrete form, which then led to Cs. Such an adventurous approach may in the end be possible. But in the meantime our approach was to follow Maher (1974) who argued that clients attempt to understand and attach meaning to anomalous experiences just like any ordinary person would. This led us to identify the voice as an A, since the voice itself is undoubtedly an anomalous experience, a true (experiential) fact *to* which the individual gives a meaning (inferential A), which triggers an evaluation at B.

This formulation (of identifying the voice as an A), however, shows the necessity of further clarifying different types of A, between those As which are pure perceptions or sensations, namely in this case an actual voice which is a physical experience, and those that are inferences about the perception or sensation. Once the inference is made, evaluations (B) will surely follow. In this formulation the cognitions about the voice then become the focus of CBT intervention, since according to our theory, it is these cognitions (evaluations of inferences) that cause emotional distress and behavioural disturbance, rather than the voices *per se*. In theory at least, the voices can be reduced to a mild irritation, and may then fade away. But the main aim is not to get rid of the voices, but to challenge the inferences and evaluations about the voices, in order to reduce distress and dysfunctional behaviour.

In order to put these ideas to the test (that voices were perceptual As about which people made interpretations, and that it is these interpretations, *qua* beliefs, that lead to emotional Cs), Chadwick and Birchwood (1994) and Birchwood and Chadwick (1997) got 67 individuals with a diagnosis of schizophrenia and who heard voices, to complete questionnaires which enquired about the meaning the voices had for them. The authors found that these beliefs about the voices were highly predictive of affect and behaviour, whereas voice form or topography bore no relationship with affect and behaviour. Furthermore, the role of cognitive mediation was borne out by the fact that in nearly three-quarters of participants there was either no relationship with content or an inference from content was the main correlate of affect. This is strong support for an ABC rather than a biological A–C model of voices.

The next main finding from these studies was the identification of the types of meaning individuals had about their voices. Four types of belief were found to be of particular importance – those about the voices' identity, purpose ('is it trying to hurt or help me?'), power or omnipotence (including 'omniscience' or being all-knowing), and beliefs about the consequences of obedience and disobedience. Results showed that 45% regarded their voices as malevolent, 27% as benevolent and 27% as benign. In addition 89% of the malevolent voices were regarded as 'very powerful', as were 82% of the benevolent voices and 64% of the benign voices. Generally speaking, the malevolent voices were 'resisted' and were distressing, whereas the benevolent voices were 'courted' and resulted in a more positive affect. There was a particularly strong correlation between power and depression and malevolence and depression.

It is important to emphasize that these beliefs – the identity, purpose and power in particular – are construed by the voice hearer not as beliefs about the voice but as synonymous *with* the voice. We are accustomed in REBT with the practice of unpacking As into levels of inferences and finally evaluations, but in voice work the implicit inference is uniquely concretized – it as if the client 'knows' it is X talking to them (e.g. the Devil) and thinks they can hear the power and malevolence in the voice, and certainly regards the identity, power and malevolence as facts, not beliefs. It is not only the mental health professional who usually thinks in A–C terms, but the client themself. Added to this, the 'fact' that the Devil talks directly to the client and has absolute power (i.e. the extreme nature of the A) makes it very difficult to adopt the usual REBT strategy of 'let's assume you are right, why would that be so awful?' In this case a better strategy, I believe, is to loosen the inferences around the voice first. This helps to bring the client's experiences more into the normal range of human experience where elegant interventions are often the appropriate intervention. Indeed it is the initial part of a process of 'normalization' in which we approach the psychotic client as a normal screwed-up human like any other neurotic client, but we have to get beneath the initial psychotic, concretizing interpretations to do this.

Having realized the voice is an A we then realized that voice and voice hearer had a type of relationship, and this puts the phenomena on the level of any kind of relationship, and of course squarely in the domain of REBT work. The client personifies the voice, then appraises them as malevolent or benevolent, and finally as powerful. Admittedly, as pointed out earlier, these attributions are often extreme – the voice is the Devil or Jesus, the malevolence is extreme and the power is total – but the characteristics are typical of those that might be attributable to significant others in the client's life, and particularly those that exist in high 'expressed emotion' (EE) relationships, where hostile, critical comments from powerful relatives are common. Indeed, we found good evidence that the relationship with the voice is a paradigm of social relationships in general (Birchwood et al., 2000b).

The pattern of relationships discussed here can be most clearly seen in command hallucinations, for not only do the personified voices often criticize the hearer, but in 40 to 60 per cent of cases they command them to do things. These potentially dangerous hallucinations can, in their most extreme form, command the individual to kill themself or others. The perceived power of the voice is one of the most important predictors of acting on such commands. So, putting all this together, the research finds:

1. Voice hearers construct the link between themselves and their voice as having the nature of an intimate interpersonal relationship, and often one that is inescapable.
2. Over 85% of voice hearers saw the voice as powerful and omnipotent, whereas the hearer is usually weak and dependent, unable to control or influence the voice. The greater the perceived power and omnipotence of the voice, the greater the likelihood of compliance, though this relationship is not linear and is moderated by appraisal of the voice's intent and the consequences of resisting.
3. Voice hearers perceived the voice as omniscient (e.g. knew the person's present thoughts and past history, was able to predict the future, etc.); this was seen as evidence of the voice's power.
4. Some voice hearers construed their voice as benevolent, others as malevolent and persecutory.
5. Those with benevolent voices virtually always complied with the voice, irrespective of whether the command was 'innocuous' or 'severe',

whereas those with malevolent voices were more likely to resist, and this resistance increased if the command involved major social transgression or self-harm. However, subjects predicted the malevolent voice would inflict harm whenever they resisted, and, if they continued to resist, felt compelled to appease the voice by carrying out an alternative action.

6.   A belief in control (i.e. power) over voices was associated with reduced compliance with *all* types of commands.

It will be obvious to the reader by now that the voice-related cognitions we have discussed resonate strongly with social rank theory. This theory not only gives a good account of post-psychotic depression, but also of the interpretation of voices. Indeed, the theory brings into sharp focus the nature of the relationship between the voice hearer in the role of the subordinate and the personified voice in the role of the all-powerful dominant, whether malevolent or benevolent. We found in a sample of 59 voice hearers that not only was there the predicted relationship with perceived low social rank and voice power and associated subordination/domination, but that this was paralleled in other social relationships in the client's life. In this research low social rank included a range of qualities on which the client felt inferior, including confidence, respect, competence and attractiveness.

In REBT terms, most of the cognitions we have been discussing – identity, purpose and power in particular – are inferential As and not Bs. Undoubtedly they are often critical As, for example, malevolence ('he thinks I am evil and should die') and power ('he is powerful and I am powerless and weak'). Since beliefs that voices are malevolent and all-powerful are formally speaking secondary delusions, I will discuss the content of the self-downing beliefs (one of the irrational derivatives) that these inferences evoke in the next section on paranoid delusions.

However, there are two points to be made about evaluations before concluding this section. First, the perceived power differential between voice hearer and voice – the voice being omnipotent and all-knowing – means that what the voice says carries great weight, and consequently conviction levels in the truth of voice pronouncements is characteristically very high, if not total. Thus the transition from a critical A such as 'you are evil' to the corresponding self-downing belief 'I surely am' is powerfully facilitated. Indeed, the almost automatic transition from the one to the other is probably far more pronounced than in most other disorders, since few other disorders have this psychotic quality of their adverse events, where the hostile other is virtually supernatural in its force and potency. This presents more of a problem, of course, for REBT disputing, and I have earlier suggested that inferences about the voice may better be weakened (i.e. the supernatural voice dethroned as it were) before tackling the belief.

A second point concerns the implication of our inference-level findings for the primary irrational belief, the must. Participants in our current study on command hallucinations almost universally say that they have a sense of compulsion to obey the command, and although they are sometimes able to resist carrying out the precise action commanded (especially when it is dangerous or anti-social) they nonetheless usually feel compelled to carry out a less serious action by way of appeasing the voice. It is clear that compliance is often driven by a 'must' belief, and there is a clear role here for a cognitive intervention, not only directly aimed at the must ('where is it written that you must obey?') but also at the derivatives (e.g.'how does disobeying show you are bad?'; 'even if the consequences for you are bad, how can they be awful?'; 'the evidence shows you are standing it when you resist'). However, as I suggested earlier, challenging the must can most often be facilitated inelegantly by first challenging the omnipotence of the commanding voice.

Delusions

Earlier I claimed that, within a biomedical model, voices were conceptualized in an A–C framework, but that we could reconceptualize them coherently in a cognitive ABC framework. The question now is, if voices can be conceptualized as As in an ABC model, what about delusions? Traditional psychiatry regards delusions much as it does hallucinations, as symptoms of an illness and therefore best construed in an A–C model. For example, Berrios (1991) argues that delusions are not beliefs, but 'empty speech acts, whose informational content refers neither to self or world'. However, at the very least we have already seen that clients can take up a meta-level attitude towards their symptoms, and this would treat delusions as an A. But (to challenge Berrios's claim) do delusions have meaningful content? Clearly they have understandable content ('people are plotting against me') but not in the form of perceptions or sensations which characterize voices, but, as DSMIV states, are beliefs ('erroneous beliefs that usually involve a misinterpretation of perceptions or experiences'). In REBT terms then, delusions are As, but inferential and not perceptual As.

Delusions are in principle understandable inferences, and only differ from normal inferences in that they often take a very concrete form ('my thoughts are being transmitted to others') and are held with much stronger levels of conviction. It is precisely because of this very concreteness and high level of conviction (the client regards them as 'facts', and they are usually expressed linguistically as facts) that delusions have only comparatively recently been considered as inferences, amenable to cognitive intervention. The ABC model is helpful because it clarifies that the delusion starts with a perceptual-level observation about which the delusional inference is made. The observation could be an event (hears man say what he was thinking), or even a voice ('give up smoking'), and the inference drawn ('my thoughts are being transmitted'; 'the spirits are looking after me'). Furthermore the ABC model also shows that implicit within the delusions is also an evaluation – to be discussed next.

Paranoia

One of the most important categories of delusion is the paranoid delusion, and indeed paranoia has long been recognized diagnostically as one of the major types of schizophrenia. Here again, we and others have made considerable progress in our cognitive approach, in our case again utilizing the ABC framework. The aspect we have focused on is the content of the paranoia delusion, with a particular interest this time not only in the inferences drawn, as discussed earlier, but particularly the core evaluations that drive the paranoia.

The main theme in any paranoid delusion at point A is a threat – the inference that there is a conspiracy among others who intend harm to the individual. This results in unhealthy affect and self-defeating behaviour at C. But what are the iBs at the heart of this threat interpretation? As Ellis has often said, once you have the A and you have the C, it is not difficult to identify the iBs. In paranoid delusions we know the As – that the FBI is plotting against me, that that man over the road is a spy watching me, that this voice is the voice of the Devil punishing me, etc. We also know there is affect and behaviour involved at C – there always is in delusions (anger or anxiety and depression, aggression or avoidance and withdrawal), we know there has to be an irrational belief, or several, and we should be able to get to them in the usual way by inference chaining.

Among the most obvious of the iBs in paranoid delusions is the self- or other-devaluing belief. Zigler and Glick (1988) proposed that paranoia is a defence against attacks against the self, which if undefended would result in lowered self-esteem and depression. How does this defence work? Perhaps by believing concretely in a fiendish plot, these individuals can believe they are not only innocent but also important. So, what cognitive mechanism is at play here? One line of thought is that they are attributing blame externally to malevolent others for all the bad things happening to them, and taking credit for the good things that happen. This attributional style is well recognized in the social psychology literature – the self-serving bias – which functions to maintain my self-esteem. Richard Bentall and his colleagues (e.g. Bentall et al., 1994) have found that paranoid participants had an attributional style characterized by an extreme self-serving bias and that this was accompanied by higher self-esteem than average.

Two types of paranoia

One problem that emerges from the research on the self-serving bias in paranoia is that the findings aren't that consistent. In fact, these clients do not form a homogeneous group. While Bentall and colleagues found the externalizers had high self-esteem, others found the opposite – that they had low self-esteem. Indeed, our own research showed some didn't even show a self-serving bias. Are Zigler and Glick and Bentall wrong after all?

We propose another explanation – that in fact there are two types of paranoia (Trower and Chadwick, 1995). One type is the classic type as described by Bentall – bad people are plotting against them; they are basically good, and others are to blame for everything. The other type also think others are plotting their downfall, but this time they are better than them and they are bad, and deserve it. The distinction can best be described in terms of the concepts of poor me and bad me, eloquently spelled out by Paul Hauck (1976) in his self-help book *Overcoming Depression*, and more theoretically by Wessler and Wessler (1980) and elsewhere. Poor-me or persecution paranoids believe they are being wrongfully persecuted by malevolent others, and bad-me or punishment paranoids believe they are being deservedly punished for their badness. Conceptualized in REBT terms, the poor-me individuals would be high on 'other-downing' but low on 'self-downing' (confirmed in several studies), would have low frustration tolerance and would be awfulizing (not yet empirically examined). Bad-me individuals on the other hand would be high on 'self-downing' and low on 'other-downing' (confirmed in several studies), but would also have low frustration tolerance and would be awfulizing (not yet empirically examined).

What's the evidence? In a recent study (Chadwick et al., in submission) findings showed both groups expressed negative other-to-self person evaluations as would be expected in paranoia. However, the 'poor-me' group showed a higher level of negative self-to-other evaluations, and a lower level of negative self-to-self evaluations than the 'bad-me' group. The 'poor-me' group was further associated with higher self-esteem, and lower level of depression and anxiety than the 'bad-me' group. Contrary to expectation, no difference was observed between the groups in the level of reported anger. However, overall the findings support our hypotheses concerning the two types.

The self and psychosis

Most researchers and practitioners in psychosis, and indeed much of mental health, uses the concept of self-esteem when referring to issues concerning the self. A central tenet of REBT is that we should abandon the concept of self-esteem. Indeed, Ellis has written that self-esteem is a form of disturbance, since it is a form of global self-rating which he rejects, and promotes *conditional* self-acceptance which he rejects. So we too have adopted the idea of person evaluation, where whole-person devaluation is the iB, and unconditional self-acceptance is the rB. And towards that goal we have promoted the concept of person evaluation as a core concept in schizophrenia research, and have published the Evaluative Beliefs Scale as a measure of it (Chadwick et al., 1999).

However, we have proposed a further development in the concept of self which forms the basis of a tentative alternative psychological level of explanation for the development of schizophrenia (Harrop and Trower, in press). This is based on our 'theory of self construction' that we put forward to explain the two types of paranoia (Trower and Chadwick, 1995). Drawing on a rich legacy of philosophical and psychological work on the concept of self (including Ellis's), we propose that there is no such 'thing' as the self, as some kind of inner object which can be measured, but rather the self has to be continuously constructed and is never secure. To construct a self an individual has to perform a series of self-presentation behaviours, and these self presentations have to be recognized as such by the 'audience' of significant others, who thereby reify the self as presented into a social object (or, better, give ontological status to the presented self).

There are (according to our theory) two opposing imperatives involved in the process of self construction. The existential imperative is the proposition that the making of a self is the most fundamental human motive – as the existentialists put it, no less than the motive *to be*. Since the self has to be constructed, the individual experiences emptiness, or, as Laing (1960) put it, 'ontological insecurity', if they fail to construct a self.

On the other hand, the moral imperative is the moral coercion of the individual ('he') to construct a self which the other wishes him to construct. In other words, the other may evoke the moral imperative in order to try to make sure that the individual will present himself in the way they want and he *ought*. The punishment for refusing to conform is that the other is more likely to refuse to give recognition, or may attempt to redefine the actor as bad – two types of threat described below. The problem with the moral imperative, then, is that it can be in direct conflict with the existential imperative. To interpret Sartre (1943/1957) this is because I wish to found my own being – to be the author of my own self construction – but the other (whom I need to achieve this) may wish to be the author of my self construction, and uses the moral imperative to try to achieve this control.

There are thus two ways that the other can thwart an individual's existential imperative to construct a self (Dagnan et al., 2002). The first is what we have termed the 'insecurity threat'. In this situation the other is serially indifferent, negligent, rejecting or absent, so that the individual cannot gain the crucial recognition that gives him ontological security. Clients often use such terms as 'worthless', of 'being nothing'. We have found that clients will call up their voices as a substitute for real people to fill the 'void', because, as one client put it, 'they need me and give me a sense of security'. Another client had a complex delusional world of little people for whom he was God. We speculate that these would be the 'benevolent' voices identified by Chadwick and Birchwood (1994).

The second type we have termed the 'engulfment threat' where the other is excessively present and intrusive, and tries to take control of the self, by means, we would argue, of the mechanism of the moral imperative. The individual who succumbs thus constructs not his authentic self but a self that is alien to him. He may feel his self is possessed by the other. In our experience psychotic clients often report this experience of 'possession' – omnipotent and omniscient voices control an individual's movements, read his thoughts, extract thoughts from and insert thoughts into his head and so on. We speculate that such voices would be of the 'malevolent' type as identified by Chadwick and Birchwood (1994), and would include command hallucinations which the individual feels compelled to obey.

The engulfment threat may also help to explain what Frith (1992) calls the disorders of willed action including abulia (no will), alogia (no words) athymia (no feelings), inability to generate appropriate behaviour of their own will, behaviour elicited by irrelevant external stimuli. Frith suggests how specific features of schizophrenia such as the above might arise from specific abnormalities in 'metarepresentation', which he attributes to a hypothesized neural deficit. This is the cognitive mechanism that enables us to be aware of our goals, our intentions, and the intentions of other people. We have already discussed the nature of consciousness as intentional. The lifelong experience of being intrusively controlled, and of having an alien and not an authentic (self-constructed) self, and the concomitant loss of a centre of initiative, is indeed likely to cause profound dysfunction in the normal operation of consciousness. We suggest that this may be the psychological origin of Frith's failure of willed explanation.

We suggest, therefore, that at least some psychotic experiences, both positive and negative, emerge from one or other (or both) types of threat to self construction, severe enough where normal social self construction actually fails, where either a social world is invented or the world implodes on the person's very sense of being.

Our theory has similarities to but also differences from REBT theory. First, it is similar in that both theories propose there is no such entity as the self which can be globally rated. Our theory is in effect a phenomenological account of the self, in which the self is no more than the totality of appearances and not an entity behind those appearances. This is similar to the REBT position that we can rate our behaviour but not the self and that the self cannot be reduced to any one behaviour (or group or set of behaviours).

However, there is a difference between the theories in the treatment of the must. Our theory in effect is claiming there are two musts, the existential imperative (or must) and the moral imperative (or must), whereas REBT does not make any such division.

The existential must might include such beliefs as 'I must do X (e.g. achieve) to be worthwhile, and if I don't, I will be worthless'. In the terms of our theory this means I must present myself in a way that gains me the recognition that makes me true-to-myself (i.e. authentic) being-in-the-world, and if I am not so recognized I am nothing, i.e. not a being. The word 'worthless' here is taken to refer to an ontological issue – the experience of nonbeing – and not a moral issue.

The moral must, on the other hand, might include such beliefs as 'I must do what others want me to do to be morally good, and if I don't, I will be judged (and therefore be) morally bad, wicked, evil'. In our theory this means I must construct my self in the way others want and I *ought* (or should), and not the way I want, otherwise they will define me as morally bad, and I will be constituted that way in my essence, if they so define me. In other words, I have the (in REBT terms irrational) belief that the other can constitute my very essence, in this case as morally bad, simply by defining me that way, and I have the false belief that that defines me in my totality – in attribution theory terms, globally and stably. It is interesting to note that Higgins (1987) also makes a distinction between the failure to achieve what I want to be and what I ought to be. He describes it as the distinction between the ideal self (one's hopes, aspirations and wishes) and the ought self (one's sense of duty, obligations or responsibilities), and is a distinction that, as Higgins points out, has been made by a number authors.

In REBT terms, the terms 'must', 'should', 'ought' and 'have to' are grouped together as more or less synonymous under the concept of the demanding philosophy. However, we make a distinction between the meanings of these terms. The term 'must' (and probably the phrase 'have to') is general, means 'imperative' and therefore applies equally to the existential and moral imperatives. However, the terms 'should' and 'ought' apply strictly speaking to the moral issue, though they are often used more loosely to mean the equivalent of must. However, I believe it is clearer and more accurate to limit their use to the moral issue. Furthermore, the terms 'should' and 'ought' are not, strictly speaking, synonymous with must, since we often dispute the belief that 'I must do what I ought'.

I do not believe that the distinction we draw between the existential and moral imperatives clashes with REBT theory – it is simply that in REBT no such distinction is drawn. Indeed, REBT theory can easily accommodate this distinction without questioning the validity of the irrationality assumption of the must. The distinction would be helpful, I believe, in that the existential issue of worthlessness is quite different from the moral issue of badness, and requires a different assessment and disputational strategy, particularly in psychosis. The thrust of the existential must dispute is that my worth and therefore existence does not depend on affirmation by specific significant others, while the aim of the moral must dispute is that disapproval by the other does not render me intrinsically bad and evil but at the worst can only be evidence of my fallibility as a human. From our self-construction theoretical point of view, the aim of both musts is to enable the person to restore their self-construction capability which had been blocked by one or other (or both) musts. We describe the principles and practice of this theory in our forthcoming book (Harrop and Trower, in press).

Conclusion

In this chapter I have argued that REBT theory, adapted and enlarged in various ways, can provide a powerful therapy for most of the cognitive, behavioural and emotional problems associated with schizophrenia. This is true not simply at a surface or meta level, in which schizophrenia is treated simply as an adverse life event, but can be applied to the various positive and negative symptoms, and in combination with other theories, particularly social rank theory and self construction theory, provide the basis for exploring a psychological model to complement the biological model of schizophrenia. The points raised in this chapter are suggestive and far from definitive, but we have already carried out a number of empirical studies that support various of the assertions, particularly with regard to voices and paranoia.

Acknowledgements

I am indebted to Chris Harrop, Paul Chadwick and Max Birchwood for their contributions to this chapter.

References

American Psychiatric Association (1994) *Diagnostic and Statistical Manual of Mental Disorders* (4th edn). Washington, DC: American Psychiatric Association.

Bentall, R.P., Kinderman, P. and Kaney, S. (1994) Cognitive processes and delusional beliefs: attributions and the self, *Behaviour Research and Therapy*, *32*, 331–341.

Berrios, G. (1991) Delusions as 'wrong' beliefs: a conceptual history, *British Journal of Psychiatry*, *159*, 6–13.

Birchwood, M.J. and Chadwick, P.D.J. (1997) The omnipotence of voices: testing the validity of the cognitive model, *Psychological Medicine*, *27*, 1345–1353.

Birchwood, M.J., Mason, R., Macmillan, J. and Healey, J. (1993) Depression, demoralisation and control over illness: a comparison of depressed and non-depressed patients with a chronic psychosis, *Psychological Medicine*, *27*, 1345–1353.

Birchwood, M., Iqbal, Z., Chadwick, P. and Trower, P. (2000a) Cognitive approaches to depression and suicidal thinking in psychosis: 1. Ontogeny of post-psychotic depression, *British Journal of Psychiatry*, *177*, 516–521.

Birchwood, M.J., Meaden, A., Trower, P., Gilbert, P. and Plaistow, J. (2000b) The power and omnipotence of voices: subordination and entrapment by voices and significant others, *Psychological Medicine*, *30*, 337–344.

Bleuler, E. ([1911] 1950) *Dementia Praecox or the Group of Schizophrenias* (English translation by J. Zinkin). New York: International Universities Press.

Chadwick, P.D.J. and Birchwood, M.J. (1994) The omnipotence of voices. A cognitive approach to auditory hallucinations, *British Journal of Psychiatry*, *164*, 190–201.

Chadwick, P., Birchwood, M. and Trower, P. (1996) *Cognitive Therapy for Delusions, Voices and Paranoia*. Chichester: Wiley.

Chadwick, P., Trower, P. and Dagnan, D. (1999) Measuring negative person evaluations: the Evaluative Beliefs Scale, *Cognitive Therapy and Research*, *23*, 549–559.

Chadwick, P., Trower, P., Juusti-Butler, T.-M. and Maguire, N. (in submission) Phenomenological analysis of poor me and bad me paranoia.

Dagnan, D., Trower, P. and Gilbert, P. (2002) Measuring vulnerability to threats to self construction: psychometric properties of the Self and Other Scale, *Psychology and Psychotherapy: Theory, Research and Practice*, *75*, 279–293.

Drake, R.E. and Cotton, P.G. (1986) Depression, hopelessness and suicide in chonic schizophrenia, *British Journal of Psychiatry*, *148*, 554–559.

Frith, C. (1992) *The Cognitive Neuropsychology of Schizophrenia*. Hillsdale, NJ: Erlbaum.

Gilbert, P. (1992) *Depression: The Evolution of Powerlessness*. Hove: Erlbaum.

Harrop, C. and Trower, P. (in press) *Why Does Schizophrenia Develop at Late Adolescence?* Chichester: Wiley.

Hauck, P. (1976) *Overcoming Depression*. Philadelphia: Westminster Press.

Higgins, E.T. (1987) Self-discrepancy: a theory relating self and affect, *Psychological Review*, *94*, 319–340.

Hirsch, S.R. and Jolley, A.G. (1989) The dysphoric syndrome in schizophrenia and its implications for relapse, *British Journal of Psychiatry*, *155* (supplement 5), 46–50.

Iqbal, Z., Birchwood, M., Chadwick, P. and Trower, P. (2000) Cognitive approach to depression and suicidal thinking in psychosis: 2. Testing the validity of a social ranking model, *British Journal of Psychiatry*, *177*, 522–528.

Laing, R.D. (1960) *The Divided Self*. Harmondsworth: Penguin.

Maher, B.A. (1974) Delusional thinking and perceptual disorder, *Journal of Individual Psychology*, *30*, 98–113.

Price, J. and Sloman, L. (1987) Depression as yielding behaviour: an animal model based on Schjelderup-Ebbe's pecking order, *Ethology and Sociobiology*, *8*, 85–98.

Rooke, O. and Birchwood, M. (1998) Loss, humiliation and entrapment as appraisals of schizophrenic illness: a prospective study of depressed and non-depressed patients, *British Journal of Clinical Psychology*, *37*, 259–268.

Sartre, J.-P. (1943/1957) *Being and Nothingness*. London: Methuen.

Siris, S.G. (2000) Depression in schizophrenia: perspective in the era of 'atypical' antipsychotic agents, *American Journal of Psychiatry*, *157*, 1379–1389.

Trower, P. and Chadwick, P. (1995) Pathways to defense of the self: a theory of two types of paranoia, *Clinical Psychology: Science and Practice*, 2, 263–278.

Wessler, R.A. and Wessler, R.L. (1980) *The Principles and Practice of Rational-Emotive Therapy*. San Francisco: Jossey Bass.

Zigler, E. and Glick, M. (1988) Is paranoid schizophrenia really camouflaged depression? *American Psychologist*, 43, 284–290.

Index

Note: Page numbers in *italics* refer to figures/tables

Advancing Theory in Therapy
Series Editor: Keith Tudor

Most books covering individual therapeutic approaches are aimed at the trainee/student market. This series, however, is concerned with *advanced* and *advancing* theory, offering the reader comparative and comparable coverage of a number of therapeutic approaches.

Aimed at professionals and postgraduates, *Advancing Theory in Therapy* will cover an impressive range of individual theories. With full reference to case studies throughout, each title will

- present cutting-edge research findings
- locate each theory and its application within its cultural context
- develop a critical view of theory and practice

Titles in the series

Body Psychotherapy
Edited by Tree Staunton

Transactional Analysis: A Relational Perspective
Helena Hargaden and Charlotte Sills

Adlerian Psychotherapy: An Advanced Approach to Individual Psychology
Ursula E. Oberst and Alan E. Stewart

Rational Emotive Behaviour Therapy: Theoretical Developments
Edited by Windy Dryden

Rational Emotive Behaviour Therapy

Rational Emotive Behaviour Therapy: Theoretical Developments is a cutting-edge examination of the theory behind this popular approach within the cognitive-behavioural tradition.

Distinguished practitioners and authors discuss the relevance of:

- Cross-disiplinary factors affecting REBT
- REBT as an intentional therapy
- Differentiating preferential from exaggerated and musturbatory beliefs in REBT
- Irrational beliefs as schemata

Thought-provoking presentation of case studies and the latest theory revision give *Rational Emotive Behaviour Therapy: Theoretical Developments* a distinctive slant: a challenging discussion of the approach's openness to revision from within and outside the ranks of REBT, and its implications for the future.

Windy Dryden is Professor of Psychotherapeutic Studies at Goldsmiths College, University of London, and an international authority on Rational Emotive Behaviour Therapy. He has written or edited numerous books including *Four Approaches to Counselling and Psychotherapy*, *Adult Clinical Problems* and *Life Coaching*.